Kicking
and Screaming
Ivana Bacik
Dragging Ireland into
the 21st Century

THE O'BRIEN PRESS

DUBLIN

First published 2004 by The O'Brien Press Ltd,
20 Victoria Road, Dublin 6, Ireland.
Tel: +353 1 4923333; Fax: +353 1 4922777
E-mail: books@obrien.ie
Website: www.obrien.ie

ISBN: 0-86278-860-9

British Library Cataloguing-in-Publication Data
Bacik, Ivana
Kicking and screaming : dragging Ireland into the 21st century
1.Ireland - Social conditions - 21st century
2.Ireland - Social conditions - 20th century
I.Title
306'.09417'0905

1 2 3 4 5 6 7 8
04 05 06 07

Editing, typesetting, layout and design: The O'Brien Press Ltd
Photograph of author, back cover and page 2: Amelia Stein
Printing: Nørhaven Paperback A/S

DEDICATION
To my mother, Rina.

ACKNOWLEDGEMENTS
My sincere thanks to all at The O'Brien Press, particularly Michael O'Brien, Íde ní Laoghaire, Emma Byrne and Lynn Crampton for all their help and encouragement. Special thanks to Rachel Pierce at O'Brien for her expertise and seemingly endless supply of patience at the editing stage! Thanks also to my family and friends, to Hilary Delany, Catherine Finnegan and other colleagues at Trinity Law School and at the Bar for their support. I am especially grateful for political and moral support to Paul Daly and other Labour party comrades and colleagues. Finally, my love and gratitude to Alan, without whom this would not have been possible.

CONTENTS

INTRODUCTION

Ireland has changed dramatically in recent decades. In the 1950s this was an intensely Catholic society, a little impoverished island off the west coast of Europe, which became, in the 1970s, an unremarkable and somewhat peripheral member of the European Economic Community (now European Union). But by the 1990s, and into the present decade, we have witnessed the emergence of a much more progressive and diverse society, a symbol of economic success for all small states in Europe. Now, in the twenty-first century, we are faced with new challenges and opportunities, we are about to become a net donor to the EU rather than a net beneficiary, and, for the first time, we belong to a country that people are more likely to immigrate into than to emigrate from.

This book is an admittedly selective account of some key issues in Irish society where significant social change has occurred in recent years, and where campaigns have sought to liberalise and reform the law accordingly. As this is a subjective and not a comprehensive choice, many topics are left out – one of the most obvious being the criminal justice system. It would, however, take another full book to describe the social changes, political campaigns and necessary law reform related to that area.

The central theme of this book is that the law, like many other institutions, is resistant to change, which is why it must be dragged forward, 'kicking and screaming', in order to force it to reflect real shifts and movements in Irish society. Over the years, activist political campaigns have had many successes in dragging forward the law, but there are still some important ways in which the law remains impervious to change. In many aspects, the Catholic Church retains great authority within our structures of power, and a theocratic conservative morality continues to wield strong influence nationally. I argue that liberals, feminists, socialists and progressives must seek the genuine separation of Church and State, and must challenge the enduring power and influence of the Church.

In an increasingly prosperous and multicultural Ireland, albeit a country in which the gap between rich and poor has grown larger in recent years, we must also strive for a more equal and a more pluralist society – but not for a more consumerist one. I believe we need to base campaigns for change upon a new set of secular values, drawn not from religious teachings or Papal encyclicals but from the principles of humanism: the core values of equality, respect for the dignity of others, pluralism and tolerance of diversity. I am advocating a new constitutional order in which equality becomes the core norm, and in which enforceable rights are guaranteed to disadvantaged groups rather than just to individuals.

A rights-based culture of this kind means a legal and political system in which substantive social and economic rights are guaranteed, for example, the rights to housing, to healthcare, to childcare. Such a system would be a State built on a social-democratic economic model, where the provision of adequate public services is guaranteed. Where there is a failure to provide adequate services, then the citizen may seek redress before the courts as a last resort, through the rights enforcement process.

This may sound unfeasibly idealistic – and I do not pretend that any law reform or constitutional amendment can offer a blueprint for the perfect society. But while we must recognise that a guarantee of rights is not necessarily a guarantee of reality, in order to make our aspirations real we must keep striving for progressive legal and constitutional change.

We have come a long way – from a country where, for many decades, Ministers for Justice feared criticism by Catholic bishops, through our membership of the European Union, to the present climate of social and economic change, with many positive developments in law reform along the way. We still have some distance to go before achieving a more equal society, but the cycle-path ahead is straight, and all we need is a good set of wheels and a clear view.

CHAPTER 1
Ireland in Context

Viewed objectively, the island of Ireland is a little piece of land set into the Atlantic Ocean halfway between Europe and America, populated by not quite six million people, a small player in global terms and geographic significance. But then, we Irish people have never viewed ourselves objectively.

In Irish eyes, Ireland has immensely inflated global and geographic significance. The importance of Ireland[1], according to our own view, lies in a wide variety of factors: in many aspects of our diverse and important history; in our past incarnation as 'the land of saints and scholars'; in our status as a bastion of the Catholic Church; in our extensive influence on other countries and other cultures through our far-flung diaspora; in the evolution of the Irish Free State over the decades after 1922 into an independent, post-colonial Republic; in our leading position in Europe, despite being on the periphery of the European Union; in our recent reincarnation as the 'Celtic Tiger' model for other small economies, with our remarkable economic boom sustaining rapid growth in the mid- to late 1990s. This widely prevalent view we hold about ourselves is also bolstered by international views of Ireland, which often go even further in eulogising the role of Ireland and Irish people in world history.

INTERNATIONAL VIEWS OF IRELAND

There are two conflicting international views of Ireland: first, that of a country which has made a significant cultural contribution in world terms, and continues to do so now economically; but second, a country which allows a large section of its population to be left far behind in social and economic terms, creating a largely voiceless underclass.

The former might best be described as the emerald-tinted view, illustrated by American author Thomas Cahill's US best-seller, *How the Irish Saved Civilization: The Untold Story of Ireland's Heroic Role from the Fall of Rome to the Rise of Medieval Europe*.[2] Cahill writes that Ireland played the key role in maintaining Western culture during the Dark Ages (usually given as AD500–1500) in Europe. According to Cahill, St Patrick, in particular, had an extraordinary influence on the subsequent history of civilisation. He brought Christianity to Ireland and also developed a culture of literacy and learning that created the conditions within which Ireland became the celebrated 'land of saints and scholars'. Irish monks and scribes, working within the Patrick-inspired hierarchy of monastic settlements, painstakingly copied the classic works and sacred texts which were rapidly disappearing from continental Europe, thus preserving Western culture while the rest of Europe languished in the dark shadow cast by the marauding barbarians. Without Patrick, Cahill argues, there would be no record of Plato, Ovid, or Homer. Furthermore, Irish missionaries, inspired by St Patrick, travelled to continental Europe, educating the barbarian hordes and bringing the light of learning and civilisation to the world at large.

A delightful account. But this story of the 'unsung heroes' from Ireland who rescued European civilisation ultimately leaves a cloying feeling, similar to that evoked by misty-eyed reminiscences of 'the oul' sod' by those who have never lived in this country. We know it is stretching the green fabric of patriotism beyond its elastic point. Yet this account of the unique Irish civilising influence holds sway with a large section of the Irish-American diaspora, in whose eyes we often see ourselves reflected from abroad. We may well be cynical about their romantic notions, but this highly skewed take on Irish history retains its influence and even thrives in some places, which means it is an image we must contend with. There is, for whatever reason, an international tendency to be well-disposed towards Ireland – a tendency that elevates us beyond our actual standing on the world stage – and there would seem to be commentators and writers in every nation willing to collude in this. And while we as Irish people don't really buy it, nor do we strive too hard to disabuse our international friends of their unfounded ideals.

Alongside the image of Ireland as a galvanising force historically, painting the world green, there is the equally flattering view of modern Ireland as an exemplary model in terms of economic performance – something for which we have become well-known internationally. Foreign commentators point to the 2004 Globalisation Index, which ranks Ireland first as the most globalised country in the world, according to their criteria of economic integration, technological connectivity, personal contact and political engagement.[3] They also point to the praise showered upon Ireland by international bodies, like the Organisation for Economic Cooperation and Development (OECD), which reported in 1999 that Ireland had had 'five straight years of stunning economic performance. No other OECD member country has been able to match its outstanding outcomes in a variety of dimensions.' A range of figures may be used to back up this analysis. For example, the growth rate per annum of the Irish economy was significantly ahead of the OECD average throughout the 1990s; between 1993 and 2000 the level of employment increased in Ireland at the highest rate in the OECD. From being a net beneficiary within the European Union, a needy and grateful recipient of structural funds, Ireland has become the economic success story of the EU, moving from 18% unemployment in the late 1980s to a rate of just 4.6% in 2004. Indeed, journalist Fintan O'Toole has noted that Ireland has now achieved no less than 'iconic status among the neo-conservative champions of small government and despisers of the interventionist State' – albeit, as he points out, that the Irish economic model has been developed through significant State intervention.[4] So Ireland now has a brand new image, that of international go-getter: entrepreneurial, ambitious and successful.

However, we do not come up smelling of roses on every front. Despite the glowing praise for the Irish economic miracle of the 1990s, there also exists a second international view of Ireland that is less complimentary and, some would argue, closer to the truth. According to the

2003 *United Nations Human Development Report,* for example, Ireland ranks second lowest among seventeen OECD nations in terms of poverty and inequality levels, only beaten to bottom place by the USA. The percentage of Gross Domestic Product (GDP) spent in Ireland on social protection measures is the lowest in the EU at 14.1%, compared with an EU average of 27.3%; Sweden, for example, spends 32.3%.

So two Irelands appear to coexist, despite their apparent mutual contradiction. We have here an Ireland capable of being a force for progress, for betterment, at home and abroad, beloved of other nations and blessed from on high; and alongside that an Ireland that is deeply polarised between rich and poor, where capitalism and aggressive *mé féinism* have created an appallingly unbalanced society in which different classes lead separate and vastly different lives: gross affluence on one side and desperate poverty on the other. Which, then, is the real Ireland?

IRELAND: THE VIEW FROM WITHIN

Despite the buoyant economy and our increasing confidence on the global stage, many individuals and organisations within Ireland have highlighted the problems inherent in our society, and are striving to bridge the gap between rich and poor. Groups which have offered strong critiques of what they see as an unequal and uncaring society include Combat Poverty, a leading Irish Non-Governmental Organisation (NGO). It found that in 2000, at the height of the economic boom, more than 8% of Irish children were living in 'consistent poverty' (ie, income deprivation combined with lack of basics, such as heating) and that roughly 24% of Irish children were living in 'relative income poverty' (ie, on incomes of less than 50% of the median).

A recent Conference of the Religious in Ireland (CORI) Justice Commission report showed that the tax take nationally in Ireland after

Budget 2003 is the lowest in Europe, at just 27.7% of GDP and 33.9% of Gross National Product (GNP). Worldwide, according to CORI, only three other OECD countries collect less tax than Ireland: Korea, Japan and Mexico – even the USA collects more tax from its citizens. So despite complaints from those in the Irish high-earners' tax band of 46%, the tax they pay does not prevent them from living a very comfortable lifestyle, and is proportionately far less than the tax they would have to pay in other neo-liberal economies.

More recently, the Economic and Social Research Institute (ESRI) reported in 2003 that relative poverty in Ireland has more than doubled since 1994, that is, the proportion of people in median relative income poverty has doubled during that time, from 6% in 1994 to 12.9% in 2001. Although the report found that consistent poverty had been greatly reduced, down from 15% of households in 1994 to 5% in 2001, and that real incomes had significantly improved during the same period, it noted the increased risk of relative poverty for social welfare recipients, older people, particularly women, those with disabilities and those tied to the home, such as single parents. In essence, while social welfare benefits had risen during the period, they had not risen enough to meet inflation.[5]

This means that poverty and social exclusion remain a reality in Ireland; that many people have reaped no benefits from recent national prosperity. There are just under 50,000 households, representing approximately 150,000 people, on waiting lists for social housing; unacceptable, lengthy waiting lists for medical treatment for those who cannot afford private healthcare; continuing problems for parents in disadvantaged areas in accessing affordable pre-school and childcare facilities ... the list goes on. It is clear that notwithstanding the 'Celtic Tiger', or, more accurately, because of the way in which the Tiger economy developed, the rich have been getting richer and the poor, while admittedly reduced in number, are getting poorer. There is still real poverty amid the plenty in Irish society today.

How do these social problems inform the view we have of ourselves? Apart from the figures contained in UN and other official reports, and despite critical accounts in some sections of the Irish media, it is generally difficult to find an account of Ireland in popular writing that is less than complimentary. The reason for this may lie in a reluctance to criticise ourselves publicly; a tendency, perhaps derived from past experience of colonisation, to band together collectively and defensively against any perceived external critique. As Frank McCourt found after the publication of *Angela's Ashes*, offering even mild criticism of particular Irish towns in years gone by may expose the critic to severe scolding from his native land. On the other hand, Bill Cullen's more anodyne account of growing up in poverty in Dublin, *A Far Cry from Penny Apples*, has been far better received in some quarters because it 'doesn't let us down'.

Of course, the rose-tinted view of Ireland as a role-model nation – held not only by others looking in but by ourselves too – grossly exaggerates our importance in the world. It also conveniently overlooks the partition of the island and the very different cultures that prevail north and south of the border. There are many Irelands, just as there are many different facets of Irish identity, and to attempt to describe a collective form of 'Irishness' represents an exercise in gross generalisation.

So if this book is not painting a portrait of Irishness, what is it aiming to do? From inside this island, efforts have been made to document and analyse recent changes in Irish economy and society – some have been less than complimentary, and some have been highly critical, particularly from a left-wing viewpoint. But to date no one has attempted an overview of recent social and legal change in Ireland, and indeed in some cases stasis or lack of change, from an unashamedly liberal, activist campaigning perspective. That is what is attempted in this book.

THE POLITICS OF SOCIAL CHANGE

It is important to place this discussion of the ongoing social change in Ireland in its political context. Upon achieving independence in 1922, Irish society was deeply divided, not just along the faultlines of the Civil War, ie, opposition to, or support for the 1921 Anglo-Irish Treaty, but also along ideological lines of a different kind. There was a split in the new State between those of a conservative persuasion who favoured maintenance of the economic status quo but wished to see the Catholic Church play a stronger role in shaping society, and those who held either liberal or socialist views. There were liberals who favoured retention of the economic status quo, but who wished to see a more secular society develop, with an emphasis on the rights of the individual. There were other liberals, and socialists, many of whom emerged from the trade union movement, who believed in a secular society but wished to see changes in the economic system so that workers' rights would take priority over the interests of capital. After the Civil War it gradually became apparent, as successive conservative policies were adopted by the government and as the influence of the Catholic Church in the political life of the nation grew, that the forces of clerical conservatism had won out over those of liberalism, or indeed socialism. The tension between these conflicting ideologies is apparent in the 1937 Constitution, as discussed below.

These conflicting ideologies deserve clearer explanation. To speak of 'conservatism' in an Irish context refers to a view of society that is essentially fearful of change, that seeks to preserve class and gender divisions and that takes as the source for its morals the teachings of the Catholic Church. In terms of party politics, this type of outlook is most associated with the Fianna Fáil party, although many within Fine Gael would equally share these views. In this context, it is worth noting that Fianna Fáil is the largest and by far the most dominant political party in Ireland, having been in government for over fifty years out of the past eighty-two years since the State was founded, in 1922

This form of conservatism may be contrasted with a more progressive, or forward-looking, political view put forward by those from a broadly liberal perspective. A 'liberal' in Ireland is someone who may be left-wing on economics – favouring State intervention, adequate public spending and public ownership of services like education and health – but who believes in greater individual freedom on social issues around sexuality, marriage, crisis pregnancy and rights of speech. Thus many Irish liberals are to be found in the Labour party because most socialists are also liberal on social issues. But, confusingly, some liberals may also be found within the Progressive Democrat party, currently in a coalition government as junior partner to Fianna Fáil, which holds a classically liberal (in a right-wing sense) view on economic policy, ie, *laissez-faire* economics, limited taxation, restricted public spending and the privatisation of traditionally State-run services.

Those of a liberal persuasion, whether on the left or right economically, by definition stand for a more secular Ireland: for the separation of Church and State, and for the curtailing of the Church's role in the provision of basic education, health and social services. Thus to speak of the 'liberalisation' of Irish society is, by definition, to speak of its secularisation. Over the years, there have been many liberal- and socialist-led campaigns to achieve greater secularisation in Ireland, but these have only recently begun to achieve any sort of visible success, such as the development of multidenominational schools, the legalisation of contraception, the decriminalisation of homosexuality and the introduction of divorce.

However, the tussle between the old and the new, the traditional approach and the reform movement, still goes on. Social changes on the ground provoke political change as the next generation comes of electoral age, and this in turn provokes change at higher levels. In the 1990s, rapid economic change was accompanied by rapid social change, putting pressure on politicians and legislators to recognise and accommodate these changes. Up until then, however, the forces of the religious conservatives held immense power – and they haven't gone away, you know, even now. Their influence is still very much in evidence: in the initiation of a referendum in 2002 to further restrict the law on abortion; in the backlash against the introduction of sex education programmes in schools; in the sacking of a teacher in an interdenominational school in 2002 after he took a more flexible approach to religious instruction than the school board would permit.

However, despite the continuing resistance from conservative groups and individuals, from the start of the 1990s it was clear that things were starting to change. In 1990, feminist lawyer Mary Robinson was elected the first woman President of Ireland in a hugely important victory. In a landmark legal ruling in the 1992 *X* case, the Supreme Court held that a pregnant, suicidal, fourteen-year-old rape victim could have an abortion as her right to life prevailed over that of her foetus; this ruling was undoubtedly influenced by the huge public outcry after the High Court had earlier refused the girl permission to seek an abortion. In 1992 also came the full legalisation of contraception; in 1993 the decriminalisation of homosexuality. In 1995 the people voted, albeit by a slim margin, to legalise divorce by amending the constitutional provisions on the family, thus breaking the traditional link between Catholic marriage and civil marriage.

In other ways too at that time the model of the perfect Catholic family came under attack. In the 1996 Sophia McColgan case, a father was given a custodial sentence for brutal sexual assaults on his children. Around the early 1990s, people began to speak more openly about child sexual abuse, especially in relation to the religious orders. In 1998 and 2000, legislation was passed prohibiting discrimination on a range of grounds, including sexuality and family status. In 2002, a referendum that would have overturned the precedent established by the *X* case – by ruling out suicide risk as a ground for abortion – was defeated in a major blow for the hitherto all-powerful anti-abortion movement.

So the tide does appear to have turned – even with the continued dominance of Fianna Fáil, who have been in government for fourteen of the last twenty years. These key events occurring throughout the 1990s and into the present decade symbolise significant shifts in thinking, both in matters of personal morality and in perceptions of the common good. They represent a definite movement towards a more liberal and a more secular society in which individuals may be freer to reach their true potential, no longer willing to live their lives under the radar of social stigma or Church disapproval.

THE IRISH LEGAL SYSTEM

The push for change is still far from over, however. While social changes and progressive movements have begun to generate political responses, the legal system has yet to catch up as it remains out of step with the times, and with the needs and concerns of Irish citizens in the twenty-first century. The response of legislators to social change can be maddeningly slow, often failing to go far enough to reflect the reality of life in Ireland today. The law can remain impervious, rooted in past certainties and resistant to shifting realities.

A review of the Irish legal system will assist in understanding the state we are in as a nation. The laws of a particular nation may never be universally supported among its citizens, but they do at least reflect the collective values of a society in a way that nothing else can. Where a country has a written Constitution, as Ireland does, that fundamental law of the land should represent the closest thing possible to a national consensus on social mores. This book will show that in Ireland this is simply not the case; rather that there is an often disturbing conflict between the provisions of our Constitution and life on the ground for the Irish citizen.

In order to understand the significance of the Constitution, it is necessary to review its place as the most important source of law within our legal system. Bunreacht na hÉireann, our national Constitution, is the fundamental law of the land and the primary source of Irish law – to which all other domestic law, both legislation and judges' decisions, must be subject. The only way to amend the Constitution is by popular referendum.

Aside from the Constitution, there are other important sources of law in our legal system: first, legislation – Acts or Statutes passed through both Houses of the Oireachtas, or national Parliament, ie, the Dáil (lower house) and the Seanad (upper house), and signed into law by the President; secondly, secondary or delegated legislation – that is, Orders or Statutory Instruments, passed by Ministers under authority given to them by the legislature or Oireachtas; and thirdly, judges' decisions, which in the Irish legal system form binding precedent to be followed by judges in other, similar, cases. Another important source of law on human rights is the European Convention on Human Rights, containing a bill of rights enforceable in Ireland through the European Convention on Human Rights Act 2003. Finally, EU law is also directly enforceable in Ireland and binding upon our legal system. Since Irish entry to what was then the European Economic Community in 1973, EC and EU law has had increasing importance, with the result that much of the legislation passed by the Oireachtas is now pursuant to EU mandate. Irish law on issues of gender equality, workers' rights, environmental protection and competition policy has been particularly influenced by EU directives and regulations. However, except in those areas where the EU has made law, the Constitution remains the primary source of law in the land.

Of all the outdated laws still on our statute books, it is the text of our Constitution, which was adopted in 1937, that most strongly represents the time lag between social change and legislative change. As will be demonstrated throughout this book, the personal rights guaranteed in the Constitution are products of another time and of a particular brand of Catholic Church-inspired morality.

The present Constitution contains fifty Articles, most of which relate to the functioning of the State apparatus – matters such as the structure of the Dáil, voting age and the national flag. There have been a total of twenty-two successful amendments to the Constitution as a whole since 1937, but the text has otherwise had enduring effect. It is worth pointing out here that the original text of Bunreacht na hÉireann was written primarily by Éamon de Valera, then leader of Fianna Fáil and of the Irish government of the time, with considerable input from John Charles McQuaid, Roman Catholic Archbishop of Ireland.

Within the text of the Constitution, importantly, there is also a bill of rights, Articles 40–44, which more than any other part of the document reflects the mores and aspirations of the society of that time (for full text of these Articles, see Appendix). Throughout this book, reference will be made to relevant provisions of the bill of rights, thus it is useful at this stage to examine the ideology behind these rights Articles.

ARTICLES 40–44: THE CONSTITUTIONAL BILL OF RIGHTS

Articles 40–44 of the Constitution guarantee certain personal rights which are enforceable by the people of Ireland through the courts. Where an individual believes that her constitutional rights are being violated, she may take legal action against the violator and obtain a legal remedy, such as damages, if she can prove the violation. However, only a limited set of rights is guaranteed in Articles 40–44. These are mostly the traditional civil-political rights associated with a neo-liberal political ideology, that is, rights which are really more like freedoms for the individual, with which the State cannot interfere, but which impose no positive obligation upon the State nor require any significant spending of State resources. Thus, the rights to liberty (Article 40.4), privacy in one's home (Article 40.5), the freedom of expression (Article 40.6.1.i), the freedom of assembly (Article 40.6.1.ii), the freedom to own private property (Article 43) and the freedom of religion (Article 44), among others, are protected.

There is, however, another type of rights recognised in international human rights law and usually associated with socialist or communitarian ideology. These are known as 'social and economic rights'; to guarantee them would impose a positive financial burden upon the State. They include the right to healthcare, to education, to housing, to a job and to social benefits. But apart from the right to education (which is guaranteed in Article 42 of the Constitution), these rights are not guaranteed in the Irish Constitution.

Reference to this type of right is relegated to Article 45, which is not part of the bill of rights *per se*, but simply tagged onto the end as a concession to a socialist, or social democratic, view of society. This Article is entitled 'Directive Principles of Social Policy', and is supposed to act as guidance to the legislature, but does not allow citizens to enforce the Principles through the courts. Article 45 expresses a commitment to ensuring that:

> ... the ownership and control of the material resources of the community may be so distributed amongst private individuals and the various classes as best to subserve the common good.

This noble phrase has been largely ignored. No court has directly sought to hold the State to its pledge to 'safeguard with especial care the economic interests of the weaker sections of the community' nor to 'protect the public against unjust exploitation'.

Articles 40–44, the enforceable rights provisions, are thus based upon a different set of values from those underlying Article 45. The rights provisions are strongly influenced by liberal-democratic values, emphasising the autonomy of the individual and ensuring the protection of classic civil and political freedoms, like freedom of conscience or religion (Article 44.2).

However, the influence of communitarian values is strongly evident in Articles other than Article 45. Similar values are also identifiable in the wording of Articles 41 and 42, which, unlike Article 45, do contain enforceable rights. Article 41 bestows group rights upon the 'Family' as 'the natural primary and fundamental unit group of Society', while Article 42 guarantees the right to education, clearly a socio-economic right, the enforcement of which requires significant State expenditure. However, the communitarian values informing these Articles, unlike Article 45, are discernibly derived from a conservative theocratic ideology rather than from a socialist tradition, since their effect is to bestow rights only upon the patriarchal and marital Family (Article 41), not upon any other model of family; and to recognise this narrowly defined Family as the 'primary and natural educator of the child' (Article 42). Rights are not bestowed on any social group, other than the 'Family', to the same extent.

Thus, the fundamental rights Articles of the Constitution have their genesis in an uneasy blend of Catholic social teaching and a late nineteenth-century liberal philosophy. The conflict between these ideologies has never been fully resolved. As leading constitutional lawyer Gerard Quinn writes, 'Our Constitution pays homage to the ideology of theocracy as well as to the ideology of liberal-democracy.' He asserts that while the ideological tensions between these competing belief systems were only implicit in the past, they are coming increasingly to light as 'the economic conditions come into existence that make liberal-democracy a credible ideology in this country ... as a market society comes to maturity'.[6]

Theocratic principles have, in short, become marginalised due to increased economic prosperity and greater acceptance of a market-generated philosophy of individualism, ie, capitalism. It is therefore true that social changes generated largely by economic prosperity have meant greater emphasis on the rights of the individual, yet the text of the Constitution remains defined by the values of the 1930s, and conflict persists between the rights and freedoms of the individual and of the community.

In this book it is argued that, at present, despite the influence of neo-liberal ideology within the text, and despite increased prosperity, the balance of rights remains weighted against the exercise of individual liberties and in favour of a very narrowly moralistic view as to what represents the common good. Overall, it is argued, the legacy of theocracy persists and a conservative morality and political outlook continue to hold immense power in Irish society. How liberals, feminists, socialists and progressives generally can challenge that outlook is the central question.

NOTES FOR CHAPTER ONE

1.   'Ireland' is used throughout to describe the State of Ireland, rather than the whole island.
2.   Cahill, Thomas, *How the Irish Saved Civilization: The Untold Story of Ireland's Heroic Role from the Fall of Rome to the Rise of Medieval Europe.* (New York: Doubleday, 1995.)
3.   The A.T. Kearney/*Foreign Policy* Globalisation Index. (See www.foreignpolicy.com)
4.   O'Toole, Fintan, *After the Ball*, p.17. (Dublin: New Island, 2003.)
5.   *Monitoring Poverty Trends in Ireland: Results from the 2001 Living in Ireland Survey.* (ESRI, 2003.)
6.   Quinn, G., 'The Nature and Significance of Critical Legal Studies', in *Irish Law Times* 282 (1989).

CHAPTER 2
Church and State

THE ENDURING INFLUENCE OF THE CATHOLIC CHURCH

In order to understand the make-up of Irish society today, it is necessary to understand the enduring influence of the Roman Catholic religion. The Catholic Church has enjoyed a long history in Ireland, where it has wielded considerable power for centuries. In the late 1800s and early 1900s, the drastic restrictions imposed upon the rights of Catholics by the British government through the Catholic Relief Acts merely served to strengthen the Church's position in society, and the will of the people to practise their chosen faith. Catholicism thus became the religion of social and political defiance, of nationhood and patriotic identity – a heady cocktail indeed.

Catholic Emancipation was formally secured in 1829. Since then, the Church has amassed significant power in Irish society. Although this was especially notable after Independence in 1922, the Church was placed in a powerful position much earlier, with the passing of the Charitable Bequests Act, 1844, for example, recognising it alongside the established Church (the Church of Ireland). This granted the Catholic Church the power to have ownership and control of many schools, hospitals and social services across Ireland, confirming its role as a social services provider in the absence of a national government.

Post-1922, in the formative years of what became the Republic, the Church moved into an alignment with those in power in the new Free State, and with successive governments, making its influence felt in every sphere of public life. As academic Maura Adshead has written, 'The Irish State, from the beginning, was ostentatiously Catholic.'[1] The power of the Church reached its peak during Éamon de Valera's first term of office as head of the Irish government (1932–1948), when he famously consulted Catholic Archbishop John Charles McQuaid for help in drafting the 1937 Constitution. The Archbishop's input into the wording of the fundamental rights Articles is especially notable. Even though the reference to the 'special position' of the Catholic

Church as 'the guardian of the Faith professed by the great majority of the citizens', originally contained in Article 44, was removed in 1972 by referendum, the strong influence of Catholic doctrine and religious belief is still clearly evident throughout the text, the Preamble of which begins, 'In the name of the Most Holy Trinity, from Whom is all authority and to Whom, as our final end, all actions both of men and States must be referred', and which goes on to 'humbly' acknowledge 'all our obligations to our Divine Lord, Jesus Christ'.

For the past eighty years, then, the Catholic Church has enjoyed a unique position in the power structures of the State. It is no coincidence, in the land where the President, every member of the Council of State and all judges are required to take an oath beginning, 'In the presence of Almighty God ...' and where the national broadcaster still carries a denominational religious message (the *angelus*) at 6pm every evening, that when we speak of 'Church and State', Church always comes first.

In part, this is due to sheer force of numbers, as Catholicism has always been the religion of the vast majority of the population. Even now, most recent Census figures from 2002 indicate that 88% of the population still identifies as Roman Catholic (although this represents a significant drop from almost 92% in 1991). That means that out of a total population of just over 3.9 million people, almost 3.5 million belong to one religion. The vast majority of the remaining 12% is drawn from the Church of Ireland or other Protestant Churches. Only 0.04% of the population (139,792 people) describe themselves as having no religion, or as being agnostic or atheist. A mere 590 people categorise themselves as 'lapsed Roman Catholic'.

Apart from its numerical strength, the Catholic Church has also maintained significant power in Ireland through its substitution for the State in the provision of social services, particularly in education, health and welfare. The importance in Ireland of the 'third sector', or community and voluntary sector, in delivering social services usually provided by the State in other systems is well known. The Community and Voluntary Pillar is even regarded as one of the Social Partners during national pay and partnership negotiations. The Catholic Church has long had a key role in providing such services, in lieu of the State, a fact acknowledged in the Government's *White Paper*, published in 2000:

> Voluntary activity, especially by religious orders and their concern with charity and the poor, played a major role in providing supplementary welfare provision. The church-based education system – at primary and secondary level – and voluntary hospitals, predate the foundation of the State. The primary role of church-based voluntary organisations and services provided by religious orders in meeting education and social welfare needs continued after the foundation of the State.[2]

As the *White Paper* points out, the roots of the voluntary sector in Ireland today can be traced back to the Church-based philanthropic organisations of the eighteenth and nineteenth centuries, such as the St Vincent de Paul Society, set up in Ireland over 150 years ago. The State gradually began to take on a wider role in funding voluntary activity after the 1950s, notably with the enactment of the Health Act 1953, and it is increasingly filling the gaps that have appeared in voluntary service provision due to the decline in religious vocations. Nonetheless, religious groups continue to play a strong role in service provision throughout the voluntary sector. A 1993 study in the Eastern Health Board area around Dublin found that 57% of voluntary groups displayed multiple forms of religious involvement.

In the areas of education and health, in particular, the institutional Church continues to have great input, with both control by the Church and indirect subsidy of the Church by the State built into the structures of our education and health systems. In welfare provision, too, through its lay organisation the St Vincent de Paul Society, the Church continues to act as a sort of 'shadow welfare State'. The Catholic bishops also continue to wield huge power within Irish society, despite scandals over extensive sexual abuse of children in the care of Catholic religious orders until recent times, and despite grave public concern over the way in which the Church attempted to deal with that abuse and to protect those alleged abusers within its ranks.

It is obvious that the powerful influence of Catholicism continues to this day, albeit not to the same extent as before. To those who claim, in despairing tones, that our society has become 'Godless' as a result of the decline in religious vocations, the answer may be that it is simply the nature of the Church's role that is changing – changing, rather than actually reducing. Whether or not we are aware of it, the Church continues to exert an influence on the everyday lives of all Irish citizens.

There is a further problem with the dominance of the Roman Catholic Church in Ireland. Although one could be forgiven for thinking of Ireland as a 'one-faith State', there are, of course, many other religions actively organised in the country, several of which have increased their numbers in the last ten years, according to the 2002 Census figures. The Church of Ireland, for example, has gained 26,400 new members; the Methodist Church more than 5,000, doubling its membership; Muslim numbers have risen from 3,900 in the 1991 Census to 19,000 in 2002; and the Orthodox community has grown remarkably, from 400 to 10,400. All religions organised in the State may avail of the guarantee of religious freedom contained in Article 44, allowing them to manage their own affairs, to own, acquire and administer property, and even to found and run schools. So far so good, at least in terms of apparently recognising all religions equally. But the sheer size of the Catholic majority means that other religions have only minimal influence by comparison. There is even a hint of a theological position particular to Catholicism in the wording of Article 44.1, which provides that 'the State acknowledges that the homage of public worship is due to Almighty God. It shall hold His Name in reverence, and shall respect and honour religion.'

Religious practice is a comfort and a necessity to a huge number of people, regardless of their beliefs, and they all have the right to practise their chosen religion. The nub of the problem with the role of religion in the Constitution, however, is this: that the State continues to 'respect and honour' the Catholic religion, above others, to an unacceptable degree, allowing one ethos to have a disproportionate influence on civil matters. In today's pluralist Ireland, a multicultural society with an increasingly secular population that is growing ever more disillusioned with revelations about abuses of power perpetrated by those in the institutional Catholic Church over the years, this is quite simply an antiquated and unsustainable state of affairs.

RELIGION AND EDUCATION

The continuing power of the Catholic Church is nowhere more readily observed than in the basic structures of the Irish education system. The National School system was founded in Ireland by the English government in 1831, and it was originally intended that the schools would be multidenominational, with religious instruction to take place separately. However, the main Churches did not support this, and the system very quickly became denominational, with each organised religion given the freedom to establish and manage primary schools under its own patronage, to be attended by members of its own faith. The right to education is guaranteed in Article 42, which emphasises the central role of the family in educating the child – meaning that families may educate children at home. It also protects the right of parents to send their children to a school of a particular religion; Article 42.3.1 protects parents' right not to send children to State schools 'in violation of their conscience and lawful preference'. And Article 42.4 goes on to assert that:

> The State shall provide for free primary education and shall endeavour to supplement and give reasonable aid to private and corporate educational initiative, and, when the public good requires it, provide other educational

facilities or institutions with due regard, however, for the rights of parents, especially in the matter of religious and moral formation.

The emphasis throughout these provisions is on the need to ensure that the child is educated within the faith of her parents. Nowhere in this Article, nor in Article 41 dealing with the family, is it recognised that the child should have the right not only to receive an education but also to freedom of belief as an individual.

Perhaps unsurprisingly given the wording of the Constitution and the historical development of primary schools, to this day the very structure of the Irish primary education system remains based on religious denomination, and support for this denominational structure may be found in constitutional law. This may sound contradictory, given that Article 44.2.2 of the Constitution states that 'The State guarantees not to endow any religion', but the implicit support derives from Article 44.2.4, which provides further that:

Legislation providing State aid for schools shall not discriminate between schools under the management of different religious denominations, nor be such as to affect prejudicially the right of any child to attend a school receiving public money without attending religious instruction at that school.

The practical effect of Article 44 has been that every religious denomination has the constitutional right to establish primary schools, and to ensure that a particular religious programme is followed in those schools. In total, excluding special schools, there are 3,156 national schools in Ireland, the vast majority of which (2,919, or 92%) are Roman Catholic. There is also a network of 184 Church of Ireland schools, and a number of other minority religion schools, including one Jewish and one Methodist school, and two Muslim schools. There are thirty-one multidenominational schools and six interdenominational schools. Because the vast bulk of schools nationally are under Catholic control (ie, over 90%), many parents of minority religions, or of no religion, may have no choice but to send their child to a Catholic school, since there is often no other school available within a wide radius.

Most of the teacher-training schools are also Catholic-run; the Church of Ireland College of Education in Dublin describes its own main function as providing a supply of teachers for primary schools under the management of the Church of Ireland or other Protestant denominations. Thus religion permeates the entire primary school structure, even in terms of teacher-training.

Ownership of schools

Although major reforms to the education system were introduced in the Education Act, 1998, the Act preserves the system of 'patronage', so that schools are still obliged to uphold the religious ethos of their patron; in most cases the local bishop. The vast majority of schools are also privately owned by the different Churches, but the State generally funds and supervises the system of education overall. Out of a total of 3,156, less than 120 schools are under sole State ownership.

The State pays the bulk of the building and running costs in national schools, and ongoing local contribution is made towards the running costs. In 1999 changes were introduced to the way the building costs of new schools are paid by the State. For new national schools, the State pays the full cost of the site, although the patron still has the choice of funding the site cost. If the State does pay, then the State owns the school building and leases it to the patron under a lease or a deed of trust; this arrangement does not change the identity or status of the patron. If the patron pays, however, the patron owns the school building.

In effect, this means that national schools are now almost all privately owned – in general by the relevant Church authorities. In the case of Catholic schools, the owners are usually the diocesan trustees; the same is true for Church of Ireland schools. Other denominational schools usually have a board of trustees nominated by the Church authorities. Multidenominational schools are usually owned by a limited company or a board of trustees, which is identified as the patron. About thirty newly established Gaelscoileanna (Irish-language schools) are vested in the Minister for Education and Science. These schools may be denominational and come under the same patronage as Catholic schools, but can opt to be under the patronage of Foras Pátrúnachta na Scoileanna Lán Ghaeilge, a limited company set up for the purpose.

The Education Act 1998, which, as explained above, gives a statutory basis to the role of the 'patron', also sets out the rules for determining the identity of the patron. A register of patrons is kept by the Department of Education and Science, so it is possible for any member of the public to check the identity of the patron of any national school. In general, the patron of a school is a representative of the owners. In practice, the Catholic Church and Church of Ireland bishops are the patrons of the schools within their dioceses, with the parish priest usually carrying out the patron's functions on behalf of the bishop. The patron has immense power within the school; most importantly, the patron appoints the statutory board of management and has the power to remove it. After much controversy over the structure of the board, at primary level it now comprises the principal and a teachers' representative, two parents, two community representatives and two nominees of the patron.

Despite the fact that the vast majority of primary schools are thus privately owned and managed by different Churches, they are all referred to, under a somewhat misleading common title, as 'national schools'. In reality, the distinction between public and private education is somewhat blurred. The education system generally could most accurately be described as 'semi-public', or 'State-aided' rather than fully public or fully State-run. There is also, of course, a further distinction between fee-paying (private) schools and non-fee-paying (public) schools, both at primary and secondary level. This distinction perpetuates a glaring inequity, a class divide within the education system, with approximately 25,000 students in private secondary schools paying day fees of €4,500 per annum, or more. Students from fee-paying schools tend to do better in State exams and have a greater chance of going on to third-level education. Some universities and colleges have introduced access programmes seeking to tackle the low numbers of students from disadvantaged backgrounds, but concerns remain about the apparent bias in the system.

The system of control and ownership of schools is no more clear-cut with regards to post-primary education. In 1967, Minister for Education Donogh O'Malley introduced the right to free post-primary education for every child. Until then, the bulk of secondary schools had been run by different Churches, and this has remained the case in practice. From the 1970s onwards, the Irish State has become more centrally involved in the provision of secondary education, and this is reflected in the establishment of Comprehensive and Community schools, which supplement the pre-existing system of voluntary secondary schools. The State also established vocational schools. However – and again confusingly – even comprehensive or community schools are not in the legal ownership of the State, instead being vested in Trustees under Trust Deeds. In fact, these State schools are also mainly denominational, and each one has a chaplain who teaches religious instruction and who receives a salary from the State in common with other teachers.

Religious instruction and the National Curriculum

The State provides a national curriculum to ensure that children receive 'a certain minimum education, moral, intellectual and social' (Article 42.3.3). A revised primary curriculum, to be followed by all national schools, was introduced in 1999. However, because the ethos of Catholic schools requires that a 'religious spirit' should permeate the entire school day, Article 44.2.4 is arguably not being fully observed in respect of pupils of minority religions, or of no religion, who attend Catholic national schools. Even if these pupils withdraw from formal religious instruction, they are still receiving some incidental religious instruction during the school day, as well as being surrounded by religious iconography in the form of statues, crucifixes, or religious pictures. In Catholic schools, the iconography is particularly prevalent: 'Religious pictures and icons are displayed in the school halls and corridors and all classrooms have some religious symbol, such as a crucifix or statue. Many classrooms have an altar that is used for prayer services during the year.'[3]

Although not all denominational schools display this much religious iconography, the central problem remains that all national schools, even multidenominational schools, must have an ethos defined by religion or religious belief. This means that, astoundingly, even today it is simply not possible for a school to be set up on a non-religious basis. The 'Rules for National Schools', contained in the 1998 Act, still provide that religious instruction may take place within the school day, although parents may withdraw their child from religion classes. But Rule 68 provides that, 'Of all parts of the school curriculum religious instruction is by far the most important ... Religious instruction is, therefore, a fundamental part of the school course, and a religious spirit should inform and vivify the whole work of the school.' Schools do generally recognise the need to accommodate diversity, and do so in different ways. A recent INTO (Irish National Teachers' Organisation) report, *Teaching Religion in the Primary School*, found that in Catholic schools, 'Children of other faiths may be engaged in another activity during religious instruction, within the classroom', but noted that 'Catholic religion lessons are taught daily and short prayers may be said during the school day'. Thus it can be very isolating for a non-Catholic child in a Catholic national school to have to sit and study apart from her peers who are engaged in, for example, preparation for Holy Communion in the same classroom.

The position is also difficult for teachers, who must teach religious instruction according to the religion of the school, regardless of their own personal beliefs. The INTO has called for a change in the teaching of religion in denominational schools, arguing that the failure to accommodate children of minority religions in such schools may be incompatible with Ireland's obligations under Article 14 of the International Convention on the Rights of the Child, which provides that 'parties shall respect the right of the child to freedom of thought, conscience and religion'.

Ongoing problems with the Education System

The laws upon which the Irish education system is based thus facilitate the ongoing dominance of organised religion and allow the Catholic Church to retain overall control of the majority of schools. But whatever the dominant religion (and 88% of the population identify themselves as Catholic), there are undeniable problems with allowing any one religion to permeate the workplace or the classroom. When one belief system is given priority over all others, it creates an unhealthy imbalance; when this is allowed to occur in a pluralist society, it can create resentment and the isolation of certain sections of society. Catholic Church-owned and run schools do not promote an integrationist approach, and therein lies the problem. A few case histories illustrate the seriously negative impact that Catholic Church dominance of the system of education has had, both for individuals and for society.

It is now many decades since the sacking of Waterford teacher Frank Edwards in 1936 for his political beliefs – he had gone to fight against Franco and Fascism in the Spanish Civil War; but it is not so long since Eileen Flynn, a teacher in the Holy Faith Convent in New Ross, County Wexford, was sacked, in 1982. The grounds of Flynn's dismissal concerned her relationship with a married man with whom she lived and by whom she had become pregnant. Flynn challenged her dismissal as unfair, but, astonishingly, the High Court ruled, in 1985, that the school had acted legally because there were certain 'long-established and well-known aims and objectives as well as requirements' that teachers in religious schools had to abide by; Judge Costello said Ms Flynn's conduct amounted to 'a rejection of the norms of behaviour and the ideals which the school was endeavouring to instil in' its pupils. In short, the decision established that a teacher whose private 'lifestyle' does not conform to the ethos of a Catholic school can legally be dismissed by the school, regardless of how well she has performed her duties as a teacher.[4]

Even more recently, in 2002, Tomás O'Dulaing, then principal of the Dunboyne Gaelscoil in County Meath, was dismissed over a dispute regarding religious instruction during the school day and the difficulty of accommodating a child of minority religion in a school with an 'interdenominational' ethos. Under such an ethos, teachers are expected to teach two different religious doctrines (those of the Roman Catholic Church and of the Church of Ireland) as if both were Truths – despite the obvious difficulty for teachers that in some important aspects, such as the theory of Transubstantiation, the two doctrines diverge fundamentally. O'Dulaing's fair-minded attempt to accommodate religious difference by having religious instruction for those Catholic children preparing for Holy Communion take place outside school hours was not backed by the school patron, and he was dismissed from his position. Although he received the backing of the majority of parents and there was a huge public outcry, O'Dulaing was not reinstated. (He later withdrew his unfair dismissal claim having obtained a position as principal in a different school.) Religious instruction in two different faiths, to the same group of children, by the same teacher, continues to take place during school hours in so-called 'interdenominational' schools.

Apart from the difficulties it imposes upon teachers, the other consequences of religious influence in schooling are many and varied. For instance, there have been numerous practical difficulties with implementing the State-initiated 'Stay Safe' programme, designed to inform children in primary schools about risks to their personal safety, such as sexual abuse and 'stranger danger'. Objections were raised to the programme on the grounds that children might feel obliged to report on their parents. Even greater difficulties have arisen with establishing the Relationships and Sexuality Education (RSE) programme in schools – the first attempt to institute sex education in Irish schools. Again, it has been opposed by many of those who are really in control of State-funded schools. As UCD sociologist Tom Inglis showed, attempts to develop an effective sexuality education programme in Ireland have been hampered by the Catholic Church's monopoly on morality.[5] As recently as autumn 2003 an attack was launched by ex-Taoiseach John Bruton TD, of Fine Gael, on a series of Irish Family Planning Association (IFPA) sex education booklets aimed at teenagers. These booklets, funded by the health boards with the aim of distribution through schools, were attacked as being too liberal because they presented the facts about sex in a non-judgmental way.

When she was Minister for Education between 1992 and 1997, the Labour party's Niamh Breathnach attempted to reduce the control of religious denominations over the education system through legislative reform of the composition of boards of management of schools. However, her moves towards a more secular system were strongly resisted by what Andy Pollak, religious affairs correspondent of *The Irish Times*, described at the time as an 'unprecedented alliance' of the main Christian Churches together with the Muslim community. Since they won concessions from the Minister over the system of school management, religious denominations have gone on to win further political successes. After extensive lobbying by religious bodies, the Employment Equality Act 1998 – despite generally outlawing discrimination on grounds of religion – contains a provision (section 37) that allows employees to be discriminated against in religious, educational or medical institutions, where 'it is reasonable to do so in order to maintain the religious ethos of the institution'. This provision was widely condemned by trade unions and civil liberties groups. Its effect, of course, is to retain the principle established in the *Eileen Flynn* case, so that teachers can still be legally dismissed where their private lifestyle conflicts with the religious ethos of the school. So much for equality legislation.

This is not the only provision in the equality legislation that preserves discriminatory rules. Under section 7(3) of the Equal Status Act 2000, primary and post-primary schools are also allowed to discriminate, by giving preference in admissions to children of a particular denomination, or by refusing to admit a child where such refusal is essential in order to maintain the ethos of the school. These provisions essentially copperfasten the existing sectarian basis of the education system, permitting schools to continue to choose whom they enrol on the basis of religious affiliation – not what one would expect of an education system in a democratic republic, but continuing the tradition of segregated education with which we have all grown up.

These issues represent only examples highlighting the deep-rooted problems remaining within the education system due to ongoing control by the Churches. Although the managerial system was modified under the 1998 Act to allow non-religious control of primary schooling, the school patron system remains in place. Any organisation or individual can be nominated as patron for a school, but the idea that the patron must, of necessity, be a religious leader is so ingrained that letters from the Department of Education to those elected as patrons of multidenominational schools can arrive addressed to 'Bishop so-and-so', because in 95% of national schools the patron is the local bishop. A second problem is that the 'Rules for National Schools', referred to above, still prevail as governing the conduct of the school day. The practical application of Rule 68, emphasising the central role of religious instruction in the curriculum, will in many cases cause some conflict with the provision in Article 44 that parents should not be obliged to have their children receive religious instruction with which they do not agree. Growing numbers of people who hold no religion means that increasing numbers of parents will be compelled to send their children to schools which uphold a religious ethos that conflicts with their own beliefs.

Where is the space in our system for the dissenter, for the non-believer? Where in rural Ireland is the recognition of children of minority religion, or of no religion? (Bearing in mind, of course, that 'minority religion' in the Irish context simply means every religion, except Catholicism.) It is clear that radical review of the education system is required. The current system is unfair, discriminatory and indeed cruel to children of minority beliefs, or of no religious faith who have to attend a school of a particular religion, where that religion infuses the entire school day and where religious instruction is an integral part of the curriculum. It is time to assert the rights of our children. In a system where out of over 3,000 schools less than forty are multi- or interdenominational, there are clearly many children and teenagers whose education does not respect their views, or the views of their parents.

Attempts at change

Generally speaking, the last two decades have seen a gradual but growing resistance to the domination of and influence over the State apparatus by the Catholic Church. Many proactive attempts have been made over the years to challenge the structural power of the Church and to encourage a more secular approach in some key social areas, in order to reflect the increasing diversity of Irish society. A humanist group, the forerunner of the present Irish Humanist Association (IHA), was established in the late 1960s, and in 1987 some of those involved in that group set up the Campaign to Separate Church and State, with the aim of seeking separation of the religious and the civil in the critical spheres of education, health and welfare. This group attempted to achieve its aims through a combination of political lobbying and legal action, and its members became active in a range of successful campaigns, notably the campaign to legalise contraception.

In 1996, however, the Campaign received a blow when it lost a High Court action against the State. It had challenged the practice whereby the State paid the salaries of school chaplains in Comprehensive and Community schools, on the basis that it was in conflict with Article 44.2.2 of the Constitution, which provides that 'the State guarantees not to endow any religion'. An appeal to the Supreme Court was dismissed in 1998 on the grounds that the aim of the Article was to prohibit the permanent vesting by the State of property or income in a religion, but not to prohibit State payment of money to a denominational school for education purposes.[6] Current and future campaigns by those involved in the Humanist Association centre on the provision of alternative humanist ceremonies around life events like birth, marriage and death.

Recently a member of the Irish Humanist Association, Brendan Sheeran, took a case to the Equality Tribunal complaining that the ringing of the *angelus* bells in a building run by the State's Office of Public Works (OPW), namely, the chapel at Dublin Castle, was an inappropriate use of public property. However, on 18 February 2004 the Tribunal ruled that the OPW was entitled to ring the bell, since this was part of the maintenance of the building's traditions. It also found that the State is 'not obliged to adopt a secularist approach' to matters of religion, but under Article 44 is required 'to respect and honour religion' (*Sheeran v. OPW*, DEC – S2004/015).

The multidenominational group Educate Together has also been seeking reforms of the schooling system. Set up twenty-seven years ago, it now operates thirty-one schools nationally, with several more in the pipeline, providing an alternative to a school ethos defined in religious terms. Educate Together schools operate under a charter that obliges them to ensure that all children have equal access to education, irrespective of their social, cultural or religious background. This ethos guarantees that the individual identity of each child is equally respected in all aspects of school life. Recently the organisation has sought changes in State policy to allow for the establishment of more multidenominational schools, and ultimately for State support for the development of a national network of State-owned schools which are legally obliged to positively acknowledge the religious, or non-religious identity of all citizens. This campaign actively continues.

It is very difficult to establish new schools without the support of a particular Church, as Educate Together has found. Parents who wish to have their children educated in a way that is not compatible with local schools must first seek out other local families with similar views, organise a local management body, source suitable temporary accom-modation, either create a patron body or apply to a patron body for patronage, and then apply to the Department of Education for recogni-tion. Until the school has been open for a probationary period it will not qualify for the Department's building aid programme, with the result that many schools – fifteen out of the total of thirty-one run by Educate Together (according to their own criteria) – remain in tempo-rary and often highly unsatisfactory accommodation.

Yet despite the existence of all these motivated, articulate individu-als and groups seeking to challenge the present denominational struc-tures on which our education system is based, despite the changes in our society generally, and despite increasing disillusionment with organised religion, the religious-dominated education system remains deeply entrenched. The Church still owns vast tracts of land on which schools are situated, and highly valuable school buildings – main-tained and kept in good condition for decades at taxpayers' expense – remain in its portfolio.

In order to develop a truly pluralist and child-centred education system, radical reform is necessary. The ownership of all national school buildings should be vested in the State, which, after all, has paid for their upkeep and maintenance over the years; the requirement for a 'patron' should be abolished; and control of the management of schools should be left entirely to elected representatives of the parents, teachers and local community. No form of denominational religious instruction should take place during school hours; rather, all schools should be truly multidenominational, with a common programme of religious education introduced that would inform pupils about all world religions, and teach them to respect those of other religions, or of no religion. Such a model might take some time to achieve given the ingrained power of religious organisations in education, but we could look to other countries, like Sweden, where secular schooling is the norm, and where the freedom of thought and conscience of children and young adults is genuinely respected. The ethos of such a system is: 'In school, you teach, and in church, you preach, you shouldn't mix the two.' An eminently sensible approach.

RELIGION AND HEALTH

The Irish health system is the subject of heated debate and frustrated criticism on an ongoing basis. Ministers for Health routinely battle with the twin demands of a growing population and subsequent increasing pressure on the system, and the realities of cutbacks and budgetary constraints. So why are badly needed changes not being made?

In terms of structuring, the health system remains unjustifiably fragmented, as the Brennan Commission report on the health service (2003) found, with sixty-five different agencies currently managing the health services on a day-to-day basis, yet no 'head office' acting in a unifying, supervisory role. The Brennan Commission recommended the development of a national health strategy, and the appointment of a national chief executive of the health service. More recently, the Hanly Report (also published 2003), with its recommendations for a more centralised approach to specialist hospitals and the inevitable implications for local hospitals around the country, has been particularly contentious.

However, that some kind of revised approach to healthcare is necessary seems obvious. Most importantly, there are grave inequities in the two-tier system, where those who have private health insurance have access to private facilities in hospitals, while public patients often languish for years awaiting treatment through the medical card system. Apart from this significant inequity, there is also the ongoing problem of religious dominance of healthcare. Like education, healthcare in Ireland has traditionally been controlled and run by the Catholic Church. This has had a huge impact both on the way the health service is structured and on the way individual hospitals are run. The fact that any sort of national direction has been lacking from our health system until now may well be a legacy of the handing over of control for hospitals and nursing homes to a myriad of religious orders, each of which brought different management structures to bear. What each had in common was the Catholic ethical code, and this in turn influenced, and limited, the types of service made available to patients.

This has been true for a very long time. The most famous, or notorious, example is, of course, the Church's role in cutting down Minister for Health Noel Browne's proposed healthcare scheme, the Mother and Child Scheme, in 1949. The letter sent to the Taoiseach by the Catholic Bishops opposing the scheme is breathtaking in its arrogant assumption of authority over the government:

> The [Catholic] Hierarchy cannot approve of any scheme which, in its general tendency, must foster undue control by the State in a sphere so delicate and so intimately concerned with morals as that which deals with gynaecology or obstetrics and with the relations between doctor and patient.[7]

The success of the Church in forcing the government to abandon a health programme that would have vastly improved the health of mothers and children caused Browne to write bitterly in his autobiography, *Against the Tide*, that 'The hierarchy had become the factual instrument of government on all important social and economic policies in the Republic. Our prospects for the preservation of an effective Cabinet and a badly needed health scheme were now changed utterly.' So as early as the 1940s, senior political figures were deeply concerned about the influence of the Catholic Church on the health system. Obviously an organisation primarily concerned with the health of the soul could not prescribe accurately and objectively for the health of the physical body, nor, for that matter, for the body politic.

One of the biggest problems arising from Church influence in medical matters was, as with the Mother and Child Scheme, the curtailing of medical procedures made available to patients. In particular, the Church's influence on dictating the kinds of reproductive health services available persists to this day, but happily not to the same extent as in the past; although this limiting of the Church's role has been very hard won, and there have been many casualties in the process.

The barbaric practice of symphysiotomy, for example, was apparently routinely carried out in some Irish maternity hospitals right into the 1980s for so-called ethical reasons. This procedure, performed during childbirth, involves sawing through the pelvis so that it opens like a hinge. Many of the women upon whom it was performed have suffered lifelong incontinence, difficulties in walking and other physical and psychological effects as a result. According to the support group Survivors of Symphysiotomy (SOS), very few of the women were consulted before the performance of the symphysiotomy, and none was asked for her consent.

The procedure, allegedly carried out for Catholic doctrinal reasons, was performed where otherwise a birth would have had to be by way of Caesarean section. The symphysiotomy procedure facilitated future vaginal births, avoiding repeat Caesareans – an unwelcome prospect that, it was feared, might induce women to resort to contraception, or sterilisation. Because women can deliver only a small number of children by way of Caesarean section, Survivors of Symphysiotomy claims that the procedure was viewed as preferable by some Catholic doctors because it enabled a woman to give birth an unlimited number of times. The attendant pain, discomfort and damage to the health of the women who underwent the operation were all overlooked by those ruling over the hospitals' all-powerful ethics committees. How this barbaric, and usually unnecessary practice could have persisted in Ireland until the early 1980s, when Caesarean section offered an infinitely better alternative for women's health, is a question that remains unanswered, since the Minister for Health has ruled out a public enquiry, despite ongoing lobbying by the support groups representing over 200 women affected by the procedure.

Other effects of Church influence in reproductive health services have been more persistent. Well into the 1990s, for example, male vasectomy operations were performed at only one hospital in Ireland – a hospital known for its Protestant ethos. Female sterilisation remains difficult to obtain, and abortion unavailable. Contraceptives have been fully legally available only in the last decade. Prenatal screening to detect foetal abnormalities is not available in Irish hospitals to the same extent as elsewhere in Europe, apparently in case detection of an abnormality might cause some women to consider termination of their pregnancy. In 2002, during the course of the Government's ill-conceived referendum aimed at rolling back the X case (see chapter 5), it was revealed that women were being forced to carry dead foetuses to term because some doctors were refusing to terminate pregnancies even when they knew that there existed a foetal abnormality inconsistent with live birth.

Ethics Committees still operate in many hospitals, and to this day many of them specifically refer to an underlying Catholic doctrine informing their policy decisions. For example, the website of the Mater Hospital, one of Dublin's largest public hospitals, states that:

> The Ethics Committee is a sub-committee established by the Board of Management to define and specify ethical policy for the hospital and to offer guidance on ethical questions and procedure. A code of ethics was formulated to which all members of the hospital must conform. The Code of Ethics recognises the special objectives of the Sisters of Mercy and it incorporates the "Ethical Code for Hospitals" published by the Archbishop of Dublin.[8]

Apparently there is no need even to point out that this refers to the Roman Catholic Archbishop of Dublin.

In addition to the insidious and often overt religious influence on the structures of and service delivery within the health system, religious influence is also highly visible in practical terms. Most hospitals continue to use religious iconography throughout their premises: pictures, crucifixes and statues. Most also employ religious nomenclature, with wards named in honour of individual saints. Religious control over those who are dying is particularly noteworthy, although there is only one reported case of a hospital employee refusing to take part in a religious ceremony for a dying patient. In the 1986 case of *Merriman v. St. James' Hospital*, a hospital orderly was dismissed because she had refused to carry a crucifix to a dying patient's bedside.[9] Unlike the *Eileen Flynn* case, however, the employee in this instance won. Her dismissal was held to be discriminatory on the grounds of religious belief, and she was re-engaged on the understanding that she would not be asked to take part in religious ceremonies again.

Extensive reform of the healthcare system in Ireland in accordance with the Brennan and Hanly reports is promised. It is also to be hoped that the grossly inequitable two-tier structure may be replaced with a system of universal health insurance. But whatever structural changes are carried out in the future, the ongoing influence of the Catholic Church on the provision of health services ought to be reviewed at the same time. The serious impact of religious teaching and ethics codes upon the health of women, in particular, should not be allowed to endure any further. As vocations fall away the influence of the Church on the health system is gradually diminishing, but the issue must be properly addressed and an alternative, secular structure carefully thought out and implemented.

RELIGION AND WELFARE

Apart from the ongoing question of religious influence within hospitals, much attention has focused of late on one very specific area of religious welfare provision: the homes and institutions run on behalf of the State by religious orders for the care of children.

Just as the Catholic Church assumed a dominant role in the provision of health and education services in the nineteenth century, so too at that time did it effectively take over control of juvenile justice institutions. Irish Catholic MPs at Westminster defeated a Bill for the Better Care and Reformation of Juvenile Offenders in 1856, 'on the basis that it did not sufficiently protect juvenile offenders from the activities of Protestant proselytising societies.'[10] This group of MPs demanded that any reform schools for juvenile offenders should be managed by people from the same religion as those offenders. As a result, in 1858 a new Reform Schools Bill was passed for Ireland, permitting religious control. From that date on, separate reformatory and industrial schools were opened and operated by the Catholic and Protestant Churches. By 1898 there were seventy-one such schools in Ireland: seventeen for Roman Catholic boys; forty-four for Roman Catholic girls; four for Protestant boys; and five for Protestant girls. There was one other, mixed industrial school – but that was mixed gender, not mixed religion.

The large numbers of children incarcerated in these institutions – more than in England, Wales, Scotland, or Northern Ireland – continued well into the twentieth century. This anomaly was due to the use of Irish industrial schools primarily to house destitute children, or children whose parents could not adequately care for them for whatever reason; children who had committed a criminal offence constituted just one-tenth of those incarcerated. The corrupting effect of poverty was recognised, as was the need to 'save the souls' of these children, particularly the girls. This was another unique feature of the Irish juvenile detention system: right up until 1969 there were always more girls detained in industrial schools than boys. Trinity College academic Eoin O'Sullivan writes that 'the production of docile females as the shock troops of a new respectable working class was integral to the mission of the Catholic female religious who operated the majority of these institutions.'

Many of these girls were also incarcerated in 'Magdalen laundries', institutions run by orders of nuns, set up to care for young women and girls who had 'gone astray' in some way and needed to be forced back into the fold. These institutions had originally been established in the eighteenth century as homes for prostitutes, but gradually they became used to house those girls and women who had had children while unmarried ('fallen women', as they were charmingly described), or who were regarded as 'wild' or uncontrollable, or who had intellectual or learning disabilities. Inmates of the institutions effectively became enslaved, often unable to leave, forced to work without pay in the laundries and subjected to brutal treatment and abuse from the nuns in charge.

Many girls and women died in the Magdalen laundries, and it has recently been revealed that not all of those who died were properly accounted for. When the remains of 133 women were being exhumed from the plot of a Magdalen laundry graveyard at Drumcondra, Dublin, in 1993, an additional twenty-two bodies were found. Death certificates existed for only seventy-five of the original 133 women; the Sisters of Our Lady of Charity has stated that it registered all of those who died in its care with the Department of Health. A campaign for an official enquiry into the deaths of these women continues.

In recent years public attention has focused on the unfortunate children who were incarcerated in this way, in industrial schools, Magdalen laundries and other institutions, as more and more revelations emerge about the extent to which they were abused, physically, emotionally and sexually, while in the care of the religious orders. Perhaps the most appalling aspect of the child abuse scandal is the negligence on the part of the State – having handed over responsibility for control of the institutions to religious orders, it failed to provide any sort of monitoring of the conditions in which the children were being kept.

However, as the full extent of abuse upon children resident in such institutions has been disclosed, there have been attempts by the State to make amends. First, in 1998 the Commission on Child Sexual Abuse (formerly the Laffoy Commission, now the Ryan Commission) was established, with an investigation committee and a confidential committee. The aims of the Ryan Commission are to provide victims of childhood abuse with a sympathetic forum to recount their experiences; to fully investigate all allegations of abuse, if the victim so wishes; and ultimately to publish an official, public report on its findings. Unfortunately, the work of the Commission soon became bogged down: over 1,800 applications were received – more than expected; and the original Chair, Judge Mary Laffoy, resigned in late 2003 citing lack of cooperation, delay in providing resources, and obstruction of her work by the Government. Taken together with ongoing legal challenges by the Christian Brothers religious order to the procedures of the Commission, even after the appointment of a new Chair, Judge Sean Ryan, it is now expected that the Ryan Commission will not be ready to publish its full report for several more years.

The Commission has no power to make any payments of compensation or redress to any individual who appears before it. Such a power was instead vested in a different and entirely separate body, the Residential Institutions Redress Board, which was established in 2002 with the role of making 'fair and reasonable' awards of money to those who were abused as children while resident in industrial schools, reformatories, or other institutions subject to State regulation or inspection. However, the deal done between the State and the Catholic Church as to who will end up paying for the redress has been subject to extensive criticism. It now appears that the State will end up footing the vast bulk of the bill, while the Church has got off exceedingly lightly.

The indemnity agreement made between former Minister for Education, Dr Michael Woods, in the dying days of the outgoing Fianna Fáil/Progressive Democrat coalition government in 2002 limits the religious orders' contribution to redress to a mere €127 million, leaving the State, ie, the taxpayer, to meet the rest of the costs. Given that over 2,500 victims of abuse have applied to the Redress Board, it now seems that the orders' contribution will be substantially less than half of the total amount that may be paid out to survivors of abuse, even though it was their members who actually inflicted the abuse upon the complainants. Prior to the indemnity agreement the Department of Finance had also recommended a 50:50 split of the costs between the religious orders and the State, but it is now estimated that the total cost of redress could be as high as €1 billion (out of which only €127 million would be paid by the orders) – which would leave a staggering bill for the State and the taxpayers.

In 2003, due to growing public concern, the Oireachtas Public Accounts Committee carried out an examination of the Church–State deal. It emerged that the first time the details of the indemnity were discussed by officials, including officials from the Attorney General's Office, was on 19 April 2002, just five days before the dissolution of the Dáil prior to the May 2002 election. Furthermore, it became clear that the Attorney General had not been represented at two key meetings between Government representatives and the religious orders in November 2001 and January 2002. These matters alone caused concern; but there is also ongoing controversy about how the orders' contribution will be paid. They have pledged to contribute around €40 million in cash, while the rest is to be paid in kind through the transfer of land and property to the State; the terms of ownership of at least some of the lands are disputed. This controversy, borne of the Government's willingness to negotiate with the Church in a unique manner, is likely to rumble on for some time.

CHURCH CONTROL OF CEREMONIES

Control by the Churches and religious denominations over the conducting of ceremonies and rituals, like weddings and funerals, has had far less serious consequences for the lives of individuals than the power wielded by the Catholic Church in other areas, particularly in the running of care institutions. Nonetheless, the role of the Church in such matters raises a serious question about individual choice. In a liberal, secular society, individual choice in key areas – how one wishes to marry; how one wishes one's child to be named; how one wishes to be commemorated on death – is an essential freedom. Other countries have sought to accommodate diverse beliefs in different ways, in Norway, for example, a 'civil confirmation' ceremony is offered by the State as an alternative to religious confirmation for children entering their teens. In Ireland, however, many people find that when it comes to such momentous events they must deal, at some stage, with the Catholic Church. The Church's control over wedding ceremonies had been enshrined in law until recently, but religious organisations have less formal control over the funeral ceremony. Although it is very rare in practice to have a non-religious funeral, the Humanist Association points out that this is a more straightforward arrangement than might be expected, since many countries have municipal graveyards in which a plot may simply be booked with an undertaker. The funeral ceremony can then be held in any venue, such as the undertaker's premises.

Marriage

Non-religious funerals are one thing, but marriage ceremonies are a different matter. Under present law, the legally recognised civil ceremony of marriage – as opposed to the religious ceremony, which is not legally binding – may only be carried out at a very limited number of civil registration offices around the country, or in churches as part of a church ceremony. When it comes to weddings, the Churches really win out. Under present law, all marriages solemnised in the State must be registered in the marriage register maintained by the Registrar-General (*an tArd-Chláraitheoir*). However, at present the register may only be signed by the parties to a civil ceremony of marriage in civil registration offices, of which there is only one in each county. (Local registrars who preside over civil registration ceremonies are appointed by the health boards.) The register may also be signed in a religious ceremony of marriage which incorporates the civil signing, and must be celebrated either through the 'rites and ceremonies of the Roman Catholic Church', or in a church or building licensed, certified or registered for the purpose of marriage. Churches of the Church of Ireland are licensed for marriages by the Bishops of the Church of Ireland, with the approval of the Minister for Health and Children. Presbyterian churches are certified by their Ministers and registered by the Registrar-General. Buildings used by other bodies (not Roman Catholic) as places of public religious worship and certified as such are registered by the Registrar-General for the purposes of marriage.

No venues other than these are generally permitted to conduct the signing of the civil register of marriage. Thus, most people conduct their religious and civil ceremonies on the same premises at the same time, so that out of over 16,000 marriages in 1996, only 928 took place in registry offices – a mere 5.7% of the total. However, albeit from a very low level, the share of civil marriages as a proportion of the total has increased. In 1970, there were only 121 civil marriages contracted in the State, 0.5% of the overall total. By 1980 this had risen to 1.8%, and it continues to rise, although figures are not available after 1996.

In recognition of this trend, extensive reform and modernisation of laws governing registration of marriage has been recommended by the Inter-Departmental Committee on Reform of Marriage Law, among others. The Civil Registration Act 2004 was introduced to reform the law on registration of births, marriages and deaths, and will radically alter the current procedures for solemnisation of marriage, doing away altogether with the need for a specific venue to be licensed. Churches will no longer have a monopoly on fancy wedding ceremonies. Instead, the Act provides that a prospective wife and husband must give three months' notice that they intend to marry (as they currently have to); they must attend together before the relevant registrar to sign a document declaring that there are no impediments to the marriage; and they can then take a marriage registration form to a venue of their choice, and sign it themselves at a ceremony conducted according to their own wishes. Once it is signed simultaneously by the marriage 'solemniser' and two witnesses, and is returned to the registrar within the required period, the marriage will be legally registered.

Initially the Act was warmly welcomed by the Irish Humanist Association, among others, as a vitally important step towards greater secularisation generally in Irish society. However, a final amendment was passed restricting the right to nominate 'solemnisers' to 'religious bodies' has been criticised by the IHA as ignoring the interests of Ireland's largest ethical minority – those of no religion. Unfortunately, the definition of 'religious body' is 'an organised group of people members of which meet regularly for common religious worship.' Does this mean that Satanists could nominate marriage solemnisers, but humanists could not?

IN REVIEW

This brief review demonstrates the negative and often malign influence that the Catholic Church has exerted until recently over our education, health and institutional childcare systems – and indeed continues to wield, albeit in a more subtle way. It demonstrates too how for many years the State effectively abandoned its responsibility to citizens and handed over control of the most vulnerable sections of our community to the Churches, and to one Church in particular. Even in less important areas, for example, control over rituals like wedding ceremonies and funerals, the Churches, and particularly the Catholic Church, clearly have retained significant power until recently. Despite welcome changes towards a more secular society, the persistent nature of Church power represents an ongoing challenge for those who wish to see more secular education, health and welfare systems developed in Ireland.

NOTES FOR CHAPTER TWO

1. Adshead, Maura in *The Encyclopaedia of Ireland*, p.172. (Dublin: Gill & Macmillan, 2003.)
2. *Supporting Voluntary Activity*, p.48. (Dublin: Government Publications, 2000.)
3. *Teaching Religion in the Primary School.* (INTO, 2004.)
4. *Flynn v. Power* [1985] ILRM 336.
5. Inglis, T., *Lessons in Irish Sexuality*. (Dublin: UCD Press, 1998.)
6. *Campaign to Separate Church and State Ltd v. Minister for Education* [1998] 3 IR 321.
7. Letter dated 5 April 1951, quoted in Whyte, J., *Church and State in Modern Ireland*, p.446. (Dublin: Gill & Macmillan, 1980.)
8. www.mater.ie
9. *Merriman v. St. James' Hospital*, in *The Irish Times*, 25 November 1986.
10. O'Sullivan, E., 'Juvenile Justice and the Regulation of the Poor' in Bacik & O'Connell (eds), *Crime and Poverty in Ireland.* (Dublin: Round Hall Ltd, 1998.)

CHAPTER 3
Family Change

THE 'IRISH FAMILY'

We are all familiar with the stereotypical 'Irish family': a martyred Mother who gives birth to a large brood of children and devotes her life to their care and well-being; a stern but kindly Father who goes out to work everyday and comes home tired but smiling, eagerly anticipating the hot dinner he knows is awaiting him, eager too to kiss the children goodnight as they troop obediently to their beds; Mass on Sundays; confession regularly; a drop of the hard stuff on special occasions; salt of the Earth.

Although this patronising 'de Valera family' description deliberately overstates the case, a romantic view of the quintessential family of yore does persist. In particular, our Constitution and our family laws, as shall be shown, are still based on the concept of the nuclear marital family: a unit comprising a mother, father and several children.

This concept is, however, greatly at odds with the reality of Irish family life, past or present. In fact, as Finola Kennedy has written in her landmark study of the Irish family, *Cottage to Crèche*[1], until 1980 marriage rates in Ireland were relatively low, and there were huge numbers of bachelors and spinsters. This pattern was due to the legacy of the Famine, whereby land was so scarce that only one child could inherit the smallholding in each family; the others had to emigrate, enter religious orders, or remain single. It was also due to economic conditions generally, as nobody got married unless they could afford to financially. Although fertility rates were high within marriage, and contraception unavailable until relatively recently, the Irish family model was never as uniform as the stereotype would have it. In his classic 1954 work, *The Vanishing Irish,* J.A. O'Brien[2] described Irish marriage patterns as the 'strange enigma of a race that believes passionately in family life and yet produces more old bachelors and more old maids than any race in the civilised world'.

Feminist academic Anne Byrne confirms that, 'Historically, Ireland has had an exceptionally high proportion of people who remained single.'[3] She points out that widely prevalent in Ireland, especially rural Ireland, throughout much of the twentieth century were the twin phenomena of 'postponed marriage' (the high proportion of those aged 25–34 who were single) and 'permanent celibacy' (the proportion of the never-married aged 45 years or older). These features of Irish life were clearly linked to the realities of land-ownership, in particular the 'stem family' system. This was the system whereby only one child from each family, usually the eldest son, would inherit the land, marry and produce the next generation – this was a widespread practice because so many smallholdings simply could not sustain more than one family. Under the more democratic 'joint family system' used in other societies, land could be held in common by larger numbers of siblings, but as this was not the prevalent land-ownership model here in Ireland, large numbers of non-inheriting children were consigned to permanent celibacy.

More sinister consequences of this family system have also been documented. According to a 1970 University of California study by Robert Kennedy, Census data shows that until 1950 female mortality was higher in Ireland than that of males. Between 1901 and 1910, the death rate for female children aged 10–14 years was 140% that of the male death rate for the same age group: a shockingly higher death rate for females, which, Kennedy suggests, was perhaps due to the level of harsh physical labour expected of girls, and less value being placed on the lives of girl children, who were therefore more likely to be neglected or become ill.[4]

Thus inheritance practices dictated marriage patterns, resulting in large numbers of single adults. How did they cope in rural Ireland? The bachelor drinking role was common among men; women usually moved out of the family home, leading to disproportionately high numbers of men in rural areas and women in urban centres. Life was grim for the large cohort of single rural women, whose lives have remained largely undocumented. No wonder that even in the 1940s, according to Anne Byrne, Ireland had 'one of the highest rates of female migration and emigration in the Western world'.[5] Those who could, or had to, leave the land either moved to the cities or emigrated, mostly to England or North America. As is well-known, Ireland's exceptionally high emigration rate at the time became a cause of great public concern, and ultimately helped to bring about change in family structures by the 1950s (see below).

For those who did manage to find a partner and settle down to live happily ever after, the truth of married life was often far from the romantic promises, and problems were compounded by the common belief that all things familial should be kept private, hidden behind closed doors. As a result, the myth of the happy family masked many real abuses, about which silence prevailed. These included silences about: women with crisis pregnancies who were sent abroad to England, or, right up until the 1970s, were placed in Magdalen laundries to 'hide their shame'; horrific levels of child sexual abuse, both within families and in institutions; domestic abuse; separation. Everyone knows of the 'Irish divorce' – married couples who lived in the same house for years, without speaking to one another, staying together for the sake of convention and fear of social opprobrium.

Following on from concern over emigration levels and despite continuing economic depression, by the 1950s public discourse had changed from actively supporting celibacy and postponing marriage to encouraging both higher rates of marriage and high fertility rates within marriage. Some years after de Valera's vision of model family life had been enshrined in the Constitution, that vision had become a reality. Research indicates that the generations which matured after the Second World War (1939–1945) began to marry at a greater rate and at a younger age, resulting in what is now seen as the typical Irish pattern of big families. By the mid-1970s, marriage rates had peaked at a level that has never been surpassed since, despite the growth in overall population over the last thirty years. In 1974, the peak year, a grand total of 22,833 marriages was recorded. From that year on, however, and particularly with economic recession in the 1980s, the pattern of early marriage and large numbers of children began to decline, and the number of 'singletons' in the population began to increase once more. Conversely, the 1990s saw a time of greater prosperity, and thus by the mid-1990s there was a slight rise in marriage rates, alongside an increase in the number of couples cohabiting without marrying and in the numbers of births taking place outside marriage. However, the figure of 20,047 marriages recorded in 2002, while it marked an increase from previous years, is still well below the sort of figures seen in the 1970s given the significant increase in population since then. Fertility levels have also fallen, from a birthrate of nearly twenty-two births per 1,000 population in 1970 to 15.5 births per 1,000 in 2002.

Thus, the Irish family has changed more over the years than we might perhaps think now, and has taken more complex forms over the past century than stereotypes, or the Constitution, would suggest. Many people, like the single rural women forced into emigration, were effectively excluded from membership of the ideal 'de Valera family'. Even for those who did grow up within large families that ostensibly conformed to the ideal model, the family was not always a happy place to be. Those who condemn current trends towards diversity in family forms and hark back nostalgically to the 'good old days' of strictly defined family life are simply deluding themselves.

The new forms of Family, or the poor relations

The 'de Valera' family model does reflect reality to the extent that, by comparison with other EU countries, Ireland has a relatively low rate of female participation in the workforce. Only 42% of our labour force is female, although women make up just over 51% of the overall population. To put it another way, according to 2003 Census figures, less than half of Irish women participate in the paid labour force, compared with over 70% of Irish men, which implies that many women continue to work, on an unpaid basis, in the home.

Whether this is as a result of a choice these women have made, or because they lack choices, is another matter. In Ireland, childcare facilities are notably poor compared to most other European countries. In fact, as the UN Committee on the Elimination of Discrimination Against Women has pointed out, the Irish State simply fails to provide sufficient support to families generally. Ireland continues to lag behind all other EU countries in maternity and parental leave provision; parental leave is unpaid; childcare provision is appallingly inadequate; and there is no statutory right to paternity leave. An Irish mother can take just eighteen weeks' paid leave on childbirth; a Danish mother about eighteen months, a French mother more than two years, a German mother three years. This means many women are forced to leave or postpone their careers because they need or want more time with their baby than the statutory eighteen weeks, or because they simply cannot afford childcare. Thus, cultural stereotypes of female carer and male breadwinner are reinforced, in theory and in formal ways, regardless of the opinions and preferences of Irish people.

On the other hand, although rates of female participation in employment are low, they are rising rapidly, and there are almost twice as many women at work today as there were ten years ago. Even five years ago, only 42% of Irish women were in the labour force, so there has been a significant increase in recent years. As a result, the house-husband – an unthinkable phenomenon fifty years ago – has become a reality in at least some Irish homes.

The other area of fundamental change is in marriage patterns – a shift largely occasioned by the changes described in work patterns. As women's independence has increased, so too have the choices available to them, and many are choosing to postpone marriage and children until later in life. As a result, the numbers of those cohabiting as 'common-law partners' have increased dramatically. In 1996, cohabiting couples made up almost 4% of all family units (31,300), but by 2002 Census figures show that this figure had more than doubled, to just over 8% (77,600). In 2002, one in five (20%) child-free couples in Ireland was cohabiting. Couples without children also constitute the type of family unit showing the fastest growth rate, up by 79% since 1981. By contrast, just over one-twentieth (5.5%) of all couples with children were cohabiting in 2002.

So what is happening to the family amidst these changes in employment and marriage patterns? While 47% of the adult population (classified as those over 15 years of age) are married, 43% are 'single' (this figure includes cohabitees), and just over 10% are widowed, separated or divorced. Divorce and remarriage rates have been increasing since the legalisation of divorce in 1995; the number of divorced persons has more than trebled in six years, increasing from 9,800 in the 1996 Census to 35,000 in the 2002 Census. The numbers of those who are either separated or divorced has risen from 87,800 in 1996 to 133,800 in 2002.

While the number of children living with cohabiting parents rather than married parents had increased from 23,000 in 1996 to 51,700 in 2002, overall the figures suggest that couples are more likely to marry when they have one or more children rather than any earlier. This is borne out by figures showing the age at which people marry – in 1996 (the last year for which figures on marriage age are available), the average age at first marriage for women was 28, while for men it was 30 years of age. Increasingly, however, even where parents marry subsequent to the birth of a child, children are being born to parents who are not married. The percentage of births outside marriage now (2002) stands at just over 31%, that is, almost one-third of births, compared with just over one-quarter (25.3%) in 1996.

These dramatic changes have been noted in many reports and by many commentators. As Fahey and Russell, authors of the leading 2001 ESRI study, *Family Formation in Ireland: Trends, Data Needs and Implications*, comment, 'The role of marriage in family formation is less dominant and clear-cut than it once was.' Similarly, in his introduction to Finola Kennedy's important book on the Irish family, Gary Becker describes family life here as having gone through a 'remarkable transformation' in the last decade. Most recently, a Government-sponsored report by Mary Daly, *Families and Family Life in Ireland* (February 2004), found that most people do not want the traditional nuclear family as a model for policy-makers, that the nuclear family itself is effectively a myth.

So the nuclear family is no longer widely accepted as the basis for policy-making; but there should be no misplaced nostalgia around its demise. Rather, the more liberated forms of family life now emerging should be celebrated, and the myth that change is negative challenged. Unusual among other commentators, social psychologist Michael O'Connell has presented a positive attitude to recent changes:

> ... the trend overall in Ireland is one where people feel less obliged to get married, are marrying later, no longer rigorously associate marriage and parenthood, or for that matter see marriage as a strict pre-condition for having a sex life. And they are less willing to simply endure a married relationship that no longer meets their expectations.[6]

Change in family forms can and should be viewed as positive because it has come about alongside a discernible shift in social attitudes in Ireland in the last decade, marked by greater tolerance of diversity generally. This shift has occurred for both internal and external reasons – the internal being largely economic, or related to land-ownership patterns, the external being changing trends internationally. The truly interesting feature of this shift in Ireland is how new it is – only a decade old, although its origins lie earlier; any divergence from the accepted model of family was still frowned upon until the late

1980s. Now, however, we are witnessing greater demand for and toler-ance of personal choice regarding life and lifestyle decisions. Individu-als no longer feel coerced into a prescribed social destiny, a change that should be welcomed as a step forward for Irish society.

THE FAMILY AND THE LAW

The Irish family in law is a paradoxical creature. 'Family' is granted a unique status in Article 41 of the Constitution as the basic unit upon which society is founded. The family therefore possesses an extraordinarily high level of constitutional recognition and protection; the language used is stronger than in any of the other fundamental rights Articles. This means that those who seek to assert their rights as a family through the courts have a much stronger basis for their case than anyone asserting an individual right under another constitutional Article.

On one reading, this is admirable. People should have the basic right to protection for their family life – after all, under Article 8 of the European Convention on Human Rights and Fundamental Freedoms, 'everyone has the right to respect for his private and family life'. How-ever, whereas the European Court of Human Rights recognises many different familial relationships as being worthy of respect – such as the relationship between a grandchild and his/her grandparents (*Vermeire v. Belgium*, 1991), or that between a natural father and his daughter (*Keegan v. Ireland*, 1994) – under the Irish Constitution protection extends to the family only when it is based upon marriage, that is, the traditional, heterosexual, nuclear, marital family, a model taken from the Catholic Church's teachings.

Within that traditional family model, Article 41 also recognises and seeks to promote a traditional, stereotypical role for women. Paragraph 2 of the Article provides that 'the State recognises that by her life within the home, woman gives to the State a support without which the common good cannot be achieved', and further notes that the State must 'endeavour to ensure that mothers shall not be obliged by economic necessity to engage in labour to the neglect of their duties in the home.' Thus, women's 'life within the home' is afforded constitutional protection, the wording of which falls just short of making it compulsory for women to spend their lives in the home. Fathers, by contrast, are not mentioned anywhere in the Constitution, except in the Preamble (apparently our 'Divine Lord' ... 'sustained our fathers through centuries of trial'). In the constitutional family model, only traditional roles for women and, by default, men, are given official recognition. No general legal protection is given to cohabiting heterosexual or gay couples, or to those who live alone, or to any other form of family unit that is not marriage-based.

Clearly a new legal framework is required that recognises the changing forms of family and accommodates those forms. Political lobby groups are attempting to bridge the gap between the constitutional model and the types of family in society today. A number of different NGOs have launched a new initiative to campaign for recognition for forms of family that do not fit the traditional model. In particular, One Family, a single parents' organisation (formerly known as Cherish), has recently called for fundamental reform of family policy to reflect changes in family structures, which reform to include amending the constitutional definition of family. Similarly, gay rights groups are lobbying for recognition for same-sex partnerships (see Chapter 6); and young and older people alike are rejecting traditional models of family life.

Yet the law of the land remains wedded to the marital family as the only officially recognised unit. To date, the huge changes that have occurred in family structures in this society have been largely ignored at an official level, although clearly apparent in official Census data. Where these changes are addressed publicly they are often expressed in a negative way, in comments bemoaning the lack of respect for marriage which new forms of family life may represent to an older, more conservative generation. For example, in an influential piece in *The Irish Times* in 1997, former Taoiseach Garret FitzGerald, writing about the change in family patterns evident from Census data at that time, commented that: 'a very disturbing picture indeed emerges ... the decline in, as well as postponement of, marriage; the large and accelerating increase in marriage breakdown ... and the huge increase in non-marital pregnancies involving births to teenage mothers.'[7]

Changing forms of family are seen as a threat to the traditional nuclear family, the breakdown of which is blamed for all sorts of ills in society. For example, in a recent collection of essays commenting on modern Irish society, editor Joe Mulholland writes of twenty-first-century Ireland that '... the social fabric has broken down. In the absence of old traditional values, customs and religious beliefs, there is a gaping void in which are pouring "*mé féinism*", irresponsibility, depression, loneliness, suicides.'[8]

The nostalgia informing these arguments is misplaced, based as it is on myth and what criminologist Geoff Pearson has described as 'moral do-doism' – the refusal to recognise that in every generation the social fabric is seen as breaking down; the youth of today are always seen as more rebellious, more destructive than yesterday's young generation.[9] The families of the past are always seen as more cohesive and stable than the families of today.

This sort of generalised disapproval of today's non-marital families is also evident in the one area where there is some form of recognition given to cohabitation, that is, in social welfare provision. Those in receipt of single-parent allowance may find themselves docked their entitlement if they are deemed to be cohabiting. They and their partner may not have any protection or ability to assert legal rights as a legally recognised unit, but ironically the law recognises the status of the cohabitee for the purpose of denying social welfare rights.

This, then, is the strange dichotomy of 'family' in Ireland: on the one hand is a rapidly modernising society where old stereotypes and roles are being redefined or rejected outright; on the other, this change is nowhere positively reflected in the laws or institutions of the State. To some extent, this is part of an international phenomenon. In many other countries there has been a gradual process of the unhooking of 'family' from 'marriage'. This has been the essential change from which many consequences have flowed, like the introduction of civil union laws allowing same-sex partners to register their relationships legally, for example. Civil union laws are now widespread throughout many European countries, such as The Netherlands, France and Belgium. In Ireland, however, social change has been particularly rapid, and the legal change that has been consequent on social change in other countries has not yet occurred.

FAILURE TO RESPOND TO CHANGE

The tide may have turned for ordinary people, but official Ireland still fails to respond positively. No move has yet been made to broaden the definition of 'family', although the State is coming under increasing pressure to do so. In the 1994 *Keegan* case, an unmarried father took a case to the European Court of Human Rights in Strasbourg, challenging the failure of the Irish State to allow him certain rights over his child. At that time, the only way for a non-marital father to obtain any rights as guardian of his child was to make an application to the court under a 1964 Act; even when the mother supported the father's application, the courts were still involved. In Keegan's case, the child's mother had sought to put the child up for adoption. Keegan argued successfully that the failure of the Adoption Acts to make provision for consulting the natural father of a child being placed for adoption infringed his rights under Article 8 of the Convention. The European Court held that the law did not give sufficient recognition to the natural father, ruling that 'family life' can extend beyond formal or legitimate arrangements. The Court stated: '... the notion of 'family' [in Article 8 of the European Convention on Human Rights] is not confined solely to marriage-based relationships and may encompass other *de facto* "family" ties where the parties are living together outside of marriage.'[10] Following the decision, the Children Act 1997 introduced a new fast-track procedure for making the natural father a legal guardian of his child – but only where both parents consent. The Adoption Act 1998 similarly gives the natural father rights to be consulted prior to the making of an adoption order.

Two years after the *Keegan* decision, the government-appointed expert Constitution Review Group (CRG) made a similar recommendation to that of the European Court on broadening the definition of family, noting that:

> The family in Ireland has been profoundly affected by social trends since 1937... The traditional Roman Catholic ethos has been weakened by various influences including secularisation, urbanisation, changing attitudes to sexual behaviour, the use of contraceptives, social acceptance of premarital relations, cohabitation and single parenthood, a lower norm for family size, increased readiness to accept separation and divorce, greater economic independence of women ... These social changes call for amendments in the Constitution, some of which raise difficult issues that require the achievement of delicate balances for their resolution.[11]

The CRG recommended that the constitutional Articles giving the marital family special protection should be deleted, and that family rights should be protected on a more inclusive basis. They recommended the Strasbourg Court's approach be taken: to grant every person respect for their 'family life', including non-marital family life, but requiring the existence of family ties between the mother and the father in cases where fathers sought child custody. This sensible recommendation would ensure that constitutional rights would only be granted to those fathers who have or had a stable relationship with the mother prior to the birth, but would exclude those biological fathers who never had any such relationship.

Unfortunately, the CRG's recommendations were not adopted by a further government-appointed, specialist Commission on the Family, which reported in 1998. In a particularly wishy-washy approach, the Commission remarked only that, 'Cohabitation is an important subject for social research'.[12]

Recent years have seen increased rhetoric around family issues. The first national Family-Friendly Day was launched on 1 March 2001 in order to highlight policies adopted by employers to help workers who combine employment with family responsibilities. In 2002 a new series of family forums was announced by the Minister for Social and Family Affairs to take place around Ireland and to investigate how the State can best support families; these forums have taken place, and Mary Daly's report, referred to above, has been launched; yet there is still no commitment to change the law.

Indeed, despite the 'family-friendly' rhetoric, many continue to criticise the official lack of recognition for diverse family forms and the continuing lack of real support for all Irish families. In April 2003 Dr Schopp-Schilling, a member of the UN Committee on the Elimi-nation of Discrimination Against Women (CEDAW), visited Ireland as part of the process around the submission to CEDAW of the fourth and fifth progress reports on Ireland. She raised concerns about the stereotypical view of the role of women contained in Article 41 of the Constitution. This, she said, 'seriously impeded' women's human rights, since such views contributed to a culture where discrimination would be tolerated. She also noted the lack of affordable childcare and paid parental leave, pointing out that this means that primary responsibility for family work and childcare is placed on women. Furthermore, this also perpetuates a situation where women hold the majority of part-time jobs and earn less than men, and are less likely than men to be involved in politics, or to hold senior management positions.[13]

So even the marital family in Ireland lacks the sort of supports available elsewhere in Europe. Although the Supreme Court has thankfully stated that non-marital children have the same rights as children born within marriage, for non-marital families there are simply no legal protections available – apart, that is, from the protection against violence in the home, created through the reforming and very important Domestic Violence Act 1996. This Act aside, lack of legal protection, or often even recognition, has created particular problems for unmarried fathers, who lack parenting rights, despite the evidence that fathers are now taking a greater interest, and indeed a greater responsibility, than ever in parenting.

Lack of legal recognition also creates fundamental problems and disadvantages for unmarried, cohabiting partners on a whole range of critical personal issues: child custody, adoption, healthcare, taxation, maintenance, citizenship, property and inheritance rights. Joint adoption of a child by a couple, for example, is only possible where that couple is married and living together; cohabiting or same-sex couples may not jointly adopt a child. Nor may a cohabiting partner who is not the natural parent of their partner's child obtain parental leave from work to look after that child. When unmarried parents separate, there is no legal provision for seeking financial maintenance. Under pension and death benefit schemes, non-marital partners are generally excluded from benefits, and a same-sex partner or unmarried heterosexual partner has no right to a legal share in the estate of their deceased partner. Married partners, on the other hand, are entitled to many advantages in taxation of their income and assets, entitlements which are not available to non-married partners. Finally, non-nationals involved in non-marital relationships with Irish citizens may not acquire citizenship on the basis of their relationships – unlike those who are married to an Irish citizen.

In October 2002, in recognition of such problems facing many families, a new campaign, the Family Diversity Initiative, was launched by a number of NGOs working with single-parent families, and this was followed by the One Family initiative referred to earlier. These campaigns aim to promote understanding and acceptance of family diversity and to work towards necessary social and legal changes to ensure equality for all families – a vital goal in a changing society.

A VIEW TO THE FUTURE

There will always be those who resist changes in family structures and who bemoan the passing of the traditional Catholic family model. However, it is now time that the real picture of people's lives becomes reflected in official law and policy. The constitutional definition of family needs to be amended along the lines suggested by the CRG some years ago. Laws need to be introduced extending the right to marry to same-sex couples, or at the very least allowing for registration of cohabitees, whether in same-sex or heterosexual relationships. This would follow the model already adopted in many other EU countries, and in those Canadian provinces and US states which have this type of civil union law. Such laws are swiftly becoming the norm in liberal democracies internationally; but they merely provide recognition for the changing reality of family life.

There is some evidence in Government-commissioned reports of an acknowledgement at State level that families have taken on more diverse forms in Ireland; that there is no longer a 'one size fits all' model. But despite the lip-service paid to family-friendly policies, the reality is that Ireland gives less support to families, to mothers and to women and men working within the home than most other EU countries. It is time that the paradox of the Irish family is resolved by conferring official recognition on diverse forms of family, and through the provision of concrete State support for all families. The universals of adult relationships may take various forms, but all deserve equal respect in the eyes of the law.

NOTES FOR CHAPTER THREE

1.   Kennedy, F., *Cottage to Crèche: Family Change in Ireland.* (Dublin: IPA, 2001.)

2.   O'Brien, J.A., *The Vanishing Irish.* (London: Allen, 1954.)

3.   Byrne, A., 'Single Women in Ireland: A Re-Examination of the Sociological Evidence', in Byrne & Leonard (eds), *Women and Irish Society* (Ireland: Beyond the Pale Publications: 1997.)

4.   Kennedy, R., *The Irish – Emigration, Marriage and Fertility.* (USA: University of California Press, 1970.)

5.   Byrne, as at note 3, p.426.

6.   O'Connell, M., *Changed Utterly: Ireland and the New Irish Psyche*, p.80. (Ireland: The Liffey Press, 2001.)

7.   *The Irish Times*, 13 December 1997.

8.   Mulholland, J. (ed.), *Why Not? Building a Better Ireland.* (Dublin: Magill Summer School, 2003.)

9.   Pearson, G., *Hooligan: A History of Respectable Fears.* (London: Macmillan, 1983.)

10.   *Keegan v. Ireland* [1994] 18 EHRR 342.

11.   Constitution Review Group, *Report of the Constitution Review Group.* (Dublin: Government Publications, 1996.)

12.   Final Report of the Commission on the Family, *Strengthening Families for Life.* (Dublin: Government Publications, 1998.)

13.   *The Irish Times*, 8 April 2003.

CHAPTER 4
Gender Equality

Inequality takes many different forms in any society. There are gender inequalities between men and women; class inequalities; inequalities on grounds of age, family or marital status, ethnicity, nationality, sexuality, disability ... the list goes on. And of course inequalities affect people in different ways: socially, economically, culturally, legally. However, across continents, across classes and across other forms of inequality, structural discrimination against women persists and has persisted for a very long time, in every society.

In Ireland, discrimination against women takes many guises, and is evident in the legal system, as is the case in other countries. Indeed, women have always had an uneasy relationship with the law in Ireland. Until very recently, women and men had never been regarded as fully equal before the law, with women always occupying an inferior position, both long before and long after Irish Independence in 1922. Even today, despite years of equality legislation and some huge steps forward for equality campaigners, women collectively continue to occupy a position of disadvantage in Irish society relative to men.

Surprisingly, this was not always the case. Before the Norman conquest of Ireland in the twelfth century, a system of indigenous laws, known as Brehon Law, was in place throughout the country. Under this system, women had many rights within the marital relationship which were not afforded them under the common-law system later introduced into Ireland. For example, under Brehon Law a woman was entitled to inherit a life-interest in family land when her father had no sons to whom he could bequeath it. If she then married a landless man or a stranger from another area, the normal roles of husband and wife were reversed and she made the decisions and paid his fines or debts. Within the marital relationship, both husband and wife were permitted to divorce for a wide range of reasons, and it was possible for a 'marriage of joint property' to exist, whereby each partner could retain the property that they had brought into the marriage after they divorced. A wife was legally entitled to divorce her husband on grounds of cruelty, failure to provide and even impotence.

By contrast, after the introduction of the common-law system, which gradually gained sway over the whole island of Ireland after the Anglo-Norman invasion of 1170 and had fully replaced the native law system by the end of the sixteenth century, women's legal status was greatly diminished. According to common-law rules, some of which were legally applicable right into the twentieth century, women could not vote or hold property, and married women had no right to enter contracts, to divorce their husbands, nor even to have the legal guardianship of their children. Within marriage, they also had a duty to submit to sex with their husbands; according to Sir Matthew Hale's 'classic' eighteenth-century legal text: 'A husband cannot be guilty of rape upon his wife for by their mutual matrimonial consent and contract the wife hath given up herself in this kind to her husband, which she cannot retract.' This outrageous notion – that a husband could not be guilty of raping his wife – remained part of the law of the land until as late as 1990, when it was finally abolished by the Criminal Law (Rape) (Amendment) Act 1990 after extensive lobbying by the rape crisis centre movement. However, it should be said that change occurred earlier in Ireland than it did in England, where the House of Lords finally abolished the 'marital rape exemption' only in 1991.

As this brief overview shows, the seeds sown in the twelfth century with the introduction of the common law to Ireland bore fruit that would affect women's lives for centuries to come.

THE FIRST-WAVE WOMEN'S MOVEMENT

The modern campaign for women's equality in Ireland began in the late nineteenth and early twentieth centuries when, alongside the emerging struggle for Independence, the women's liberation movement developed, with the aim of securing the vote for women and of challenging the discriminatory nature of the law. However, at that time there was palpable tension between those espousing the cause of feminism and those pushing the cause of nationalism. Up until the creation of the Irish Free State in 1922, the fight for women's suffrage and the difficult question of links with the nationalist cause dominated this first wave of the women's movement. To put it bluntly, some women were content to wait for the vote until after the nationalist cause was realised; others resented always being told, 'Wait until after the revolution.'

After the creation of the Irish Free State in 1922 and the ensuing Civil War, the women who had been most prominent in the independence struggle – like Constance Markievicz, an officer in the Irish Citizen Army during the 1916 uprising and later the first woman elected to the House of Commons (in 1918) – became less influential and gradually faded from public view. Many of these women opposed the Anglo-Irish Treaty of 1921 (which created the Free State), took part on the anti-Treaty side in the Civil War, and were thus not included in the Cumann na nGaedheal government, first elected in 1923, which subsequently remained in power until 1932. Indeed, few women were involved at a policy-making level in the first governments of the new State, and policy on gender issues bore little sign of any feminist influence, with successive post-Independence governments adopting a conservative approach to social issues, an approach heavily influenced by the Catholic Church. For many decades after Independence there was little sign of an organised 'women's movement', nor were many laws passed after 1922 which could be described as emancipatory of women. Thus the women's movement is widely believed to have been dormant at this time, marginalised in Irish public life, until a new generation of more vocal feminists began to emerge in a second wave fifty years later.

This widely held view is not entirely accurate, however. UCC academic Linda Connolly and others have argued that women did continue to be politically active after Independence, but at a different, more local level, for example, through organisations like the Irish

Housewives' Association (IHA). Connolly also asserts that '... a core cadre of feminist women ... continued their activism in smaller numbers from the 1920s on'.[1] The collective voice of the women's movement would occasionally revive, as with the Irish Women Workers' Union (IWWU) laundry workers' three-month strike in 1945 for better conditions, led by suffragette activist Louie Bennett; it resulted in the right to two weeks' paid holiday leave being granted to laundry workers. This landmark agreement, negotiated by the IWWU, eventually made similar holiday entitlements the norm for industrial workers. Apart from such notable exceptions, however, women's public voice remained silent for many decades following Independence.

Some of the women's organisations active during this period, like the Irish Countrywomen's Association (ICA) and the IHA, mentioned above, sought to develop women's role within the family in order to influence society as a whole. These associations took on a campaigning role at times; the IHA, for example, actively supported Noel Browne's proposed Mother and Child Scheme, which would have provided immense health benefits for many women and children, but which eventually failed to be adopted by the government following bitter opposition from the Catholic Church and the medical profession. Other organisations, like the women graduates' associations from the National University of Ireland and Trinity College Dublin, campaigned to remove the obstacles facing women in the workplace. Despite these early campaigning efforts, the accepted social function for women remained firmly located within the home: expressed through Catholic Church teaching and through the law, most notably through the 1937 Constitution (see below). Of course, women had made some important gains at the birth of the new State, particularly with the extension of the franchise in 1922 to all women and men over 21 years of age. But a cynical commentator might describe this as the last piece of progressive legislation for women in Ireland for over fifty years.

Equality in the 1937 Irish Constitution

Certainly, there is little that is positive for women in the Irish Constitution. It provides an equality guarantee in Article 40.1, which reads:

All citizens shall, as human persons, be held equal before the law. This shall not be held to mean that the State shall not in its enactments have due regard to differences of capacity, physical and moral, and of social function.

While this wording may sound progressive, it has been interpreted very restrictively, primarily because of that qualifier in the final line regarding 'social function'. When this is linked with the particular 'social function' prescribed for women in Article 41, one can see the problem. The latter Article expresses woman's social function in terms of her 'life within the home', and refers to mothers (but not fathers) having 'duties in the home'. Even in 1937, when the Constitution was being debated in the Dáil, the wording of Article 41.2 led to women's groups protesting outside the debating chamber. But inside the chamber, of the 152 deputies who took part in the debate, only three were women; they have been described by Professor Yvonne Scannell of Trinity College Dublin as the 'silent sisters' because they made no meaningful comment on the provisions in question, despite the Article's undoubted significance in defining women's role so narrowly.[2]

This, then, goes some way to explain why, while there has been increasing reliance by aggrieved citizens on the fundamental rights Articles in the Constitution since the 1960s when a more activist judiciary emerged in the courts, the equality guarantee itself has generated relatively little case law – and has not been a particularly useful tool for feminist legal activists. Even where campaigners have tried to use it in legal argument, and it has formed the basis for a judicial decision, it has been subjected to a restrictive interpretation by the courts.

The delimiting effect, legally, of the particular social function ascribed to women by Article 41.2 was seen, for example, in the *de Búrca* case ([1976] IR 38). Here, two women journalists, Máirín de Búrca and Mary Andersen, were on trial for criminal contempt of court arising out of newspaper articles they had written. They challenged the Juries Act 1927, which provided for the random selection of men (subject to certain property-ownership criteria) from the electoral register for jury service, but which excluded women from jury service generally; individual women had actively to apply in order to become jurors. The journalists argued that this was in breach of the equality guarantee since it meant that, unlike men charged with a criminal offence, they would not be tried by a jury of their peers, an implicit constitutional right. The Supreme Court ruled in their favour, although not all the judges relied directly upon the equality guarantee; two of the judgments were based upon the requirements of trial 'in due course of law' under Article 38.5 of the Constitution. Moreover, in an infamous passage in his judgment, Chief Justice O'Higgins remarked that some women, namely mothers with young children, should be collectively excused from jury service because of their constitutionally recognised 'social function'.

Similarly, the social function proviso in Article 40.1 was used to neutralise the effect of the equality guarantee in the *Norris* case ([1984] IR 36), where the Supreme Court held that nineteenth-century legislation criminalising homosexual intercourse between men, but not between women, was not discriminatory. In the words of (again) Chief Justice O'Higgins, the legislature was 'perfectly entitled to ... treat sexual conduct or gross indecency between males as requiring prohibition because of the social problem which it creates, while at the same time looking at sexual conduct between females as being not only different but as posing no such social problem.' Thus, because of different social aspects or functions ascribed to men and women, male homosexuality could be treated differently in law from lesbianism. Norris took his case on to the European Court of Human Rights, which subsequently ruled that the ban was in breach of the Convention (see Chapter 6).

The idea of different 'social functions' justifying what would otherwise be unconstitutional discrimination has popped up in several other cases too, and sometimes to the detriment of men rather than women, for example in *Dennehy v. Minister for Social Welfare* (High Court, 26 July 1984). Here the applicant, a deserted husband, challenged as discriminatory legislation that provided for the payment of social welfare to deserted wives, but not to deserted husbands. Judge Barron upheld the law, referring particularly to Article 41.2 and the 'common good' of women's 'life within the home' as entitling the State to protect financially deserted wives as opposed to husbands. In *MhicMhathúna v. Ireland* ([1989] IR 504), the High Court also held that the State was entitled to give certain tax and welfare benefits to single parents, since their position was regarded as different from that of two parents living together.

This is an interesting feature of equality cases in Irish courts – that many of the judgments have been based upon other constitutional Articles, not on the equality guarantee in Article 40.1. This is apparent even in those cases, like *de Búrca*, where equality claims have been successful. It would appear that Irish judges have a particular aversion to basing decisions upon the equality clause, perhaps due to a conservative politics prevailing among the judiciary, and would rather find other reasons to rule in favour of a claimant, even where the real issue in the case is that of sex equality, or gender discrimination. For example, in *Murphy v. Attorney General* ([1982] IR 241), the Supreme Court struck down a tax law that discriminated against married couples, but again not because it was in breach of the equality guarantee. Rather, the Court held that it offended the provisions of Article 41, the family rights clause, under which the State must 'guard with special care the institution of Marriage'. Similarly, in *Murtagh Properties v. Cleary* ([1972] IR 330), where a union representing male bar staff took industrial action against their employer because they objected to the employment of women lounge-workers in the same pub, the Supreme Court held that the union's action was unlawful because it breached the right of the women to earn a livelihood – not because it infringed the equality guarantee. There is, or at least was, a distinct tendency among the judiciary to sidestep the equality clause in favour of reliance upon other, perhaps less controversial, provisions of the Constitution.

Apart from the obvious problems with the idea of gender-specific 'social function', and with judges' apparent reluctance to tackle the equality issue directly, there is also another restriction inherent in the language of Article 40.1, since it provides only for 'equality before the law'. This conception of equality, common to neo-liberal democracies worldwide and enshrined in international and transnational instruments like the European Convention, is often referred to as formal or juridical equality, meaning that the State may not discriminate against people of a particular race, for example, but not allowing for the State to recognise pre-existing inequalities based on race. Formal equality does not recognise the famous adage that 'sometimes the greatest inequality lies in treating unalike cases alike'.

In contrast, substantive equality – the form of equality associated with socialist or social democratic political systems – allows for positive action measures to be taken to remove or lessen the effect of pre-existing inequalities. Such measures might include the provision of training programmes exclusively for people with disabilities, or the setting of quotas in government departments providing that at least a certain percentage of those employed must be employees with disabilities. However, no express protection for such measures is provided in the Irish equality guarantee.

Other restrictions in the equality guarantee are more obscure, but have nonetheless contributed towards the lack of effectiveness of the Article. In particular, the phrase 'as human persons', regarded by contemporary academics as mere 'pious padding', has been used bizarrely by the courts to restrict the guarantee only to those areas where discrimination is experienced in relation to a human attribute. So, for example, a company which claimed that it should have the same right as another company to trade on a Sunday could not rely on the equality guarantee since it was not a 'human person' (*Quinn's Supermarket v. Attorney General* [1972] IR 1). While this interpretation of the phrase might seem rational enough, the Courts later extended it further, so that, for example, in the *Murtagh Properties* case cited above, the women lounge-workers discriminated against by their male colleagues could not rely on the equality guarantee since it applied to them only as 'human persons' and not as workers. This sort of decision appears to have been arrived at gratuitously by judges, simply to limit the application of the equality guarantee even further. There has been some evidence recently that this restrictive approach has fallen out of favour with the judiciary; but no court has yet overruled the *Murtagh Properties* decision.

THE SECOND-WAVE WOMEN'S MOVEMENT

Notwithstanding the clear limitations of the Constitution as a guarantor of equality, the unwillingness of judges to allow claims to succeed on equality arguments, and the absence of a public women's voice through much of the mid-twentieth century, legal and substantial change for Irish women did begin to occur slowly, with a second-wave feminist movement emerging in the 1970s and 1980s. This movement was strongly influenced by the civil rights movements developing in different countries internationally at that time. The general upsurge in political awareness was reflected in Ireland by the emergence of a strong, more determined voice for women as a new breed of campaigners took up the fight for equal rights.

UCD academic Ailbhe Smyth has documented the four different phases of the feminist movement in Ireland between 1970 and 1990.[3] First, she describes a growing mobilisation and politicisation of women between 1970 and 1974, spearheaded by the founding of the Irish Women's Liberation Movement (IWLM) in 1970 and the 'contraceptive train' event in 1971; the establishment of the Council for the Status of Women in 1972, and the 1973 abolition of the 'marriage bar', which had prohibited women from continuing to work in the civil service, local authorities and health boards upon marriage. In 1973 also the 'unmarried mother's allowance' was introduced, easing considerably the difficult social position of female single parents. The year 1973 was a watershed for the development of equality law in Ireland generally, since Irish entry into the EEC (European Economic Community, now European Union) that year became a significant catalyst for change in this area. Given the shortcomings of the Irish constitutional equality guarantee, the laws of the EU are generally viewed as offering greater scope for the achievement of equality by Irish women than what is available at national level.

Entry to the EEC obliged the State to enact employment, equality and maternity protection legislation, for example, and the Anti-Discrimination (Pay) Act, 1974 and the Employment Equality Act, 1977 were passed due to the necessity to comply with EC Directives on equal pay and discrimination in employment, respectively. The 1974 Act prohibited discrimination by employers in rates of pay between male and female employees, while the 1977 Act was directed at discrimination on the grounds of sex or marital status in the conditions of employment more generally.

Ailbhe Smyth describes the years between 1974 and 1977 as marking a second phase in the development of the feminist movement; a period of high energy and radical action defined by the emergence of the radical feminist organisation Irish Women United (IWU) in 1975. This group adopted direct action tactics by invading male-only pubs, sports clubs and swimming areas; it was avowedly left-wing in politics, and called for equal pay, free legal contraception and rights for lesbians.

The years between 1977 and 1983 represent a third phase in this development, with a consolidation of the movement towards greater status for women. During these years the Women's Right to Choose campaign was established and in 1979 called for the legalisation of abortion; and the Rape Crisis Centre network and groups like Women's Aid, offering support to women who had suffered violence in the home, were set up by activists. The academic discipline of women's studies began to develop within colleges and universities, and women became more sexually liberated, with a distinctive lesbian voice emerging within Irish feminism during the 1970s.

The years between 1983 and 1990, Ailbhe Smyth's fourth stage, were very different, marked by a succession of personal tragedies and notorious political defeats for the women's movement. A defeat with significant lasting effect was the passing of the Eighth Amendment to the Constitution in 1983, giving the foetus an equal right to life with the pregnant woman (see Chapter 5). This provision was used for many years by anti-abortion campaigners to take legal action against those women's clinics and students' unions which were providing information on how to obtain abortion in England, effectively silencing many organisations. Other setbacks included the defeat of the divorce referendum in 1986, and the *Eileen Flynn* case in 1985, in which a teacher was dismissed from her job in a convent school in County Wexford after becoming pregnant (see Chapter 2).

In terms of personal tragedies, in 1984 Ireland was deeply shocked by the case of fifteen-year-old schoolgirl Ann Lovett who died in childbirth, along with her newborn child, in a graveyard grotto in Granard, County Longford; and by the death of Sheila Hodgers, a pregnant woman with cancer who was denied potentially life-saving medical treatment because she was pregnant, and who died in hospital in Drogheda in 1983 (as debate raged around the anti-abortion amendment) along with her prematurely born baby.

These were bleak years for feminism in Ireland, but change was to come. Since 1990, with increasing economic prosperity and a general liberalisation of society, the women's movement has entered a new phase, becoming mainstreamed in policy-making at every level. A political turning point was the election of Mary Robinson as President of Ireland in 1990, after a lively and upbeat political campaign. In 1992 came the Supreme Court ruling in the X case, placing the woman's right to life over that of her foetus where there is a threat of suicide, followed, in November 1992, by referenda guaranteeing the freedom to obtain information on abortion and the right to travel abroad for abortion – both were passed. That same month, November 1992, a record number of women were elected to the Dáil – twenty female TDs out of 166, up from thirteen in 1989.

The new Fianna Fáil/Labour government formed in January 1993, after the 1992 election, established for the first time a Department of Equality and Law Reform, the aim of which was to oversee legal change in the area of equality. In 1995, at the instigation of this Department, a referendum to permit divorce was put to the people and finally passed, enabling no-fault divorce legislation to be enacted (although the amendment requires that couples have lived apart for at least four out of the previous five years before they may divorce). Other progressive Acts passed in the 1990s included laws liberalising the sale of contraceptives, and more far-reaching equality legislation, developed by the new Department and introduced to replace the Equal Pay and Employment Equality Acts of the 1970s. This new Employment Equality Act, and a complementary Equal Status Act, were initially declared unconstitutional by the Supreme Court in 1997, but were later re-enacted by the subsequent Fianna Fáil/Progressive Democrat government in 1998 and 2000.

One of the reasons for the Supreme Court decision was that the new employment equality law would have obliged employers to make 're-asonable accommodation' in order to employ persons with disabilities. The Court held that although the employment of people with disabilities was a worthy social goal, the expense involved in accom-modating them could not be placed entirely on the private sector since this infringed the employers' constitutional rights to private property (ie, profit). Following this decision, the legislation was altered so that a watered-down version of disability protection was introduced instead. The right to private property had effectively beaten the right to equal-ity, much to the disappointment of disability rights campaigners (see Chapter 9).

MOVING INTO THE TWENTY-FIRST CENTURY: THE EQUALITY LEGISLATION

The new, re-enacted equality legislation comprises two Acts: first, the Employment Equality Act 1998, which prohibits workplace discrimination on nine grounds: gender, marital status, family status, disability, age, race, religion, sexual orientation, or membership of the Traveller community; second, the Equal Status Act 2000, which bans discrimination on the same nine grounds in the provision of goods and services, such as entry to bars or clubs, hotel bookings, supply of goods under contracts, etc. Discrimination on any of the nine grounds laid out in the Employment Equality Act is forbidden in relation to advertising of jobs, access to employment, conditions of employment, training or experience, promotion or regrading, classification of posts.

Direct and indirect discrimination are both prohibited. Direct dis-crimination occurs where one person is treated differently than another, because of their gender. Indirect discrimination is more com-plex, but it can be broadly defined as occurring where a condition is applied to everyone in an apparently neutral way, yet the proportion of those who are disadvantaged by the condition is substantially higher in the case of persons from one category than those of the other, and that the condition cannot be justified by objective factors unrelated to any of the discriminatory grounds. In other words, if an employer requires that all of those working as cashiers are at least six feet tall, this

apparently gender-neutral requirement will be indirectly discriminatory because more men than women can comply with the condition;
women are disproportionately disadvantaged. Nor can the employer
argue that a height requirement is justified objectively for the job of
cashier.

The approach adopted in both pieces of equality legislation is
premised upon a formal conception of equality (like the conception in
the Constitution), thus providing for the removal of discriminations
rather than for the adoption of positive action policies. This means that
although the Acts prohibit discrimination, they do not impose positive
obligations on employers or other establishments, and little if any provision is made for positive or affirmative action. Rather, the enforcement of the Acts has always been dependent upon individuals taking
actions against their employers, or against clubs or other
establishments.

Problems with the Equality Legislation

This limited conception of equality is one weakness of the legislation;
but there are also other areas where the equality laws do not go far
enough to protect against discrimination. Many potential claimants
have fallen at the first hurdle of taking a claim, which requires the
existence of a 'comparator', ie, somebody of the opposite gender, or of
a different family status, for example, in the same or similar position as
the claimant, but who does not suffer the same discrimination. That
means the employment equality legislation often cannot tackle the
general problem of low pay, or 'glass ceilings and sticky floors',
because in a workplace where all the women are shop-floor workers
(stuck to the sticky floor) and all the managers are men (who have risen
above the glass ceiling), for instance, then none of the shop-floor
workers will have a suitable comparator: they cannot point to a male
shop-floor worker whose salary is higher than that of his female
co-workers, or who has better conditions than theirs. In such situations

there is no provision in the legislation for a 'hypothetical comparator'. A claimant cannot argue that a hypothetical man working in a similar job to hers would get higher pay – she must be able to measure her position against that of an actual fellow employee.

Another problem – a very fundamental one at that – is that the equality legislation actually permits discrimination in some instances, an anomaly that continues to be the subject of much heated debate. Section 37 allows religious-run medical or educational institutions to discriminate on the religion ground in order to retain their religious ethos: a principle that has been strongly criticised by teachers' unions and civil liberties groups, since it enshrines in law the decision in the *Eileen Flynn* case, referred to above. Furthermore, employers can also invoke a solid defence where a 'genuine occupational qualification' can be said to exist. This means that employers may discriminate in relation to entertainment (where they need to hire a woman to play a woman's role in a film), or the performance of work outside the State, which allows oil companies, for instance, to send only male executives from Ireland to negotiate deals in countries like Saudi Arabia. Discrimination is also permitted (on the gender ground only) in the provision of personal services, for example, by live-in nursing staff, or where communal sleeping or sanitary facilities are provided. The existence of this defence has been criticised by equality law expert Professor Deirdre Curtin on the grounds that the only two jobs where gender is really a genuine occupational qualification are those of sperm donor and wet-nurse.[4]

The gap between law and reality

The aspect of the equality legislation that deserves most criticism is its lack of effectiveness. Although some sort of employment equality law has been in place for over thirty years, there is a continuing – and according to some studies, a widening – gap between legislation and actual practice, as figures on pay differential, in particular, continue to show. Anti-discriminatory legislation has simply not been enough to tackle deep-rooted gender discrimination, and the Government has simply failed to introduce any other policies to improve the position of women collectively. Ireland signed up to the UN Convention on the Elimination of All Forms of Discrimination Against Women in 1985, but since then progress on gender equality has been slow. In January 2004, for instance, the Women's Human Rights Project published a report that is extremely critical of Irish government inaction on gender initiatives promised at the UN Women's Conference in Beijing in 1995.

Statistics and figures on the relative positions of women and men in the workforce are highly revealing. Women still account for only 5% of senior management positions in private and public sectors, and 28% of members on State boards. The majority of low-paid workers are women, and there are ongoing problems with occupational segregation, often caused by lack of access to education and training. Three times as many women as men work in 'education and health'; one-and-a-half times as many in 'hotels and restaurants'.

The gender pay gap is particularly striking, according to a very recent report by the Irish Congress of Trade Unions (ICTU).[5] In 1974, the difference between the average hourly earnings of women and men was as high as 40%. By 1979 it had dropped to 33%, then it took twelve years to reduce by 1% further; but then raced down by 16% in the early 1990s. The gap currently stands at just under 15%, a wider gap than exists in most EU states. A significantly wider gap exists in the private sector than in the public sector, partially due to the higher rate of unionisation in the public sector. A major cause of concern noted by ICTU was that the gap has actually widened in some areas, like hotel and restaurant work. Census figures for male and female hourly earnings between 1996 and 2001 further illustrate that the gender gap in pay is actually widening. In 1996 the difference was IR£2.16, but by 2001 it was IR£2.47. Similarly, the *Statistical Yearbook of Ireland*

2003 shows that in manufacturing industries the average weekly earnings for women are only 67% of those for men; women's average hourly pay rate is only 75% that of men. ICTU identifies three main factors as contributing to the gender pay gap: occupational segregation; 'reduced labour market attachment' (ie, women are more likely to take time out, or career breaks in order to have children); and discrimination in recruitment, training and pay systems.

ESRI research published in 2002 shows other disparities in pay exist, based on marital status. While single women tend to earn the least (5% less, on average, than single men), married men tend to be the highest earners, earning 25% more, on average, than single women. In another study, economist Alan Barrett called the gender pay gap the 'sex discrimination index'[6] – to put it simply, women would earn 15% more for their work if they were men. So, after thirty years of equal pay legislation, we still have a huge pay differential between men and women.

Among the professions, too, there is marked gender disparity. According to a recent survey conducted among Irish lawyers, for example, men overwhelmingly outnumber women at the top levels – only 21% of judges and 9% of senior counsel among barristers are women – despite the fact that women have been studying law in larger numbers than men for some years; two-thirds of law students nationally are now women.[7] It was also found that over one-third of women lawyers had experienced the use of sexist or inappropriate language; 30% felt excluded from social networks essential to furthering their careers; and 14% had been harassed or bullied in the workplace.

This study, like so many others, identified childcare as a major issue for women in the workplace. Parenting responsibility is still disproportionately borne by women rather than men, and the State offers little support to mothers or fathers in Ireland, in comparison to other European countries. Although maternity leave is paid, it is only provided for at the bare EU minimum of eighteen weeks; parental leave is unpaid. Fathers do not get any specific recognition in the Irish work-place – and few can afford to take up their entitlement to unpaid parental leave. Parents in Germany, France, Spain, Austria, Finland and Sweden, by contrast, all receive more than eighteen months' leave, and parental leave is offered on a paid basis in most EU countries (Austria, Finland, Denmark, Germany, Italy, Luxembourg, Sweden and Belgium – in certain circumstances). Ireland also has one of the poorest levels of childcare provision in Europe; parents here spend an average of 20% of their earnings on childcare, compared with an average of 8% across the EU.[8]

Discrimination against women is not confined to the workplace. In January 2004 the National Women's Council of Ireland launched a campaign to highlight sex discrimination in the social welfare system, arguing that it is still based on the model of the male breadwinner and fails to recognise women as adults in their own right. In 2002, for example, only 25% of women, compared with 67% of men, got a State pension based on their own PRSI contributions. In certain categories, such as farming, or where women are involved in a family business, the percentage who have no personal pension is as high as 90% and more. Ninety-five percent of 'qualified adults', in other words those claimed for as dependants by other adults receiving welfare support, are women. In most cases even the limited allowance for these women is not paid directly to them, but to their husbands, meaning that women are dependant on their husbands to survive economically.

One of the reasons why so much of our social welfare legislation and other laws have an adverse effect upon women may be the small proportion of women among Irish legislators. Since the historic election of Constance Markievicz in 1918, there has been no remarkable increase in the number of women TDs. At 13% (twenty-two out of 166 TDs), the proportion of women now in the Dáil has increased by only 1% since the previous election in 1997, when twenty women TDs were elected. In the 2002 elections, there were fewer women candidates than in 1997, and no female candidates ran at all in ten constituencies. According to a 2002 report by the National Women's Council of Ireland (NWCI), the current figure of 13% is among the lowest in Europe for female parliamentarians, and way off the UN target of 30%.[9] Ireland now ranks 59th out of 120 nations in the world when it comes to women's parliamentary representation, and the NWCI estimate that at the current rate it would take 370 years for the percentage of women in the Dáil to reach 50%. The Irish percentage is lower than the European average (17%), lower than the average for the Americas (16%), lower than the Asian average (16%) and equal only with the average for sub-Saharan Africa (13%). By comparison, the percentage of women in the Australian Parliament is now 23% (up from 1% sixty years ago); in Sweden women make up nearly 45% of parliamentarians; in Denmark, 38%; and in Finland, 37%.

The Irish figures are no better at local level – just 15% of local government representatives are women, and this percentage has not increased in ten years. But why are things so bad in Ireland? Largely because nothing has been done to change the situation. Men have traditionally dominated Irish politics, business and the professions; the working culture of the political system and of most decision-making bodies is not family-friendly; and there is inadequate provision of childcare for women seeking to participate in these processes. It is no coincidence that in countries such as Scandinavia, where the figures for women's political representation are the highest, proactive steps, including the introduction of quotas, have been taken to ensure higher representation rates for women. In some countries, political parties are required by law to put forward an equal number of male and female candidates, or risk losing their State funding. In France, for example, a parity law of this kind was introduced in 2000, which resulted in a noticeable improvement in the numbers of women entering politics, particularly at local level. Other steps that could be taken include education measures; the establishment of 'talent banks', or databases of women qualified for appointment to boards; the funding of women's groups to support women in going forward for election. But changes to increase the numbers of women in Irish politics have never been encouraged by political parties, or brought about through proactive means; rather, where change has occurred, it has happened very slowly, and there is no sign that women's political representation levels are likely to improve in the future.

LOOKING TO THE FUTURE

Although there are many and obvious flaws in the equality legislation, its enactment is nonetheless highly significant for Irish society. The Equal Status Act 2000 has extended the concept of equality beyond the workplace for the first time, and both new Acts have increased the grounds of discrimination beyond sex and marital equality. With some imagination, and creative use of the legislation, it may be possible to develop a more genuinely effective equality policy that is not premised on outdated views of the 'social function' of different groups within society.

Despite the bleak statistics listed in the previous section, the years since 1990 must be acknowledged as having marked a generally positive fifth stage in the development of feminism in Ireland, marked by a great move forward in the liberation of women, economically, socially and sexually; and the mainstreaming of the concept of gender equality through legislative and policy developments. It is undeniable that women have made very considerable advances in a relatively short time. Ireland has had two women Presidents since 1990; a woman is currently Tánaiste in the Government; two out of eight Supreme Court judges are now women; and ordinary women are more independent, more liberated and more in control of their own lives than ever before in our history.

Since the second-wave women's movement first became organised in Ireland and Britain in the 1970s, feminist concepts have become mainstream. But the reality is that mainstreaming has not achieved substantive change for the majority of women, who remain infinitely less powerful than men, economically, politically and socially.

Many of the legal changes brought about have not been really effective – either for women or for other disadvantaged groups. The forms of inequality may have changed, and some individual women may have achieved positions of power, but the substantive inequalities remain. The largest proportion of low-paid workers are women, and there are ongoing problems with occupational gender segregation. The victims of domestic violence are overwhelmingly female, and after nearly thirty years of equal pay legislation a huge gender pay differential remains; proper childcare remains unaffordable for most, and abortion unavailable. Real equality for women remains an aspiration; the feminist struggle is far from over.

Future campaigns should focus on the need for paid parental leave, and for fathers to have a right to paternity leave; for an entitlement to decent, affordable childcare; for proactive measures to ensure greater representation of women in politics and decision-making; and for an end to the gender pay gap through strengthening of legislation and enforcement procedures. Perhaps most importantly, focused education and training are needed to break down gender stereotypes and to help build a society where all are judged on equal terms, according to merit and regardless of gender.

NOTES FOR CHAPTER FOUR

1.   Connolly, L., *The Irish Women's Movement*, p.67. (Dublin: Lilliput Press, 2003.)
2.   Scannell, Y., 'The Constitution and the role of women', in Farrell, B. (ed.), *De Valera's Constitution and Ours*. (Dublin: Gill and Macmillan, 1988.)
3.   Smyth, A., 'The Women's Movement in the Republic of Ireland 1970–1990', in Smyth, A. (ed.), *Irish Women's Studies Reader*. (Dublin: Attic Press, 1993.)
4.   Curtin, D., *Irish Employment Equality Law* (Dublin: Round Hall Ltd, 1989.)

For further analysis of the legislation, see Bolger, M. and Kimber, C., *Sex Discrimination Law*. (Dublin: Round Hall Ltd, 2000.)

5.   *Gender and Pay*. (ICTU report, 2004.)

6.   Barrett *et al, How Unequal? Men and Women in the Irish Labour Market*. (Ireland: Oak Tree Press/ESRI, 2000.)

7.   Bacik, Costello & Drew, *Gender InJustice – A Report on Women Lawyers in Ireland*. (Dublin: TCD Law School, 2003.)

8.   NWCI, *Women's Manifesto*, 2004.

9.   NWCI, *Politics in Ireland; Jobs for the Boys*, 2002.

CHAPTER 5
Reproductive Rights

Ireland has a unique legal approach to matters pertaining to reproductive health. This is the only country with a constitutional provision giving equal rights to life to a pregnant woman and to the foetus she carries; ours was the last country in Europe to legalise contraception, yet there is still no clear legal basis for emergency contraception (ie, the 'morning-after pill'); this is also the State where recent innovations in reproductive health, like IVF services (*in vitro* fertilisation) and sperm banks, are simply unregulated.

Our unique approach to matters sexual has deep-rooted origins. Through most of the twentieth century, Ireland was a seriously sexually repressed society, and we experienced the sexual revolution much later than anywhere else in Europe. Now, however, the sexual landscape looks very different. A much freer and more liberal sexual culture is emerging, fertility rates are falling and phenomena like 'postponed parenting' are becoming the norm, so reproduction now means something very different for twenty-first-century women and men in Ireland. Unfortunately, these changing attitudes to sex and reproduction are not yet reflected in the legal system. There has been huge resistance from religious and other conservative forces in this area, perhaps more than in any other, so change has been very slow to happen – and a great deal more is needed.

CONTRACEPTIVE LAWS

In one area, at least, changing sexual attitudes have brought about and been matched by substantial legal reform. As a result of extensive litigation and political lobbying by family planning groups, progressive legislation has been introduced to legalise and regulate contraception. Resistance to such legislation persisted for many, many years, with the Catholic Church leading a vigorous campaign to prevent the legalisation of contraception, opposition based on the Church's teaching that sex should take place only within marriage and then only for the purpose of procreation. The only form of family planning permitted under Catholic dogma is the notoriously unreliable natural or 'rhythm' method, which allows a couple to have sex only during 'safe' times, ie, when the woman is not ovulating. Catholic morality was enshrined in law soon after the emergence of the Irish Free State. Under 1935 legislation, the sale, import and advertising of contraception were all criminalised.

The impetus for change in the law began with the new ideals of love and sex generated in the 1960s, and slowly made its way to Irish shores. In 1971, the Irish Women's Liberation Movement (IWLM) manifesto, *Chains or Changes? The Civil Wrongs of Irish Women*, stated that legalisation of contraception was a key aim. That same year, on 22 May, members of the IWLM and many other women travelled to Belfast and back to Dublin on a 'Contraceptive Train', importing con-traceptives illegally in a public act of defiance. This direct-action tactic prompted huge controversy and many resigned from the IWLM in pro-test, but the legalisation of contraception became a core demand for a whole range of individuals and organisations. Mary Robinson, then a Senator, introduced an unsuccessful contraceptive bill in the Seanad in 1971; feminists rallied around to support the *McGee* case in 1973, which established the right of married couples to import contraceptives for their own use (*McGee v. Attorney General* [1974] IR 284); a new alliance called CAP (Contraception Action Programme campaign) was formed in 1976.

These concerted campaigns paid off to a limited extent, precipitating the introduction of the Health (Family Planning) Act in 1979, which legalised contraceptives, including condoms, and made them available on prescription for 'adequate' medical reasons, or for '*bona fide*' family planning purposes (ie, for use by married couples). This Act was infamously introduced in the Dáil by then Taoiseach Charles J. Haughey as an 'Irish solution to an Irish problem' – it allowed enough contraceptive use to keep some of the campaigners happy, but did not offend the Catholic Church's sacred cow that sex should only take place within marriage.

Further legislative reform was introduced by the Fine Gael/Labour coalition government in 1985, with a range of outlets being permitted to sell condoms and spermicides to persons over the age of 18 without a prescription. It was not until 1992, however, that the selling of condoms was finally deregulated, so that condoms may now be sold in shops and dispensed through machines without any minimum age restriction. The contraceptive pill remains available on prescription only, but again without any age restriction. The Health (Family Planning) (Amendment) Act 1992 and the further amending Act of the following year also legally oblige health boards to provide family planning services. Although a study of women with crisis pregnancies demonstrated that contraception is still difficult to access in more rural parts of Ireland[1], undoubtedly its use has now become widely acceptable socially and politically. In the mid-1990s the Health Promotion Unit of the Department of Health even ran public information campaigns promoting the use of condoms to prevent venereal disease and HIV infection. Changed times indeed.

Problems persist, however, as regards emergency contraception (the morning-after pill). Like the contraceptive pill, the morning-after pill is available only on prescription from doctors. Like the pill, it is available free through the health system to medical card-holders, but unlike in England, there have been no moves here to allow the emergency contraceptive to be sold over-the-counter without a prescription. Since there is no specific legislation regulating emergency contraception, it is subject to the same rules that apply to the dispensation of the contraceptive pill. For this reason, doctors have continued to prescribe the combined oestrogen/progesterone morning-after pill, although a new emergency contraceptive, Levonelle, has come on the market – a pill that is apparently safer for women's health than the heavier dosage pill used here. Until May 2002, Levonelle was unavailable in Ireland because the Irish Medicines Board took the view that it could be classified as an 'abortifacient'. Although Levonelle has now been licensed and is available on prescription, the morning-after pill continues to be administered on prescription only, by doctors acting without a specific legal framework.

Yet despite the lack of evidence to support any claims that liberalisation of contraceptive law has brought about a moral breakdown in society, the Catholic Church remains resolutely opposed to contraceptive use. Cardinal Desmond Connell, Archbishop of Dublin, issued a statement in 1999 denouncing contraception and staunchly defending papal teaching on family planning. He said that a planned child is 'more like a technological product', and also condemned *in vitro* fertilisation and other forms of reproductive technology. In March 2004, the Vatican issued a further condemnation of fertility treatments like IVF.

More seriously again, Catholic aid agencies have refused to promote the use of condoms as a HIV-prevention measure in developing countries, citing ideological reasons. It has been argued by Mary Raftery, among others, that the Church's policy against condom use in the campaign to prevent HIV/AIDS is dishonest and dangerous, and could needlessly consign countless people to suffer preventable illness and ultimately death.[2]

IN VITRO FERTILISATION AND SPERM DONATION

Perhaps due to the fear of offending Cardinal Connell and his colleagues, legislation has never been introduced to provide for assisted human reproduction services, including sperm banks and *in vitro* fertilisation (formerly known as the 'test-tube babies' technique). None of these facilities, including IVF, is provided by the public health services in Ireland. The Government's own information website stresses that while IVF may be available from private consultants, 'any services that are provided are not currently subject to statutory control. That is, there is no law governing the provision of these services.'

The Medical Council has issued ethical guidelines for doctors concerning the provision of such services. The latest edition of these guidelines (March 2004) allows the donation of fertilised *ova* to others. In other words, there are no longer any ethical objections to an infertile couple being able to use the fertilised eggs, produced through IVF, of another couple.[3] Unsurprisingly, the Pro-Life Campaign immediately criticised this development, opposing any freezing or preservation of fertilised eggs (usually known as zygotes or pre-embryos), and also opposing the donation of frozen eggs or embryos to other couples. The recent Vatican statement on IVF goes even further than this, describing any destruction or loss of embryos in the *in vitro* process as 'a true massacre of the innocents'. Strong words, and no compassion for those unable to conceive, for whom the IVF procedure can offer a real hope of parenting.

A Commission on Assisted Human Reproduction was established in 2000 to prepare a report on how this complex area might be regulated. The Commission's report is due to be published sometime in 2004: another lengthy consultation process on a subject that political parties generally just do not want to touch. The fact is that politicians have been so intimidated by the anti-abortion lobby that they are now reluctant to broach any issue pertaining to reproduction, with the ironic result that Ireland remains a regulation-free zone as far as many reproductive matters are concerned.

The unfortunate side effect of this legal vacuum is that access to assisted human reproduction services in Ireland is now limited to those who can afford them. The cost of the treatments is very high: with a private doctor or clinic, a typical single cycle (around seventeen days) of IVF treatment can cost around €5,000. Medication is an extra cost, and women often have to undergo several cycles of treatment before success, if any, in conceiving.

The main centre for IVF treatment in Ireland is at Human Assisted Reproduction Ireland (HARI), located on the campus of the Rotunda

Maternity Hospital in Dublin. This centre was set up in 1989 to serve patients from every county nationally. Its practice is governed by the rules of the Medical Council, and it offers a range of assisted reproductive technology services, including counselling for infertile couples, *in vitro* fertilisation and intra-cytoplasmic sperm injection (ICSI), and semen freezing for cancer patients. The Irish centre gives its conception rates as less than 30%, which is not unusual for such procedures internationally.

The difficulty of availing of these services in Ireland means that people are prepared to go to great lengths to access IVF elsewhere, although costs abroad, for example in Britain and the US, can be higher. It was reported in 2002 that some Irish people were even travelling to Barbados to obtain fertility treatment; the cost for one full cycle was put at around €12,000, including flights and two weeks' hotel accommodation on the Caribbean island. In spite of the expense and lack of availability, the Commission on Assisted Human Reproduction heard, in June 2003, that over 1,000 babies have been born in Ireland using IVF, with much of the sperm coming from donors abroad, particularly from donors in Denmark.

One consequence of the absence of any legal regulation for this area is that there are no enforceable principles governing the resolution of the sort of complex problems that have arisen elsewhere. In Britain, for example, such problems arose in the case of Diane Blood, a woman who wished to use her dead husband's sperm to conceive a baby. She first approached the Human Fertilisation and Embryology Authority, created in 1991 under the English Human Fertilisation and Embryology Act 1990. Its primary function is to regulate the storage of eggs, sperm and embryos; to license and monitor British clinics that offer IVF and DI (donor insemination) treatments; and to regulate all research into human embryos. The Authority refused her permission, but she ultimately won a three-year legal battle and was granted leave by the Court of Appeal to take the sperm to Belgium for treatment. She subsequently gave birth to her dead husband's son. Had this case arisen in Ireland, where there is no legislation, no regulatory authority and no minimum legal standards governing private or public clinics, it is impossible to say what the outcome would have been.

The absence of regulation, and thus potentially of certain protection for clinics against negligence cases, may well be a factor in the inadequate availability of assisted reproduction services in Ireland. Notably, there are no 'sperm banks' as such in existence in Ireland; where there is a lack of legal certainty, professionals may be unwilling to provide services. A concession is made to men who are being treated for cancer and who may subsequently become infertile – they are given the option of banking sperm at an infertility clinic (like the one at the Rotunda Hospital) before they begin cancer treatment.

It is strangely ironic that, despite the strong guarantees of family rights in the Constitution, despite the pro-family rhetoric of Church leaders and governments, we continue to place so many obstacles, particularly the economic obstacle, in the way of infertile couples and individuals. An infinitely preferable approach would be to offer IVF and other assisted reproductive services through the public health system, allowing those indigent and disadvantaged couples and persons who are infertile the same opportunity to conceive as is presently afforded to those who can afford it.

ABORTION: CONFLICTING VIEWS

Nowhere has conservative, Catholic resistance to change been applied to such strong effect as on the abortion issue. Abortions, or deliberate procurements of miscarriage, have been a fact of life for a long time; recipes for miscarriage-inducing concoctions have been recorded as early as 2600BC. However, the issue of abortion has become the subject of much controversy and debate – one of those conversation topics guaranteed to divide any group of people. It has been a particularly divisive topic in Ireland. Pro-choice groups are campaigning for the legalisation of abortion, in order to provide a full choice of reproductive health options to pregnant women whose pregnancy is either unwanted or is causing a crisis for them. By contrast, anti-abortion activists (who call themselves 'pro-life') favour the prohibition of abortion, irrespective of the circumstances. Debate in Ireland has centred around the law and the moral/legal aspects of abortion, rather than the medical/health aspects.

Abortion is prohibited both in nineteenth-century criminal legislation and in the Constitution; doctors may only terminate pregnancies in Ireland in the very limited circumstance where the continuance of the pregnancy would pose a 'real and substantial risk' to the life of the pregnant woman. Yet thousands of Irish women have abortions every year outside the Irish jurisdiction – in England and elsewhere in Europe – and the abortion rate is rising. Clearly, prohibition does not have the effect of reducing the number of terminations, nor of addressing the real needs of women with crisis pregnancies. The futility of prohibition has been recognised in other developed countries worldwide where abortion laws have been liberalised in recent decades. American feminist lawyer Catherine MacKinnon has also commented critically that laws prohibiting abortion:

> ... make women criminals for a medical procedure only women need, or make others criminals for performing a procedure on women that only women need, when much of the need for the abortion procedure as well as barriers to access to it have been created by social conditions of sex inequality.[4]

The legal context

Abortion was made a criminal offence in Ireland in 1861, under sections 58 and 59 of the Offences Against the Person Act. Section 58 makes it an offence for a pregnant woman unlawfully to 'attempt to procure a miscarriage', ie, to undergo an abortion, while section 59 criminalises the supply of any poison or instrument, or provision of assistance to a woman in obtaining an abortion. The 1861 Act was passed by the British Parliament, but applied to Ireland both before and after Independence, and its provisions remain part of Irish law. For many years after it was passed, prosecutions were taken against persons performing backstreet abortions both in England and in Ireland. However, the law was relaxed after the 1939 English case of *R. v. Bourne* ([1939] 1 KB 687). Dr Bourne was prosecuted under the Act for performing an abortion on a young girl who had been gang-raped by a group of soldiers. The trial judge, Judge Macnaghten, directed the jury that the use of the word 'unlawful' to qualify the procurement of a miscarriage meant that there were circumstances in which it would be lawful to perform an abortion. He noted that a doctor would therefore have a defence if he or she carried out an abortion to preserve the life of the pregnant woman; or where the effect of the continuation of the pregnancy would be to make the woman or girl a 'physical or mental wreck'.

This judgment led to an increase in the availability of backstreet abortion in England, as doctors were able to rely upon the *Bourne* defence. As a result, women began to travel from Ireland to England for abortions, and the rate of Irish prosecutions for abortion and infanticide (the killing of an infant child by its mother) fell considerably. It rose again only during the years of the Second World War, when restrictions were placed on travel to England from Ireland. The last prosecution in Ireland for a backstreet abortion was the infamous *Nurse Cadden* case. In 1956 the nurse, reputed to have performed hundreds of abortions, was the last woman sentenced to hang in Ireland following the death of one of her patients; her sentence was later commuted and she died in prison.

Matters moved faster in Britain. In 1967, largely as a result of pressure from the medical profession which voiced concerns at the high death rate among women undergoing backstreet abortions in poor sanitary conditions, the British Parliament passed an Abortion Act. The 1967 Act provided, for the first time, for a range of circumstances in which abortion could be carried out legally, including where necessary to preserve the health of the woman. Once abortion became legally available in England under this Act, the number of women travelling from Ireland for terminations began to increase significantly, rising to 3,600 in 1981 – the same year that an Irish Right to Choose campaign was launched. The numbers have continued to increase since, averaging now at over 6,000 per year.

It has often been speculated that this figure, representing the number of women who register at English clinics with Irish addresses, underestimates the real number of women who travel to England, as it is believed that there must be many more who, out of fear and in order to conceal their identity, give the addresses of friends or relatives living in England. However, the figures demonstrate the extent of the need for legal abortion in Ireland. For many Irish women this need is currently addressed through the availability of travel abroad. But the needs of the most vulnerable women – the young, the poor, the unwell, or those with disabilities, for whom travel is very difficult – are simply not being met. For those who are unable to travel, but who need to obtain abortions, Irish law and society offers no remedy at present.

Right to Choose campaigns

So what, if anything, is the Irish women's movement doing to achieve legal change to address the needs of women? Twenty-five years ago a small group of feminist activists established the first Women's Right to Choose group in Ireland, in late 1979, demanding the legalisation of contraception and abortion. In March 1981 this group held a public meeting at Liberty Hall, Dublin. What happened as a result of the campaign launched at that meeting has been described by Linda Connolly thus:

The counter-right then made itself visible and increasingly mobilised ... by diverting the abortion debate into the legal/constitutional arena – an area which required extensive resources and expertise. Tactically, it aimed to block the women's movement from providing its services by actively campaigning for a constitutional referendum on the 'right to life of the unborn', which the Irish electorate supported in 1983.[5]

The establishment of the first Irish pro-choice campaign may have been a factor in precipitating dramatic legal events and extensive changes and developments in the law over the past twenty years, but more than two decades on from that significant public meeting, little has changed in reality, apart from the legalisation of contraception. Thousands of women travel every year from Ireland to England for abortions, small groups of pro-choice activists continue to hold campaign meetings, and the counter-right anti-abortion groups remain highly visible, well-financed and apparently permanently mobilised. The abortion debate, which might better have taken place in a medical or health context, has been well and truly diverted into the legal/constitutional arena. As recently as 2002, following a successful campaign by anti-abortion groups, yet another constitutional referendum on abortion was held, supported and backed by the powerful forces of Fianna Fáil and the Catholic Church, although happily, and remarkably, this was defeated. Since then the issue of abortion has disappeared from the political agenda, but meanwhile thousands of women with crisis pregnancies continue to travel to England for a medical service that remains unavailable here.

The lack of any progress towards legislating for abortion in Ireland is clearly a governmental failure, but it is also a failure on the part of the Irish women's movement. Feminists living in Ireland have failed to change the law, and have also failed to move the debate beyond the law and outside of the legal/constitutional arena, where it continues to fester. Despite our failure, the reality of women's experience of abortion remains the same, whatever the legal debates that may continue to rage.

The 1983 Eighth Amendment

Prior to the establishment of the Irish Right to Choose campaign in 1979, there had been dramatic legal change on abortion not just in England and elsewhere in Europe but also in the USA, and these changes were to have repercussions in Ireland. In 1973 in *Roe v. Wade* ((1973) 410 U.S. 113), the US Supreme Court held, building on earlier case law around the right to privacy and contraceptive rights, that women had the right to abortion under the US Constitution as a corollary of the right to privacy. This decision acted as a catalyst for reactionary forces in Ireland to lobby for a constitutional referendum to 'copperfasten' the legislative prohibition on abortion. The same year that *Roe* was decided, the Irish Supreme Court held in *McGee v. Attorney General* ([1974] IR 284) that a right to marital privacy was implicit in the Constitution, thereby enabling a married couple to import contraceptives for their own use, even where this was prohibited by statute. The *McGee* decision was described by William Binchy, a leading figure in the anti-abortion movement then and now, as being 'live ammunition', or a 'time bomb' in the hands of a court. He warned that in the 'foreseeable event of some change in attitudes in this country on the question of abortion ... the privacy concept espoused by that decision provides the key for opening that door in the future.'[6]

The decision in *Roe* and the legal reasoning of those who saw *McGee* as offering a backdoor route to the legalisation of abortion had 'a clearly visible effect on the development of Irish law and policy on abortion.'[7] It gave an impetus to the PLAC (Pro-Life Amendment Campaign), which resulted in the passing of the Eighth Amendment to the Irish Constitution in September 1983, guaranteeing the unborn an equal right to life to that of the pregnant woman.

The bitter and angry 1983 referendum campaign has been described as a 'second partitioning of Ireland'.[8] The anti-abortion campaign had successfully played one political party against another to win promises from the government to hold a referendum; and despite serious misgivings expressed by many about the wording PLAC wished to insert into the Constitution, the Fine Gael/Labour government reluctantly put a referendum to the people which the parties in government ultimately did not support. It was passed by a two-to-one majority: 67% to 33%, on a 53% turnout of the electorate.

The wording of the Eighth Amendment to the Constitution, which became Article 40.3.3, is as follows:

> The State acknowledges the right to life of the unborn and, with due regard to the equal right to life of the mother, guarantees in its laws to respect, and, as far as practicable, by its laws to defend and vindicate that right.

Article 40.3.3 remains uniquely misogynistic, even in a world of sexist laws. Ours is the only Constitution in the world to give the foetus a right to life that is equal to the right to life of a pregnant adult woman or girl-child. No other country sets up the two rights against each other in this way. Additionally, it is unique in that it expressly sets up the right to life of both the pregnant woman and the foetus that she carries as being in opposition – anticipating that a time would come when somebody else would have to decide between them. That time did come, just nine years after the passing of the referendum, but after a great deal of litigation had taken place which was to extend the effect of the provision well beyond that publicly envisaged by its advocates; PLAC members promised that they would not use the Amendment to pursue individuals through the courts, but they broke that promise.

The effect of the Eighth Amendment

Shortly after the passing of the Eighth Amendment, the Society for the Protection of the Unborn Child (SPUC), established in 1980, began to use the new provision as the basis for a series of cases it took during the

1980s against those audacious enough to provide desperate women with information on abortion facilities in England. The first move that SPUC took was to issue proceedings against two non-directive pregnancy counselling agencies, Open Door Counselling and the Well Woman Centre. Both agencies offered pregnant women information on all the options open to them, including that of termination – in particular, information on the names, addresses and contact numbers of clinics offering termination services in England. SPUC argued that the provision of this information in Ireland, to women who might ultimately decide to terminate their pregnancies in England, amounted to a breach of the constitutional right to life of the unborn, and that the State was failing in its constitutional duty to protect the unborn if it did not move to close down the agencies in question. This argument clearly required a breathtaking leap of logic in order to succeed: it involved the ridiculous assumption that women would not choose to terminate their pregnancies if they were not provided with information by the agencies concerned. Yet this argument succeeded – and SPUC also succeeded in persuading the State to take the case on its behalf. Judge Hamilton ruled against the counselling agencies in December 1986, stating that their right to freedom of expression could not be invoked to interfere with the 'fundamental right' to life of the unborn (*Attorney General (SPUC) v. Open Door Counselling Ltd* [1987] ILRM 477).

This High Court decision, subsequently upheld by the Supreme Court, established that the provision of information on abortion was unlawful under the Constitution. The agencies appealed to the European Court of Human Rights, which in October 1992 ruled that the Irish government's ban on abortion information was in breach of Article 10 of the European Convention on Human Rights, which guarantees freedom of expression, since it [the ban] was 'overbroad and disproportionate' (*Open Door No. 2* (1993) 15 EHRR 244).

The effect of the Irish courts' judgments in the *Open Door* case had a dramatic effect on the availability of information. Other counselling agencies, in fear of being injuncted and closed down, stopped providing information on abortion. An 'underground' helpline, run by the Women's Information Network, was established, which linked up with a support group in London, the Irish Women's Abortion Support Group (IWASG), to provide women with both information and more practical help with travelling arrangements. In Ireland, however, the only organisations that continued to provide information on abortion openly to their members and to members of the public were students' unions.

Shortly after it had initiated the *Open Door Counselling* litigation, SPUC began similar legal action against the officers of a number of students' unions, which were providing information on abortion in their student handbooks. The student officers, of whom this author was one, were from three bodies: six officers from the national union, USI (Union of Students in Ireland); four from University College Dublin; and four from Trinity College Dublin. Stephen Grogan, the first-named defendant in the case, was the President of USI at the time. Once again, SPUC succeeded in obtaining injunctions against the student officers from the High Court and the Supreme Court, prohibiting them from distributing this information, again on the grounds that it was unlawful under the Constitution. SPUC had at first sought to have the four officers from Trinity College jailed, as they had already distributed their student handbooks prior to the High Court case. Mary Robinson, then a Senior Counsel, defended the students in the High Court and succeeded in keeping the Trinity Four out of prison and in getting the issue referred to the European Court of Justice.

In its 1991 judgment (*SPUC v. Grogan (No. 2)* Case 159/90 [1991] 3 CMLR 849), the European Court of Justice raised the possibility that a future right to provide information on abortion might be established through EC law. The European Court defined abortion as a 'service' within the meaning of Articles 59 and 60 of the Treaty of Rome – the fundamental law of the EC, as it then was. Article 59 provided for the abolition of restrictions on freedom to provide services within the Member States, and Article 60 defined 'services'. The Court held that 'termination of pregnancy, as lawfully practised in several Member States, is a medical activity which is normally provided for remuneration and may be carried out as part of a professional activity' (para 18). Thus, it was held to fall within the definition of 'services', and prohibition of the provision of information in one Member State on a service lawfully available in another Member State would normally be in breach of EC law.

However, ultimately the Court concluded that as there was no commercial connection between the students' unions and the English clinics where abortions were performed, the information ban could not be regarded as a restriction within the meaning of Article 59 of the Treaty, so the operation of EC law was excluded in this case. The corollary of this decision is that if a counselling agency in Ireland were to be established with an economic link with an abortion clinic in England, then EC law prohibiting restrictions on information would apply to allow the provision of information about the English clinic by the Irish counselling agency.

The students' case was returned to the High Court, where, in August 1992, Judge Morris granted a permanent injunction restraining the defendants from providing information on abortion. This injunction was finally lifted on appeal by the Supreme Court in March 1997, by which time many other more dramatic legal and social developments had occurred.

In the context of EC law, two further significant developments took place following the decision of the Court in *Grogan*. First, in November 1991 the Irish government negotiated an additional clause, or protocol, to be adopted as part of the Treaty on European Union (the Maastricht Treaty), apparently to avoid the possibility of EC law overriding Article 40.3.3 of the Irish Constitution, should a conflict arise. That Protocol states: 'Nothing in the Treaty on European Union ... shall affect the application in Ireland of Article 40.3.3 of the Constitution of Ireland.' The adoption of Protocol No. 17 was barely noticed at the time, but it was to become highly controversial in the aftermath of the *X* case, which came before the High Court in February 1992.

The *X* Case and beyond

The Eighth Amendment provides that the right to life of the 'unborn' must be respected, defended and vindicated 'with due regard to the equal right to life of the mother'. It was inevitable, therefore, that where the two rights came into conflict, the courts would have the unenviable task of deciding which of them took priority. This dilemma first occurred in February 1992 with the *X* case – the facts of which are well-known, but worth recapping briefly (*Attorney General v. X* [1992] 1 IR 1). A 14-year-old girl became pregnant as the result of rape. She wanted to terminate the pregnancy, and her parents took her to England for that purpose. However, they notified the Gardaí that they were going because they wished to find out if DNA samples from the foetus could be used in any subsequent criminal proceedings against the offender. The Attorney-General, Harry Whelehan, became aware of this and took proceedings before the High Court seeking an injunction to stop the girl from travelling out of Ireland for the abortion. Judge Costello duly granted the injunction. The nightmare scenario predicted by those who had campaigned against the 1983 amendment had come to pass, and a pregnant child was effectively imprisoned in her own country. *The Irish Times'* cartoonist, Martyn Turner, famously depicted the plight of the girl in his sketch of a map of Ireland, with barbed wire instead of coastline, enclosing a young child carrying a teddy bear.

X and her parents, who were already in England when they were notified of the injunction, returned to Dublin – and political uproar ensued. A march called by a previously unknown pro-choice organisation, DARG – Dublin Abortion Rights Group, mostly made up of ex-students involved in the case against the students' unions – unexpectedly drew a crowd of 10,000 people onto O'Connell Street in Dublin. Other demonstrations were held around the country; there was popular outrage at the notion that this young girl might be prevented from travelling abroad and be forced to proceed with an unwanted pregnancy against her own wishes and those of her parents.

In the face of this mounting public pressure, the government offered to pay the legal costs of an appeal by the girl's parents to the Supreme Court. The appeal was heard within a matter of weeks, and the Supreme Court reversed Judge Costello's decision and allowed the girl to travel. The Court found that because the girl was suicidal as a result of the pregnancy, the continuation of the pregnancy would have threatened her right to life, which meant the two rights were in direct conflict. In such a situation, the Court ruled, the right to life of the pregnant girl or woman should prevail. Chief Justice Finlay stated in summary that, 'If it can be established as a matter of probability that there is a real and substantial risk to the life, as distinct from the health, of the mother, which can only be avoided by the termination of her pregnancy, such termination is permissible.'

Thus, the risk of suicide was held to have established a sufficient risk to the life of X to render lawful the termination of her pregnancy – in other words, she could legally have an abortion in Ireland. In fact, she returned to England, together with her parents, although it was reported that she miscarried before having the termination. However, despite the decision in X's favour, the corollary of the Chief Justice's test was that where a woman was not facing a threat to her life, then not only would it be illegal for her to have an abortion in Ireland, but she could also be prevented from travelling abroad to avail of legal abortion elsewhere. Further, because of Protocol No. 17 to the Maastricht Treaty, a woman in this invidious position could not rely upon the EC law guaranteeing freedom of movement to enable her to travel, since this would be overridden by Article 40.3.3 of the Constitution. When it was realised that the Maastricht Treaty might have this effect because of the Protocol, a massive campaign against its adoption was launched by the pro-choice movement and those who had demonstrated to allow X to travel.

As a result of this public outcry, and faced with the potential defeat of the Maastricht Treaty referendum, the government was again forced to take action. First, in May 1992, and again at the instigation of the Irish government, the Foreign Ministers of the EC Member States adopted a 'Solemn Declaration' in relation to Protocol No. 17. This declaration states that the operation of the Protocol in Ireland will not affect freedom to travel between Member States, or freedom to obtain or provide information relating to services lawfully available in Member States. The actual legal effect of this Declaration, which apparently contradicts the words of the Protocol, or indeed the actual legal effect of the Protocol itself, have never been tested. Nonetheless, its adoption reassured people that girls in X's position would not be prevented from travelling in future, and it thus helped to ensure that the Maastricht Treaty referendum was passed by the people in June 1992.

The second action taken by the government was to put three amendments to Article 40.3.3 of the Constitution before the people in November 1992. The aim of the first of these – known as the Twelfth Amendment, or the 'Substantive Issue' Amendment – was to rule out suicide as constituting a threat to the life of a pregnant woman while enshrining the remainder of the Chief Justice's definition of lawful abortion. This meant that, if passed, abortion would only have been allowed where necessary to save a woman's life if she had a physical illness or condition giving rise to a real and substantial risk to her life; but not allowed where she was at risk of suicide. The second amendment guaranteed the freedom (but not the right) to travel abroad, and the third allowed for the provision of information on services lawfully available in other Member States.

The so-called Substantive Issue Amendment was opposed by pro-choice groups who wished, at a minimum, to maintain the lawfulness of abortion in circumstances such as those of the X case. In a bizarre twist, it was also opposed by a number of anti-abortion groups who, while seeking to overturn the decision in X, did not think that the proposed wording went far enough, in that it still allowed for abortion in limited circumstances, ie, where necessary to save the life of the pregnant woman. Even this was too much abortion for them; they denied that abortion was ever necessary to save a woman's life. The Pro-Life Campaign, in particular, argued that termination of pregnancy should only be permissible where it was 'an unsought side-effect of medical treatment necessary to save the life of the mother'. Given that it was opposed both by pro-choice and anti-abortion groups, albeit for different reasons, it was hardly surprising that the proposed Twelfth Amendment was rejected by the people on 25 November 1992. However, in a clear victory for the pro-choice movement, the travel and information referenda were passed on the same date.

Following these amendments, the Regulation of Information (Services Outside the State for Termination of Pregnancies) Act 1995 came into force, providing for the conditions under which information on abortion may be legally provided. However, the first comprehensive study of women and crisis pregnancy in Ireland, conducted subsequent to the introduction of the Act, demonstrates the unfortunate reality that information on both contraception and abortion is still difficult to obtain for many women and girls in Ireland.[9]

When the three referenda were being held in November 1992, the government made it clear that if the Twelfth Amendment were not passed, it would introduce legislation to implement the X case, ie, legislation confirming the right to termination where the pregnant woman was suicidal, or her life was otherwise at risk. Indeed, the need for legislation had already been explicitly commented upon by the courts. In the *X* case, Judge McCarthy, one of the Supreme Court judges, had pointed out that:

> In the context of the eight years that have passed since the Amendment was adopted and the two years since *Grogan's* case, the failure by the legislature to enact the appropriate legislation is no longer just unfortunate, it is inexcusable. What are pregnant women to do? What are the parents of a pregnant girl under age to do? What are the medical profession to do? They have no guidelines save what may be gleaned from the judgments in this case.[10]

The *C* Case and beyond

Despite these strong views, yet another case of a tragic teenager came before the High Court in November 1997 – the *C* case, in which a 13-year-old girl became pregnant as a result of rape (*A and B v. Eastern Health Board* [1998] 1 IR 464). She was in the care of her local health board, which sought and was granted permission by the District Court to take the girl to England for an abortion. However, the girl's parents, having previously supported her decision to terminate her pregnancy, changed their minds 'as the result of outside influence' (according to the judge, members of the militant anti-abortion group Youth Defence had been involved in persuading them to oppose their daughter's wishes) and appealed the District Court decision to the High Court. In that court, Judge Geoghegan found on the evidence of psychiatric opinion that the girl was suicidal, and that the continuation of her pregnancy would pose a 'real and substantial risk' to her life. Thus the abortion would have been lawful in Ireland, and the health board was entitled to take her to England, which it subsequently did. Once again, however, the judge acknowledged that if there were no such risk to the girl's life, she would not have been entitled to have the abortion in Ireland, nor to travel abroad to obtain it.

It is an appalling indictment of the Irish legal system that, despite the holding of five referenda on abortion between 1983 and now, there is still no legislation in place to protect the rights of young women in the desperate position of the girl in the C case, that is, girls who are pregnant but unable to travel abroad without assistance: the most vulnerable group of pregnant women, whose present legal position is untenable. Unless they are in the care of a health board that is willing to apply to the courts for permission for them to travel, they will be forced to continue the unwanted pregnancy. Even where the health board applies on a girl's behalf for permission to travel, the court may not grant the right to travel unless the girl can prove she is suicidal, or that her life is otherwise at risk if her pregnancy continues. The freedom to travel can only be exercised by those with the means to do so; there is no enforceable right to travel. The personal stories of the many women and girls who do travel, and of the many others who would travel if they could but cannot, are never told in public – only anonymously, or under assumed names. We simply do not know how women in such situations cope.

The medical profession and the legislation vacuum

There is barely any more evidence available on how doctors cope where they have patients with crisis pregnancies. Under the Information Act 1995 they are entitled to provide patients with information on all the options available to them, including that of abortion, but they cannot provide information on abortion without also providing information on all the other choices, ie, fostering, adoption, or keeping the child. In a typically Byzantine feat of legal drafting, the Information Act does not permit doctors actually to 'refer' women patients to clinics in England; the woman must make the appointment herself. Where a woman's pregnancy poses a risk to her life, doctors are again in a legal quagmire. Apart from the Chief Justice's words in the X case, nobody has explained what constitutes a 'real and substantial risk' to life that may justify an abortion, nor has anyone decided how to establish suicide risk.

The apparent absence of any pro-choice views from within the medical profession has been a notable feature of the debate on abortion in Ireland. Whereas anti-abortion doctors have been vocal, few doctors have been willing to present themselves as being in favour of legalising abortion. In June 2001, the issue of abortion was pushed to the fore once more with the visit to Dublin and Cork of the Women on Waves ship, a boat with an abortion clinic on board, staffed by Dutch doctors and nurses, providing information about abortion to interested groups and individuals. What was most remarkable about the ship's short visit was the number of women who phoned the ship's hotline, or turned up in person at the quayside, desperate to know if they could obtain an abortion on board. The sheer scale of the problem – the needs of so many pregnant women for whom a journey to England is difficult if not impossible to arrange – had not been previously recognised. The ship's visit served as an important reminder of the reality of the experience of crisis pregnancy for so many women.

It also served to galvanise pro-choice advocates in the medical profession into action. A new group was formed, Doctors for Choice (made up of both female and male doctors); this was the first time that a pro-choice doctors' organisation had been established. Since then, doctors have intervened to a greater extent in the debate, for example, in the referendum campaign of March 2002.

The discernible shift in medical attitudes is particularly evident in the Medical Council's new *Ethical Guide* (sixth edition), published in March 2004. Previous ethical guidelines published by the Council, the doctors' professional body, had taken the view that even where abortion could lawfully be carried out within the terms of the X case, it would be professional misconduct in some circumstances. A previous version of the Council's Ethical Code held that the 'deliberate and intentional destruction of the unborn child is professional misconduct' and had only envisaged termination of pregnancy as ethical where it was a 'side effect of standard medical treatment of the mother'. This had effectively enshrined into medical practice the Catholic doctrine of 'double effect' – that termination may occur as a result of an 'unintended outcome', or 'side effect' of a medical procedure carried out for another aim, but it may not occur as the intended outcome of a procedure carried out for that aim.

This distinction appears a bizarre way to conduct medical practice – that an accident is permissible but an action is not. However, after pressure for change from among more liberal members of the medical profession, the new *Ethical Guide* reads, at para. 24.6 (under the heading 'The Child in Utero'):

> The Council recognises that termination of pregnancy can occur where there is a real and substantial risk to the life of the mother.[11]

This new provision expressly recognises the principle set out in the *X* case, and the change in emphasis in the approach to pregnancy termination taken by the Medical Council must be welcomed as a result.

Recent developments

In the years since the *C* case, there have been a number of further developments, but no legislation to clarify these issues for women or doctors has been forthcoming. Legislation had already been recommended by the Constitution Review Group, a group of legal experts chaired by TK Whitaker, which concluded in 1996 that legislation within the ambit of the existing constitutional framework was the 'only practical possibility'. The CRG considered that 'it would not be safe to rely on' the position of the anti-abortion campaign, ie, that abortion is never necessary to save the life of a pregnant woman. This view would rule out the introduction of an absolute constitutional ban on abortion.[12] During the first stage of a protracted 'consultation process' on abortion which followed the *C* case, a comprehensive and thoughtful *Green Paper* was published by the government in September 1999, presenting a total of seven options for the government, ranging from an absolute constitutional ban on abortion (which they also rejected as unsafe) to legislation allowing for abortion on request.[13]

This report was referred to the All-Party Oireachtas Committee on the Constitution (APOCC), which itself engaged in a further consultation process, holding oral hearings during 2000 and finally reporting to the Cabinet Sub-Committee on Abortion in November 2000.[14] Unfortunately, these recommendations were not as considered or thoughtful as those contained in the *Green Paper*. Although all members were agreed on the need to invest resources in a programme to tackle the incidence of crisis pregnancy, they could not agree on a single recommendation as to legal change. Instead, three alternatives were presented – none of which came close to the seventh option put forward in the *Green Paper*, that of abortion on request.

The first approach was to leave the legal position unchanged, the second to introduce legislation within the existing constitutional framework, and the third to amend the Constitution to rule out suicide as a ground on which threat to life could be established. On one point, fortunately, all members of the Committee were agreed: that an 'absolute constitutional ban' on abortion, as sought by anti-abortion campaigners, would be unsafe and would put the lives of pregnant women at risk. This at least represented a step forward from the fundamentalist position adopted by all the anti-abortion groups in the wake of the X case, and in the referenda put to the people in November 1992.

Of these three limited options, the pro-choice campaign favoured the second option, that of legislation within the constitutional framework to implement the X case test. Such legislation would at least have prevented further X or C cases from occurring, and could have safeguarded the lives of suicidal women unable to travel abroad for abortions. The pro-choice group Abortion Reform, a broad-based coalition of pro-choice organisations, such as DARG, Women's Aid and the IFPA, actively campaigned for such legislation to be introduced. The more moderate wing of the anti-abortion movement, on the other hand, actively supported the referendum to rule out suicide risk as a ground for abortion; this was effectively a re-run of the November 1992 Twelfth Amendment. Some of the more extremist members on the anti-abortion side, who had always campaigned for an absolute constitutional ban on abortion, still opposed this more limited referendum as they argued it would allow abortion, albeit on the most restrictive grounds – where necessary to save the life of a pregnant woman. Many of these fundamentalists denied that it would ever be necessary to terminate a pregnancy to save the life of a pregnant woman, despite evidence to the contrary provided in the oral submissions of doctors to the APOCC hearings.

Abortion Reform made submissions to the APOCC calling for legislation to implement the X case test for legal abortion. Due to the ongoing failure to introduce any such legislation, on 5 March 2001, nine years to the day after the Supreme Court gave its judgment in the X case, the organisation launched legislation to implement the X case. This proposed legislation outlined conditions under which a doctor might carry out an abortion, ie, on receipt of a psychiatrist's opinion that the pregnant woman concerned was suicidal as a result of her pregnancy and was likely to commit suicide if the pregnancy proceeded. If passed, such legislation would have ensured that no change was made to the existing X case test for lawful medical procedures (real and substantial risk), and would have required no referendum – but no political party would take it on at that time.

The referendum of March 2002

The wheels of the legal and constitutional consultation process on abortion law ground on, and the recommendations of the APOCC were considered by the Government later in 2001. Although there was clear disagreement, even among anti-abortion activists, as to the best approach to take in the aftermath of this process, the Fianna Fáil/Progressive

Democrat coalition Government was ultimately swayed by the intensive lobbying of the Pro-Life Campaign – the slightly more moderate wing of the anti-abortion movement. On 6 March 2002 a referendum was put to the people, the effect of which would have been to reverse the decision in the *X* case by ruling out suicide risk as a ground for abortion. The referendum contained within it the text of a whole new piece of legislation, a highly complex and technical document apparently drafted by then Attorney-General, Michael McDowell TD. This was the fifth referendum in less than twenty years on the subject of abortion, but it amounted effectively to a re-run of the 'Substantive Issue' referendum defeated in November 1992.

The campaign around this referendum was dominated by a debate on the question of whether pregnant women or girls ever really became suicidal, and if so whether pregnancy termination could ever be a way of preventing suicide. This morbid and deeply unpalatable debate carried within it a perceptibly misogynistic undercurrent – that women could not be trusted, indeed that pregnant women would pretend to be suicidal in order to obtain abortion. In order to counter this approach, the pro-choice movement, or more accurately a range of different women's groups and civil liberties groups united under the 'Alliance for a No Vote' (ANV) banner, organised a group of psychiatrists and psychologists to explain that there exist established professional methods to assess suicide risk, and that these could be applied in order to guard against any 'abuse' of the system. Many on the pro-choice movement found it deeply distasteful to adopt this strategy, but given that the referendum was really about suicide rather than abortion, it was considered necessary.

Despite the intervention of these brave members of the psychiatric profession, the anti-abortion lobby appeared to be gaining the upper hand late in the campaign. Then, just a week before the referendum, at a press conference called by pro-referendum groups, the Masters of Dublin's three maternity hospitals, despite calling for a yes vote for the referendum, gave a hostage to fortune in answer to a question from veteran feminist journalist Nell McCafferty, who asked them about their attitudes to foetal abnormalities incompatible with life. The doctors admitted that they believed abortion should be allowed in certain circumstances; that a pregnant woman carrying a foetus that had no chance of survival outside the womb should be entitled to have an abortion in Ireland.

This admission was seen as a major boost for the 'No' side in the debate. Following extensive campaigning by the ANV, the Irish Family Planning Association, the Labour party and other progressive groups, the referendum was ultimately defeated, although as with the 1995 divorce referendum the majority was tiny. Turnout was 42.8% of the electorate, of which 49.6% voted Yes, while 50.4% voted No. Unfortunately, while the defeat of the referendum was very important symbolically, demonstrating that even the combined power of the Catholic Church, the anti-abortion movement and the Fianna Fáil party could not win over changing public opinion on this issue, defeat did not mark any step forward for pro-choice campaigners. It simply stopped the clock turning backwards. The difference it made to the reality of crisis pregnancy for Irish women was negligible.

The reality of women's experience

The law on contraception may have undergone rapid change in recent years, but for the present the law on abortion remains rooted in a quagmire, with the X case representing the only circumstances in which abortion may lawfully be carried out in Ireland, but with no abortions being carried out in practice on grounds of suicide risk. After the defeat of the 2002 referendum, the Government stated that it would not bring in any legislation on the X case. Even if legislation is introduced in the future providing for the conditions under which abortion on suicide-risk grounds may be performed, the reality of Irish women's experiences of abortion will not be addressed. Over 100,000

Irish women have had abortions since 1983, the year of the Eighth Amendment, the vast majority of them on grounds other than risk to life. The Irish abortion rate now runs at over 6,000 per year – comparable to the abortion rates of most other European countries where abortion is legal. Yet the voices of these women are not heard in the debate on abortion. They have effectively been silenced under the present legal regime. One recent book, *The Irish Journey: Women's Stories of Abortion*,[15] represents an attempt to present women's experiences of abortion for the first time; yet even in this publication women provide their stories anonymously.

These are women who face a 'double crisis': on top of their crisis pregnancy, they also face the added crisis involved in the practical, financial and emotional difficulties of making the journey to England, and of the legal and social stigma still attaching. The right to choose how, when and whether they reproduce – the core principle behind any reproductive rights campaign – is denied to them. Any practical legal solution must address their needs. Indeed, any legal approach that falls short of addressing the real needs of real women is ultimately not just a Government failure, it is a failure for all of society.

One recent positive development for reproductive health has been the establishment of the Crisis Pregnancy Agency (CPA), set up in 2002. The CPA now acts as the conduit for funds to non-directive counselling organisations, like the IFPA and the Well Woman Centre, as well as to directive agencies, like Life and Cura, which do not give information on abortion. It is also developing policy on important issues, such as the existence of 'fake' counselling centres which purport to offer women information on abortion, but instead use subterfuge and shock tactics to dissuade them from terminating their pregnancies.

Unfortunately, the establishment of the CPA has not brought about any move to clarify or liberalise existing law on abortion. Nor has the CPA intervened in recent controversies surrounding the issue of embryonic stem-cell research; embryonic stem-cells are thought to have immense potential for medical research seeking a cure for conditions like Parkinson's disease. In late 2003, anti-abortion groups in Ireland and around Europe mounted a campaign to prevent EU funding being provided to support such research; at the same time, it became apparent that in Ireland there is no legislation regulating this area, just as there is no legislation on *in vitro* fertilisation, surrogacy, or sperm donation. In this crucial area, there is no legal quagmire – just no law.

FUTURE LEGAL CHANGE

Legal change is necessary not only to legalise abortion but also to establish a statutory framework within which the provision of other reproductive health services may be regulated. Undoubtedly, as experience elsewhere shows, regulation of sperm banks, *in vitro* fertilisation and other assisted human reproduction services is necessary. Similarly, legislation should govern the conduct of embryonic stem-cell research. Until now, one reason often given for the failure to legislate in this area is the presence of Article 40.3.3 in the Constitution and the legal status it gives to the foetus, which makes the legality of any procedures involving work with embryos or foetuses uncertain. This is another, practical reason for the deletion of this Article from the Constitution.

An even more important reason to remove Article 40.3.3 is that as long as it remains part of our fundamental law, it devalues the lives of women; by equating the right to life of the unborn with that of the mother, it gives unborn life an unrealistically absolute claim on the life of the pregnant woman, a claim that is, in practice, untenable. The adoption of the Article has not prevented one crisis pregnancy, nor stopped even one woman travelling to England to terminate her pregnancy. It simply serves to compound the crisis of a crisis pregnancy. Its retention allows us to maintain the hypocrisy that there is no abortion in Ireland; its deletion would remove legal uncertainty about reproductive health services and the morning-after pill and would allow us to introduce sensible legislation providing for a range of conditions under which abortion might be performed lawfully.

Pending the removal of Article 40.3.3 by referendum, limited legislation should be introduced providing for the conditions under which a pregnancy may be terminated, that is, where its continuance poses a threat to the life of a pregnant woman – the long overdue legislation under the X case test. This measure would at least address the needs of women in the most desperate circumstances. In the longer term, more fundamental, broader change is necessary to ensure the real needs of women in Ireland are met.

NOTES FOR CHAPTER FIVE

1. Mahon, Conlon & Dillon, *Women and Crisis Pregnancy*. (Dublin: Government Publications, 1998.)

2. See Mary Raftery, 'Trocáire's condoms challenged', in *The Irish Times*, 11 March 2004.

3. *Medical Council Ethical Guide* (Sixth edition, 2004).
See www.medicalcouncil.ie/professional/ethics; see also Coulter, C., 'Council's new guideline on IVF has huge implications for the family', in *The Irish Times*, 26 March 2004.

4. MacKinnon, C., 'Reflections on Sex Equality in Law', p.100, in *Yale Law Journal* 1319, 1991.

5. Connolly, L., 'From Revolution to Devolution: Mapping the Contemporary Women's Movement in Ireland', p.561, in Byrne & Leonard (eds), *Women and Irish Society*. (Belfast: Beyond the Pale Publications, 1997.)

6. Binchy, W., 'Marital Privacy and Family Law: a reply to Mr. O'Reilly', in *Studies* 330, 1977.

7. Kingston & Whelan with Bacik, *Abortion and the Law*, p.260. (Dublin: Round Hall Ltd, 1997.)

8. Hesketh, Tom, *The Second Partitioning of Ireland*. (Dublin: Brandsma Books, 1990.)

9. Mahon, Conlon & Dillon, as at note 1.

10. *Attorney General v. X* [1992] 1 IR 1, at p.90.

11. *Medical Council Ethical Guide*, para. 24.6. (Sixth edition, 2004.)

12. Constitution Review Group, *Report of the Constitution Review Group*.

(Dublin: Government Publications, 1996.)

13. *Green Paper on Abortion*. (Dublin: Government Publications, 1999.)

14. APOCC, *Fifth Progress Report: Abortion*. (Dublin: Government Publications, 2000.)

15. *The Irish Journey: Women's Stories of Abortion*. (Dublin: IFPA, 2000.)

CHAPTER 6
Sexuality and Sexual Offences

SEXUALITY IN MODERN IRELAND

Catholic Church teaching and orthodoxy has long dominated discussion of sexuality in Ireland. Extensive censorship laws (see Chapter 7) and the stranglehold of the Church on many communities meant that through most of the twentieth century issues around sexuality could not be openly debated, and the gay community in particular remained largely closeted. Only relatively recently – with a diminishing of the power and influence of the Church, the legalisation of contraception, and increased economic prosperity bringing about a liberalisation of Irish society – has it become possible to talk about sexuality more openly.

In terms of sexuality, Ireland is now a very different place from even just a decade ago. Homosexuality has been decriminalised, a confident and visible gay scene has emerged in major urban centres, sex education is finally being taught in (some) schools, and there is open discussion about hitherto hidden sexual issues. In particular, fuelled by ground-breaking media investigations, there is much public debate around child sexual abuse scandals of the past: a shockingly widespread level of abuse – within the Church, in institutions, by teachers and carers, and within families – that, until now, was swept firmly under the carpet. Abortion is now perhaps the only sexual subject about which there remains a social taboo.

In some quarters, there is grave unease at the pace of recent change, which has occurred over a surprisingly short period of time. Sociologist Michael O'Connell argues that this 'quiet sexual revolution' has only been happening in Ireland since as recently as 1993. It is no wonder then that there are those who fear liberalisation, who believe that a culture of overt sexualisation has emerged and that the loss of sexual inhibitions has somehow been a loss to society. But who would want to return to the joyless repression that characterised Irish attitudes to sexuality in the past? Loss of inhibition should be welcomed as a positive development for Irish society, a change that allows all adults, regardless of sexual orientation, to enjoy a fulfilling sex life and sexual identity.

Yet once again, as with other aspects of social relations, the law has not kept pace with rapid social changes around the issue of sexuality.

THE CRIMINALISATION OF HOMOSEXUALITY

Social attitudes may have moved on, but the criminal law on sexual offences still retains many features that owe their origins to nineteenth-century ideas of sexuality. For historical reasons, the law on sexual offences against women and girls has developed differently from that relating to offences against men and boys. This is due to very different social views of such offences, and to the differential views taken about and the treatment of homosexuality and heterosexuality in society at large. The law in this area has undergone a process of continuous and ongoing change as public attitudes have shifted and shifted again, yet it remains rooted in certain assumptions taken from Victorian ideas of morality.

The nineteenth-century legislation on sexual offences, introduced in England during the reign of Queen Victoria and applying also in Ireland, was the Offences Against the Person Act 1861. This Act, which codified pre-existing common law and older legislation on sexual offences, contained a chapter headed 'Unnatural Offences', which dealt with sexual offences by men upon other men, and a separate chapter entitled 'Offences Against Women and Girls', which related to sexual offences perpetrated upon women by men. There was no reference in the Act to sexual offences between women; Victoria is famously and apocryphally described as having refused to countenance the existence of lesbianism!

The offences of buggery and of indecent assault on male persons were dealt with in sections 61 and 62, contained in the 'Unnatural Offences' chapter of the Act. The law was amended to prohibit all forms of 'indecency' between males, under the Criminal Law Amendment Act 1885, which provided at section 11 that any male person who committed 'any act of gross indecency with another male person', in public or in private, would be liable to imprisonment for up to two years. This was the provision under which Oscar Wilde was convicted and sentenced to two years' imprisonment in 1895.

These laws remained part of Irish law upon independence from Britain in 1922, and ultimately remained in place until the 1990s. Incredibly, until 1993 male homosexual intercourse was a criminal offence in Ireland under this outdated legislation. By then, however, the emergent lesbian and gay rights movements had already had a significant impact on Irish society.

The Lesbian and Gay Rights movements

The decriminalisation of homosexuality in 1993 was finally brought about due to remarkably successful lobbying by the gay rights movement over many years. Further legal protections have since been introduced against discrimination on the grounds of sexual orientation: in the workplace (the Employment Equality Act 1998); and in the provision of goods and services (the Equal Status Act 2000). 'Sexual orientation' is defined in both Acts as meaning 'heterosexual, homosexual, or bisexual orientation.' The campaign for gay rights continues on the issue of domestic partnership law, the aim being to enable same-sex couples to register their relationships formally with the State and thereby gain many legal protections currently available only to married couples.

This has been a long campaign: the Sexual Liberation Movement had its first public meeting in 1973, the Irish Gay Rights Movement was founded in 1974, and the first National Gay Conference was held in 1981. There were many strands to the campaign, with various groups making significant contributions. The Quay Co-Op resource centre, established in Cork in 1982, fostered many initiatives and campaigns on lesbian and gay rights. Another high-profile group, Gay Health Action (GHA), published the first Irish AIDS information leaflet in 1985. For some time GHA was the only organisation providing information and advice on AIDS and safe sex to the gay community and other groups, and to professionals and the media. Its existence led to the setting up of the AIDS Alliances and the support group Cáirde (for those who are HIV+).

An equally high-profile campaign group, the Gay and Lesbian Equality Network (GLEN), which forged links with many other civil liberties organisations, took on the twin aims of ensuring both criminal law reform and legal protection through anti-discrimination legislation. There was, however, a general decline in gay activism in the mid-1980s, which might be described as a decade of 'backlash', symbolised by the burning down of the Hirschfield (gay resource) Centre in Dublin in 1988 and the tragic killing of a gay man in Fairview Park in 1983. However, the law reform campaign continued, focusing in the late 1970s and early 1980s with the constitutional case taken by David Norris.

In 1984, Norris, now a Senator and a pioneer for gay rights, challenged the constitutionality of the provisions of the 1861 and 1885 Acts prohibiting sexual relations between men. In *Norris v. Attorney General* ([1984] IR 36), he argued that as a homosexual man, the effective criminalisation of homosexuality under the 1861 and 1885 legislation amounted to a denial of his constitutional right to privacy (he argued that this was an implied constitutional right). Among other things, he also argued that it amounted to a breach of the equality guarantee since the ban did not apply to lesbians. He lost his challenge on all of these grounds, both in the High Court and the Supreme Court, which held by a 3:2 majority against him. Many passages in the judgment of Chief Justice O'Higgins for the majority make bizarre reading today, being based upon the sort of Victorian notions of morality on which the legislation itself was founded. The Chief Justice discussed at length the way in which homosexuality had traditionally been regarded by organised religions, observing that, 'from the earliest days' it had been regarded:

> ... with a deep revulsion as being contrary to the order of nature, a perversion of the biological functions of the sexual organs and an affront both to society and to God. With the advent of Christianity this view found clear expression in the teachings of St. Paul, and has been repeated over the centuries by the doctors and leaders of the Church in every land in which the Gospel of Christ has been preached. Today ... it remains the teaching of all Christian Churches that homosexual acts are wrong.

The Chief Justice then referred to the Preamble of the Irish Constitution, which, he stated, indicated the intention of the people of Ireland to adopt a Constitution consistent with Christian beliefs and he could not accept that, in the very act of doing so, 'the people rendered inoperative laws which had existed for hundreds of years prohibiting unnatural sexual conduct which Christian teaching held to be gravely sinful.'

Thus, with many more gratuitous comments on the evils of homosexuality, the Court concluded that the legislation was constitutional. The European Court of Human Rights subsequently took a different view, ruling in 1988 that the ban on homosexuality was in breach of Norris' right to privacy under Article 8 of the European Convention on Human Rights (ECHR). At the time, however, the ECHR was not part of Irish law, and so it took some years before the government finally acted to remove the ban, and only after extensive political lobbying by GLEN and others. The Criminal Law (Sexual Offences) Act 1993 was introduced by Minister for Justice Máire Geoghegan-Quinn, and it legalised homosexuality for the first time in Irish history. The 1993 Act was widely welcomed for its progressive effect, liberating thousands of gay citizens from the fear of prosecution. However, it did not retrospectively abolish the offences pertaining under the old 1861 Act, so that a person may still be charged with indecent assault if the sexual relations in question occurred before the commencement date of the 1993 Act.

Minister Geoghegan-Quinn insisted, on principle, that the age of consent for homosexual intercourse should be the same as that for heterosexual intercourse, ie, 17 years of age. That is, it remains an offence to have homosexual intercourse with a boy who is under 17 years of age; this was an important feature of the legislation. The same issue was also being debated in Britain at the time, where there was great resistance from members of the House of Lords to the introduction of an equal age of consent for both homosexual and heterosexual intercourse. Ireland, however, had a particular starting point for the debate, given that the Law Reform Commission *Report on Child Sexual Abuse* 1990 had recommended repeal of the relevant sections of the 1861 Act, and section 11 of the 1885 Act, and also that the same legal regime should obtain for consensual homosexual and heterosexual activity. In this respect, at least, Irish law was well ahead of British legal reform; an equal age of consent (now 16 years of age) was introduced much later in Britain. Thus the gay rights movement in Ireland has been remarkably successful in bringing about progressive legal change.

Although many women were and are involved in law reform campaigns and the gay rights movement, lesbians have never been as visible in Ireland as gay men. Many lesbians were and remain involved in feminist campaigns and in the women's movement, but in 1978, at Ireland's first conference on lesbianism, held in Dublin, few women participants felt able to identify themselves publicly as lesbian. In 1980, Joni Crone appeared as Ireland's first 'out' lesbian on 'The Late Late Show', but it was to be another fourteen years before another lesbian, writer Emma Donoghue, appeared on the programme. In 1991, Lesbians Organising Together (LOT) was founded – a national network of different collectives and other political and cultural groups working together to promote and support the visibility and active participation of lesbian and bisexual women in Irish society. Every year, a lesbian arts festival (aLAF) is organised in Dublin, and a lesbian and gay film festival also takes place annually. But by comparison with the growing confidence evident in the male gay community, Irish lesbians continue to be less vocal and less visible.

Present day

In recent years, a new generation of high-profile young gay Irish men have become media celebrities, such as Graham Norton, Brendan Courtney and Brian Dowling. Incidentally, Dowling became famous as a result of appearing on 'Big Brother', the British reality television show; as a result of appearing on the same show in a different year, Irish lesbian woman Anna Nolan also launched a media career. A thriving gay scene is based around a number of venues and events in different urban centres: Gay Pride (now simply Pride); the annual Alternative 'Miss' Ireland Competition; the Dublin cabarets led by Panti, Shirley Temple Bar and Veda, among others. Political campaigns continue under the auspices of the National Lesbian and Gay Federation (NLGF). There is also a strong media presence with the revamped publication *Gay Community News* – although a more glossy and less political magazine, *Gay Ireland*, launched in 2001, did not survive.

A more informed and political generation of gay women and men have embraced the emergence of bisexual and transgendered identities; sexuality is no longer perceived in either/or terms. An increased political confidence and the enhanced visibility of gay people as cultural icons has led to a common perception that homosexuality is now positively valued in Irish society.

Unfortunately, continued economic and social discriminations against gay men and women means that the campaign for lesbian and gay rights is not yet over. In particular, there is resistance to the recognition of gay rights from the more traditional sectors of society, and from the Irish-American diaspora. Although Mary Robinson, when newly elected President of Ireland, made her inclusive conception of Irish identity clear by welcoming lesbians and gay men into the Áras for the first time in December 1992, Irish lesbian and gay groups continue to be denied the right to march in the annual St Patrick's Day parade in New York City. Their vocal protests and memorable slogans ('Two, Four, Six, Eight, How do you know St Patrick's straight?') have focused international attention on a redefinition of Irishness and Irish identity.

Unfortunately, Catholic Church leaders in Ireland are not moved by these protests. They have continued to use language such as 'objectively disordered', 'deviant' and 'evil' when discussing homosexuality. Homophobic remarks are a real problem at many levels in society. This has very serious practical implications, since for both lesbians and gay men in Ireland today, homophobic physical attacks are also still a regular occurrence – gay women forced out of their home due to intimidation by neighbours; assaults outside gay bars on the streets of Dublin. Such attacks are more likely to occur in a context where Catholic Church leaders believe it is acceptable to express homophobic sentiments.

Legal discriminations against gay people also persist, especially in the context of gay partnerships and in matters relating to the custody, parenting and adoption of children. As the Supreme Court has declared the constitutionally protected 'family' to be limited to that based upon marriage, it means even non-married heterosexual couples receive little legal recognition; and there is no recognition of partnership rights in any form for same-sex couples.

The many advantages that come with recognised legal status, in terms of immigration rights, tax benefits and inheritance rights, for example, may not be availed of by lesbian or gay couples. Specific gay marriage and parenting rights remain non-existent. Senator David Norris and a group of others are actively campaigning to seek to put in place 'domestic partnership' legislation that would provide rights such as these to same-sex couples. While such legislation would fall short of providing gay couples with the right to marry, it could be introduced without constitutional amendment and would at least resolve many of the practical difficulties which can arise for couples unable legally to register their partnerships at present; it appears to have cross-Party support.

In spite of this ongoing lack of official recognition for same-sex partnerships, more generally there has been a sea change in Irish attitudes to homosexuality, a shift reflected in the extensive legal change that has occurred in recent years. Like the feminist movement, this is a campaign that has come a long way in a short time: from a criminal offence to a matter of pride in just over a decade.

SEXUAL CRIMES

In relation to sexual offences, including offences against children and offences concerning prostitution, Irish laws remain mired in nineteenth-century concepts of sexual behaviour and deviance. At a time when there is a marked increase in the incidence of reported rape, sexual assaults and child sexual abuse, it is appalling that the criminal law relating to such offences has never undergone comprehensive reform. Law Reform Commission recommendations on simplifying and codifying the law in this area have been widely ignored. Instead, changes have been made piecemeal, with amending legislation sometimes even reversing earlier reforms. The result is a complex mesh of different offences, inconsistent sentencing schemes and unwieldy amendments.

Disparity in treatment

Until relatively recently, for instance, due to the different historical developments of the laws on sexual offences against men and against women, sexual assault on a female carried a lower maximum penalty than the equivalent offence of indecent assault on a male. The Offences

Against the Person Act 1861 provided a maximum of ten years' penal servitude for indecent assault on a male, and a maximum of two years' imprisonment for indecent assault upon a female (section 52). In 1885 the penalty for indecent assault on a female was raised to five years in the case of a second or subsequent offence, and in 1981 the maximum penalty for indecent assaults on females was raised again to ten years' imprisonment. Finally, in 1990, the Criminal Law (Rape) (Amendment) Act provided that the offence of indecent assault upon any male or female person would now be known as sexual assault, and that the maximum penalty for sexual assault would be five years (effectively reversing the 1981 change introducing a ten-year maximum). These offences all related to crimes against adults or against children.

However, due to the increased seriousness with which such offences are regarded, the penalties for sexual offences committed against children of either sex have now been increased, in line with the relevant recommendations of the Law Reform Commission. The Sex Offenders Act 2001 thus changed the maximum penalty for sexual assault on a child of either sex (a child being a person aged under 17) to fourteen years' imprisonment.

But while the general scheme of sexual offence legislation has now become gender-neutral, differences of treatment between males and females remain. For example, under sections 1 and 2 of the Criminal Law Amendment Act 1935 young women are granted an immunity from prosecution where they consent to intercourse under the prescribed age, but no such immunity exists in relation to sexual intercourse with boys under 17 years of age. Leading criminal law academic Tom O'Malley suggests that:

> Despite being apparently discriminatory against males, ss.1 and 2 of the Act of 1935 have never been challenged as being inconsistent with the Constitution ...
> There may also be a belief, probably justified, among lawyers that the wording of Article 40.1 of the Constitution, which legitimates discrimination on the

basis of capacity and social function, would be fatal to any challenge to the sections in question. The immunity from prosecution granted to young women seems to be based largely on a paternalistic philosophy which is also reflected to some extent in the so-called proviso to Article 40.1 of the Constitution. As with other gender-based concessions, such as the special verdict of infanticide, this immunity may be viewed benevolently as a form of positive discrimination which acknowledges the power differential within heterosexual relations and the fact that it is the female who will have to bear the consequences of a teenage pregnancy.[1]

There remains a plethora of different sexual offences concerning children, and a range of different pieces of legislation dealing with these. The 1935 Act created the offences of unlawful carnal knowledge of a girl under 15 (punishable with life imprisonment), and of a girl between 15 and 17 (a maximum penalty of five years' imprisonment applies for a first offence, and ten years' imprisonment for a second or subsequent offence). These provisions of the 1935 Act remain in force today, but there is no equivalent of these sections for heterosexual intercourse with boys. Acts of 'gross indecency' with males under 17 are prohibited under section 4 of the 1993 Act, and then there are other offences provided for under the Child Trafficking and Pornography Act 1998. In 1990 the Law Reform Commission made the eminently sensible recommendation of redressing much of the complexity by introducing one comprehensive offence of 'child sexual abuse' or 'sexual exploitation', but unfortunately this has never been implemented in legislation.

As a result of this confusing and complex historical development, the law on age of consent for sex is far from clear-cut. No wonder the Law Reform Commission recommended clarification – it is sorely needed in this legal minefield, with its nineteenth-century attributes, its obsession with the concept of 'indecency', and its coyness about naming the actual behaviour prohibited.

Rape law and sexual offences against women

The law on sexual offences against women has evolved historically in a different way from the law on homosexuality, and indeed from the law on sexual offences against children. The offence of rape was traditionally defined as non-consensual sexual intercourse by a man with a woman; there was no equivalent offence for non-consensual intercourse committed by a man upon a man, since homosexual relations were all forbidden anyway, whether consensual or not. The crime of rape was traditionally the most serious sexual offence in the criminal law, and because of its origins, subsequently evolved as the archetypal gendered crime at common law.

Common-law rape is now prohibited in statute under the Criminal Law (Rape) Act 1981, as amended in 1990 and 1993. It is defined there more precisely as non-consensual sexual intercourse by a man with a woman where he either knows that she does not consent, or is reckless as to whether or not she consents. This is the *mens rea* or mental element of the offence, ie, the state of mind the accused must possess at the time of the offence in order for him to be criminally liable.

The definition of rape has its roots in earlier times, when it was regarded as a crime against property. The word derives from the Latin *rapere* (to seize), as the crime was seen to have the effect of forcibly seizing a valuable property from the male owner, ie, the father or husband of the female victim. Historically, rape was deemed to have occurred only where there had been emission of semen within the vagina, which put the paternity of a subsequent child born to the woman into question. The requirement to prove emission was abolished in most jurisdictions in the nineteenth century, although the emphasis on penile-vaginal penetration has persisted until recently in European systems, showing continued evidence of what Carol Smart describes as 'the dominant phallocentric perspective' on rape.[2] Any form of sexual abuse not involving penetration is instead defined in most countries as constituting the lesser offence of 'sexual assault'.

Recent changes to the definition of rape throughout Europe have meant that it is now generally defined as a gender-neutral offence, which may be perpetrated upon men and by women. In some EU countries there is just one offence – 'sexual coercion' – and this is divided into different categories to cover all forms of sexual assault, including rape or penetrative sexual assault. By contrast, the Irish reform introduced through section 4 of the Criminal Law (Rape) (Amendment) Act 1990 is unique. We have retained the common-law definition of rape as a crime capable of being committed only by a man upon a woman, but in addition we have created a second type of rape offence: 'rape under section 4'. This new and additional gender-neutral offence is committed through penetration of the anus or mouth by the penis, or penetration of the vagina by an object, again where carried out with the same level of awareness as to the victim's lack of consent. Bizarrely, penetration of the anus by an object is not included within this definition. When questioned about this exclusion during the Dáil debate on the matter, then Minister for Justice Ray Burke explained that:

> The penetration of the anus by an object will not constitute rape under section 4 because in certain circumstances such an occurrence may not constitute a serious offence. For example, one could have horseplay among schoolboys where an object, for example, a pencil could penetrate the anus and a person would not be charged with rape in such circumstances.[3]

The 1990 Act also introduced the new offence of 'aggravated sexual assault' and the Minister pointed out that such 'horseplay among schoolboys' could constitute an assault of that nature instead.

This means that two separate rape offences now exist in Irish law, both carrying the same maximum penalty of life imprisonment. It is difficult to identify a rationale for maintaining a distinct offence of common-law rape, other than the traditional premise that penile-vaginal intercourse should be regarded differently in law than other forms of penetration because it may result in pregnancy. Irish feminists had, however, called for all forms of sexual penetration to be included within one broadly defined rape offence, and remain dissatisfied with this compromise approach to reform.

Sexual offences on trial

Apart from problems with the legal definition of rape, the cross-examination of the victim during rape trials has long been a focus for feminist reformers, since the credibility and character of the victim or complainant in a rape trial are frequently undermined by defence counsel tactics. Two other issues pertaining to the testimony of the victim in the adversarial trial have been particularly contentious. The first of these is the defence's use of evidence that the victim has had sexual intercourse with others, or with the defendant, at some time in her life prior to the rape. The second is the warning traditionally given by the judge to the jury that it is dangerous to convict on the uncorroborated evidence of a rape victim ('the corroboration warning').

Evidence of the victim's prior sexual history was traditionally admissible without restriction in rape trials, unlike any other type of criminal trial, and was frequently used in order to undermine the credibility of the victim (always female, since until 1990 there was no equivalent offence of rape upon a male). Following extensive lobbying by women's groups in Ireland, such evidence cannot now be admitted at trial without the judge's permission. Defence counsel must apply to the judge, in the absence of the jury, before introducing any evidence that the victim had sex with anyone prior to the alleged rape. Under reforming legislation introduced in 2001 (the Sex Offenders Act 2001), the victim is now entitled to have legal representation to enable her or him to appoint a barrister to argue against the introduction of such evidence. Although this represents some improvement on the old law, it may still be criticised as inadequate to protect the victim's privacy.

According to the corroboration rule, again applied specifically to the complainant in a rape trial, the judge had to warn the jury of the danger of convicting the accused on the victim's evidence alone. The warning has been subject to strong criticism by feminist commentators, since the only crime it applies to is rape, and it may cast doubt upon the veracity of the complainant's evidence. In other words, it stems from the myth that women are likely to make false claims of rape. It is no longer mandatory procedure in Ireland, however, and the judge now has discretion as to whether or not to give a warning; but this provision has unfortunately not led to any change in practice. The Court of Criminal Appeal has held that it would be 'prudent' for the trial judge to continue to warn the jury in almost all cases where the victim's evidence was uncorroborated (*DPP v. Molloy*, CCA, 28 July, 1995).

It is clear that very particular and clearly gendered rules apply pertaining to the conduct of rape trials. Reform of rape law and procedures is ongoing in most European jurisdictions, including Ireland, largely due to campaigning by women's groups and rape crisis centres. The 2001 Act, for instance, introduced for a reforming purpose, initiated a sex offenders' register for the first time, imposing obligations on all those convicted of sexual offences to be registered with the Gardaí. It also introduced specific powers for sentencing judges to place restrictions and conditions on those convicted of such offences, such as, for example, in the case of those convicted of offences against children, a condition that they must stay away from schools or playgrounds after their release from prison.

Nonetheless, further reform is necessary in Ireland to clarify the law, since there remains a plethora of different sexual offences, ranging from rape; rape under section 4 of the 1990 Act (ie, oral rape or anal rape); sexual assault (formerly 'indecent assault upon a female person', or 'indecent assault upon a male person'); aggravated sexual assault (within the meaning of section 3 of the Act of 1990); incest of various forms prohibited under the Incest Act 1908; buggery with a person or an animal under sections 61 and 62 of the 1861 Act; and defilement of mentally impaired females (under the 1993 Act).

Such a multiplicity of offences contributes to the unnecessary complexity around sexual offence trials, and can lead to inconsistency in sentencing, since each offence carries a different maximum penalty. While some important reforms have been made, such as the introduction of the sex offenders' register, a wide range of changes is still required to answer the needs of victims, while respecting the rights of those accused to receive a fair trial. In a study conducted in 1998 comparing Irish laws on rape with those pertaining in every other EU country, the authors made fifty recommendations for legal change, including, for example, the recommendation that the definition of rape should become gender-neutral; that the corroboration warning be abolished; that legal representation be introduced for victims where evidence of prior sexual history is sought to be introduced by the defence (this recommendation was implemented in the 2001 Act); that training be provided to those dealing with victims of rape or sexual assaults; and that adequate facilities be provided in courthouses to ensure that victims are not brought face-to-face with alleged offenders.[4]

However, even such extensive law reform would obviously not be sufficient on its own to address the causes of rape, at a wider level, in the relations between men and women. Sexual offences committed by men against women still make up the vast majority of all sexual crimes coming before the courts, and in most cases rape and sexual assaults are carried out by persons known to the victim. A preventative approach to rape, which policy-makers everywhere should adopt, should therefore emphasise the vital role of education in changing attitudes and debunking the prevailing myths about rape – such as the myth that 'no means yes', or the myth that 'real rape' is only committed by a stranger in a dark alley – and in challenging the aggressive construction of masculinity, in order to reduce the incidence of violence against women.

PROSTITUTION AND THE LAW

A brief history of prostitution in Britain and Ireland

As with the law on rape, the criminal law on prostitution has developed historically in a clearly gendered way. Typically, only those working as prostitutes (mostly women) are penalised, while the (mostly male) customers remain outside the controls of the criminal law. The law promotes a double standard: it prohibits the public display of prostitution but not the act of selling sex. The focus is on controlling, containing and above all concealing the sale of sex. Only the public offer of sex for sale is criminalised, through the offences of 'loitering' and 'soliciting'. The offer of sex for sale in private is not criminalised, other than through laws forbidding the existence of brothels. It is not an offence for one woman to offer sex for sale in private. Until 1993, it was not an offence for a man to buy sex, either in public or in private. Even now, the purchase of sex is not an offence, except in public places. The reason for the present, peculiar state of the law lies in the historical development of prostitution offences.

Traditionally, condemnation of prostitution has been reserved for prostitutes alone: the double standards of Victorian morality meant that men could justify their use of the services of prostitutes with impunity. As women were disenfranchised and denied any legal personality, the male-dominated Executive and legislature could lay down the law on the relative characteristics of the sexes with authority and without challenge. That men's sexual impulses had to be indulged was beyond question; one justification, still in circulation, for the legal acceptance of prostitution was that it provided an outlet for those impulses that would otherwise be unleashed on respectable women. The harsh moral code in operation throughout the nineteenth century dictated that women became tainted by any contact with extra-marital sex. Women were deemed degraded by the sexual experience so that they became 'fallen women', driven by their disgrace and desperation to prostitution. While 'fallen women' were scorned by society or treated with pity by so-called philanthropists, the law was principally concerned with regulating their activities for the protection and convenience of others.

The Vagrancy Act 1824 penalised 'common prostitutes' for 'wandering in the streets or public highways', demonstrating that legislative concern centred not on the prostitutes themselves, nor on the causes behind their existence, but on the public manifestation of their activities. The Metropolitan Police Act 1839 similarly provided for the prosecution of a 'common prostitute', or 'nightwalker' for loitering or being in a public place for the purposes of prostitution or soliciting. It is significant that none of the key terms used in the laws of this period were defined in the relevant Acts. Under section 14 of the Dublin Police Act 1842, the opinion of a police officer as to whether any individual woman was a prostitute was sufficient evidence for the court. This section provided that it was an offence, subject to a penalty not exceeding fourteen shillings, for a 'common prostitute', or 'nightwalker' to loiter or to be in 'any thoroughfare or public place for the purpose of prostitution or solicitation, to the annoyance of the inhabitants or passengers.' Various other nineteenth-century public order statutes also contained measures aimed at regulating the activities of prostitutes. Loitering became an offence, as did keeping a 'disorderly house', ie, any lodging house used by more than one prostitute. Publicans were banned from allowing prostitutes to 'assemble and continue' on their premises.

It was not until the 1860s, however, that the full force of the law was brought to bear on prostitution with the introduction of the Contagious Diseases Acts of 1864–69, which introduced registration, compulsory medical examination and incarceration for prostitutes, ostensibly to protect soldiers from venereal disease; soldiers were not subject to any of these provisions. The first Contagious Diseases Act was passed in 1864 in a manner that became notorious to those who later campaigned for its repeal: introduced, surreptitiously, into the House of Commons very late at night, with few in attendance, under a title nearly identical to that of legislation dealing with livestock disease. It is possible that any confusion caused by the ambiguity of the similar titles was due to prudish drafting rather than a deliberate attempt at obscuring the nature of the Bill, although repeal campaigners thought differently.

Under the Act a woman could be summoned before a Justice of the Peace on the information of a police officer or doctor that she was believed to be a prostitute with venereal disease who had been soliciting in a public place. If the Justice was satisfied the information was correct, he could then order her to be examined in the local designated hospital, where she was to be conveyed with 'all practicable speed'; if found to be suffering from venereal disease, she would be detained for treatment for a maximum of three months. The Act applied in eleven targeted areas in England and Ireland; Cork, Queenstown (Cobh) and the Curragh were the areas targeted in Ireland. Hospitals were established in these areas, in which such women were confined and underwent mandatory treatment. The second Contagious Diseases Act introduced new powers for Justices and extended the maximum period of detention in hospital to six months. The third and final Act, in 1869, extended the application of the scheme to other areas, increased the maximum period of detention in hospital to nine months, and provided for the detention of menstruating women.

By the late 1860s public opinion on social reform was changing. A repeal movement was gaining steam, led by groups such as the Ladies' National Association for the Repeal of the Contagious Diseases Acts (LNA), founded in 1869. Branches of the LNA were established in Ireland, and Josephine Butler, the leading light of the movement, came over to speak at a meeting in Dublin in 1878. The Association succeeded in preventing the proposed extension of the Acts to the general civilian population, and the Acts in their entirety were finally repealed in 1886.

The fertile climate of moral reform, together with the 'social purity' crusades that grew from the repeal movement, led to the passing of the Criminal Law (Amendment) Act 1885, which, ironically, was as oppressive in its own way as the Contagious Diseases Acts had been. It prohibited all forms of 'indecency' between men, and gave the police extensive powers against procurers and brothelkeepers. The implementation of this new legislation was very successful in reducing the number of brothels, but this in turn had the effect of forcing prostitutes back onto the streets, where they were more vulnerable – and not just to the law.

In the late 1800s and early 1900s, the most notorious red-light district in Dublin was 'The Monto', the area around Montgomery Street in North Dublin, but the withdrawal, in 1922, of the British garrison stationed there led to a falling-off of business for prostitutes in the district. The death knell for the area was the foundation of the Legion of Mary in 1921, one of its express aims being the clean-up of the Monto. In 1925, after a two-year campaign, this was achieved. Once this was done, the policing of prostitution could no longer be confined to one area, and the identification of prostitutes became more problematic as they moved to different locations. Accordingly, the definitions in the legislation of words like 'soliciting' and 'loitering' took on a new significance.

'Loitering' and 'Soliciting'

The terms 'solicitation' and 'prostitute', central to the legislation, had been given various definitions in judicial decisions. In the 1913 decision of *Horton v. Mead*, solicitation was held to entail 'some gesture, act or words addressed to a prospective customer or contact'; solicitation by a prospective customer, however offensive, did not constitute an offence. The most authoritative definition of prostitution was given in the 1918 *de Munck* case, where prostitution was described as taking place when 'a woman offers her body commonly for lewdness for payment in return', thus it was not necessary that the woman offered herself for sexual intercourse, nor did sexual intercourse need to take place. 'Common prostitutes' were defined at common law as being women who 'offered themselves commonly for lewdness'.

These were pre-Independence cases, and after 1922 new legislation was introduced to Ireland to deal with prostitution. The Criminal Law Amendment Act 1935 was the first post-Independence Irish law dealing with prostitution, but was drafted in similar terms to the nineteenth-century statutes. It contained a comprehensive prohibition on 'indecent behaviour,' and made it an offence for a common prostitute to loiter in a public place and importune or solicit passers-by for the purposes of prostitution. After the dispersal of the prostitutes of Monto, the 1935 Act, supplemented by earlier legislation, continued to be enforced with the purpose of containing and controlling the most visible manifestations of prostitution. Beyond this minimal policing, it would appear that no developments in legislation or policy took place for over twenty years, apart from a short-lived policing initiative in 1964, whereby a number of the newly recruited Ban Gardaí (women police officers) were sent out onto the streets of Dublin to entrap would-be clients so that the men could be charged with the common-law offence of 'breach of the peace'. This experiment was discontinued after the names of a number of the men were published in the papers, and there were publicly expressed concerns about the safety of the Ban Gardaí. The need to protect the identities of some very influential male clients may also have been a less advertised factor in this decision. Following the discontinuance of this innovative policy, the practice of charging women with being 'common prostitutes' under the Criminal Law Amendment Act 1935 continued.

The treatment of prostitutes did not change for a long time, until 1981, in fact, with the landmark Supreme Court decision in *King v. Attorney General* ([1981] IR 233). King had been convicted, under section 4 of the Vagrancy Act 1824, for being a 'suspected person or reputed thief' found loitering in public. Evidence of his previous character was necessary in order to convict him, since that was the easiest way for the prosecution to show that he was 'suspected' or 'reputed'. On appeal, the Supreme Court overturned King's conviction, ruling that section 4 was 'so arbitrary, vague and difficult to rebut, and so related to rumour or ill-repute or past conduct', that it was clearly in breach of Article 38.1 of the Constitution – the provision requiring trial 'in due course of law', which protects the presumption of innocence. The term 'common prostitute' in section 14 of the Dublin Police Act 1842 was as vague and ill-defined as that found unconstitutional in King's case, and therefore the practice of charging women with loitering or soliciting as a common prostitute was ended, because a successful prosecution would require evidence predictive of the woman's behaviour.

This decision rendered much of the old legislation obsolete in practice. Instead, for a time the Gardaí had to resort to prosecuting both the woman and the client, either for the common-law offence of breach of the peace, or for the offence contained in section 5 of the Summary Jurisdiction (Ireland) Act 1871, which provides that any person who 'wilfully and indecently exposes his person or commits any act contrary to public decency' shall be liable to a £5 fine or two months' imprisonment. Clients could be charged directly under this section, while prostitutes were charged with aiding and abetting them in indecent exposure, and were subject to the same penalty.

The problem with securing prosecutions under these provisions was that in order to prove indecent exposure, it was necessary to prove that the 'person' of the defendant had been exposed. This term had been strictly construed by the courts. In a 1972 decision, which had persuasive influence in the Irish courts, the English High Court had ruled that 'person' meant penis, and that 'however deliberate be the intent to insult the female, and however great the insult she feels, the exposure of the backside is not within the section.' Thus a man could escape conviction if the garda failed to convince the court that he or she had actually seen the client's penis being exposed. Perhaps unsurprisingly, between 1984 and 1992 only ten prosecutions for prostitution are recorded in the *Annual Garda Reports*, and in three separate years – 1988, 1989 and 1991 – no prosecutions for prostitution were recorded.

In a detailed report on vagrancy offences, the Law Reform Commission recommended the need for legislative reform to enable prosecutions for prostitution to proceed,[5] and reform was finally introduced in 1993 by Minister for Justice Máire Geoghegan-Quinn. The Criminal Law (Sexual Offences) Act 1993 famously decriminalised homosexuality (as previously discussed), but also introduced important reforms to the law on prostitution. Presumably because of the potential for political controversy over the provisions on homosexuality, the Act was given a restricted two-day debate in the Dáil in June 1993. Many Opposition deputies deplored the lack of time for discussion; for instance, Liz O'Donnell TD remarked that the issue of prostitution was not getting the intellectual debate it warranted, and criticised the use of clichés like 'the oldest profession' by other TDs. In the course of the very brief debate, the provisions on prostitution were described by Joe Costello TD, among others, as 'harsh, punitive and unenlightened'.

In its favour, the 1993 Act abolished all references to 'common prostitute', repealed much of the old legislation, and for the first time created gender-neutral offences of loitering and soliciting. However, it does not define the term 'prostitution', thus retaining the definition of sexual availability given in the early cases. Perhaps its most unfortunate aspect is that it also retains the traditional terms of 'loitering' and 'soliciting' as the basis for prosecution. In practice, therefore, predictive identifying evidence must still be used to convict for prostitution. Increased penalties were also imposed for both soliciting and loitering offences, so that women are effectively forced to commit further criminal acts to pay their fines. Imprisonment may now be imposed as a penalty only for a third or subsequent offence, but it is argued that it should not have been retained at all. Instead, express provision should have been made for alternative penalties, for example, a police caution for first and second offences.

Although many of the old provisions have been repealed by the Act, various antiquated and little-used statutory and common-law offences relating to prostitution are still in force, such as the offence of keeping a disorderly house, that of unlawfully detaining a woman in a brothel under section 8 of the Criminal Law Amendment Act 1885, and the procuration of women for immoral purposes under the same Act. The retention of these offences in their present form appears pointless, particularly given their discriminatory and outdated language. Unfortunately, the new Act was rushed through with insufficient time to conduct a proper, wholescale review of prostitution law. More up-to-date laws prohibiting the trafficking in children and adults for the purpose of prostitution are required instead.

Despite the 1993 legislation, the dangers still present for those engaged in prostitution were evidenced by the murder of a young woman prostitute, Sinead Kelly, on a Dublin street in June 1998. These dangers remain even where a good relationship has developed between women and gardaí; women rarely feel safe working on the streets, as two studies conducted among women working in prostitution in Dublin by the Women's Health Project (WHP) revealed (November 1994; May 1996).

In a further study, which interviewed thirty women working as street prostitutes in Dublin about their experience of the criminal law, the participants again spoke of their fear of violence.[6] Eighty percent of the women interviewed had been subjected to violence of one form or another. All but one of the women said they were afraid for their safety while working on the street, even though they were generally positive about their relationship with the Gardaí and expressed confidence about police responses to complaints of violence. However, over 50% of those interviewed had already been prosecuted under the 1993 Act, while the others felt it was only a matter of time before they too were arrested; most favoured some form of decriminalisation.

Possible alternatives

The 1993 Act, like the earlier legislation, is clearly based upon a political concern to protect neighbourhoods and 'respectable' women from harassment through the suppression of public loitering and soliciting. It therefore proceeds from the assumption that prostitution must be contained within certain limits and hidden from public view. Yet the act of selling sex is not illegal: the double standard is obvious. Society is willing to accept that women may be paid for sex in private, as 'kept women' or 'mistresses', but will not tolerate the same commercial exchange in public. As a result, the law targets only the most visible manifestations of prostitution, not the private exploitation of women.

What, then, should be the law on prostitution? The 1996 WHP report stops short of recommending total decriminalisation, although this is clearly the preferred option of the women interviewed in the study referred to above. Any law aimed at controlling prostitution through prohibiting public solicitation will inevitably subject women to harassment. Even where the language used in the law is gender-neutral, experience shows that it is the (mainly women) prostitutes who are targetted in enforcement. Even where attempts have been made to use the law against the male customer, these have been risible.

Is total decriminalisation the legal solution? This question has exercised the feminist movement for years. Clearly, it would be far better for those women who work as prostitutes to work in a legal, safe environment. As against that, many feminists have argued that the decriminalisation of all those involved in prostitution would only compound existing exploitation and serve to further objectify women as sexual commodities.

A compromise solution might be possible through a strategy of partial decriminalisation. That would mean abolishing the offences of soliciting and loitering for both men and women, but maintaining criminal penalties for the organising and controlling of prostitution, and for the trafficking of women and men. Thus, the act of controlling the sale of sex by others, or making profit from the sale of sex by others or another, ie, pimping, would remain a criminal offence. In this way, the most extreme form of exploitation involved in the conduct of prostitution might be avoided.

Clearly, these recommendations do not provide any sort of ideal solution. Ideally, no women would work as prostitutes; ideally, sexual intercourse would only take place between free and consenting adults in a non-commercial environment. At present, however, due to the existing power structures and substantive inequalities which remain deep-rooted in patriarchal society, sex is a lucrative commodity, and so prostitution takes many forms: from the sale of oral sex on public streets by heroin addicts, to the private trading of sexual intercourse in return for expensive dinners. Whatever the form of prostitution, no solution to its causes will be found in the law alone. Until women have social and economic equality, in the workplace and in society, prostitution of one kind or another will continue to provide an obvious economic alternative for many women.

As Emma Goldman, the famous anarcho-feminist, wrote:

Nowhere is woman treated according to the merit of her work, but rather as a sex. It is therefore almost inevitable that she should pay for her right to exist, to keep a position in whatever line, with sexual favours. Thus, it is merely a question of degree whether she sells herself to one man, in or out of marriage, or to many men. Whether our reformers admit it or not, the economic and social inferiority of women is responsible for prostitution.[7]

NOTES FOR CHAPTER SIX

1. O'Malley, T., *Sexual Offences Law, Policy and Punishment*, pp.97–8. (Dublin: Round Hall Ltd, 1996.)

2. Smart, C., 'Law's Power, the sexed body and feminist discourse', in 17 *Journal of Law and Society*, 194–210, 1990.

3. Dáil debates, 13 November 1990.

4. Bacik, Maunsell & Gogan, *The Legal Process and Victims of Rape. (*Dublin: Rape Crisis Centre, 1998.)

5. *Report on Vagrancy and Related Offences*, 1985.

6. Haughey, C. & Bacik, I., *Final Report: A Study of Prostitution in Dublin*. (Unpublished: Law School, TCD/Department of Justice, Equality and Law Reform, 2000.)

7. Goldman, E., 'The Traffic in Women', in *Anarchism and Other Essays*. (New York & London: Mother Earth Publishing Association, 1917.)

CHAPTER 7
Censorship and Freedom of Expression

Debates on the issues of free speech and censorship have always been controversial, and indeed continue to generate controversy in Ireland. Despite a long-standing constitutional guarantee of freedom of expression, highly restrictive censorship laws remain in place. Extensive restrictions on freedom of information and speech are permitted on grounds of 'State security' and 'public morality', and a climate of moral paternalism holds sway, ostensibly justified on grounds of the 'common good'. In this chapter, these key aspects of the free speech debate in an Irish context will be examined.

FREEDOM OF SPEECH

The freedom of speech, or freedom of expression, is guaranteed in virtually every international human rights instrument and in the Constitution of every liberal democracy. The protection of this vital freedom is generally regarded as necessary in order for democracy to flourish, and its guarantee is seen as an essential feature of the democratic process. Without the freedom to express views and opinions that differ from those of the government, for example, no opposition parties could ever function in any political system. Despite its importance, in no country is the freedom of speech guaranteed without any restrictions.

In Ireland, although the freedom of expression is protected within the Constitution, the guarantee is much more restrictively worded than, for example, the First Amendment to the US Constitution, which states emphatically that 'Congress shall make no law ... abridging the freedom of speech or of the press.' Closer to home, the European Convention on Human Rights provides at Article 10(1), in similarly clear terms, that 'Everyone has the freedom of expression. This right shall include freedom to hold opinions and to receive and impart information and ideas without interference by public authority and regardless of frontiers.' While Article 10(2) provides for a range of conditions to which the freedom may be subjected, the language of Article 10(1) is infinitely more generous than that of its Irish equivalent.

The Constitutional Guarantee of Free Speech in Ireland

The guarantee of freedom of expression set out in Article 40.6.1.i of the Irish Constitution protects 'the right of the citizens to express freely their convictions and opinions' (for the full text, see Appendix). But this protection is limited, since 'organs of public opinion' may not be used 'to undermine public order or morality or the authority of the State'. Also, the Article further provides that 'the publication or utterance of blasphemous, seditious or indecent matter is an offence which shall be punishable in accordance with law.' The freedom of expression is thus significantly restricted – more severely, indeed, than most other constitutional freedoms guaranteed in the Fundamental Rights provisions of the Constitution (Articles 40–44). When compared to the statements (above) contained in the US Constitution and the ECHR, it is clear that a relatively grudging protection is offered to this vital freedom in the Irish Constitution.

Given the central nature of the guarantee of free speech in most human rights instruments, it is surprising that since the enactment of the Constitution in 1937, the guarantee in Article 40.6.1.i has rarely been considered by the courts. Even where the guarantee has been invoked, the imposition of extensive censorship has been upheld as lawful in a range of different areas by Irish judges. For example, leading media lawyer Marie McGonagle writes that, 'There have been relatively few instances of the courts invoking Article 40.6.1.i in support of media freedom.'[1]

Such limited Irish case law as exists under the Article has tended to emphasise the restrictions permitted upon the exercise of the freedom of expression. In 1996, the Constitution Review Group reviewed the relevant cases, concluding that, 'The relative paucity of case law in this area is such that not much would be lost if [the Article] were to be replaced.'[2] The CRG described the wording of the Article as 'unsatisfactory', and recommended that it be replaced by a new clause modelled on Article 10 of the ECHR.

Despite this strong recommendation, no change to the constitutional guarantee appears likely; and so the state of free speech law in Ireland remains 'unsatisfactory'. Restrictions continue to be permitted in a range of areas. As constitutional experts Hogan and Whyte point out, it is striking that, despite the constitutional guarantee, 'common law and statutory restriction on freedom of expression have survived intact'.[3] Some are relatively uncontroversial, for example, libel laws protect an individual's privacy rights and private reputation; contempt of court laws and restriction on the reporting of criminal proceedings protect the individual's right to a fair trial. However, more contentious issues surround those restrictions based upon two different grounds: State security or authority, and public morality.

State security or authority

Extensive limitations on free speech are contained in legislation, purportedly justified in the interest of State security. For example, section 10 of the Offences Against the State Act 1939 makes it a criminal offence to type, print, publish, send through the post, distribute, sell, or offer for sale any incriminating, treasonable or seditious document. An 'incriminating' document means any document emanating from or appearing to emanate from an unlawful organisation; a 'seditious' document is one which contains matter attempting to undermine the public order or the authority of the State. In one case, a poster of a man in paramilitary uniform bearing the slogan 'IRA calls the shots' was regarded as an 'incriminating' document within the meaning of the Act, and the defendant was convicted of the criminal offence of possession of such documents.[4] Patrick MacEntee SC, probably the best-known criminal defence barrister in Ireland, has described these restrictive provisions as having 'enormous powers of control and censorship of information'.[5]

Apart from these provisions, the best-known example of censorship law under this heading was contained in section 31 of the Broadcasting Act 1960 (as amended). Section 31(1) allowed the relevant Minister (formerly the Minister for Posts and Telegraphs, now the Minister for Communications, Marine and Natural Resources), to direct RTÉ, by order, to refrain from broadcasting any material that the Minister deemed likely to promote, or incite to crime, or would tend to undermine the authority of the State. This provision was challenged as unconstitutional in *The State (Lynch) v. Cooney* ([1983] ILRM 89), where the Minister had used the section to prohibit the transmission of election broadcasts on behalf of Sinn Féin – a legal political party – because of that organisation's association with the Provisional IRA. The applicant succeeded before the High Court in his claim that the section conflicted with the freedom of expression guaranteed in the Constitution; but he lost in the Supreme Court, which held that the freedom could be lawfully restricted in this way. Chief Justice O'Higgins gave a trenchant judgment in defence of the restriction, saying that the wording of the freedom of expression Article,

> ... places upon the State the obligation to ensure that these organs of public opinion shall not be used to undermine public order or public morality or the authority of the State. It follows that the use of such organs of opinion for the purpose of securing or advocating support for organisations which seek by violence to overthrow the State or its institutions is a use which is prohibited by the Constitution. Therefore it is clearly the duty of the State to intervene to prevent broadcasts on radio or television which are aimed at such a result or which in any way would be likely to have the effect of promoting or inciting to crime or endangering the authority of the State.

No Ministerial Order was made under this section after 1994 because of the developments in the Northern Ireland peace process, and the section was eventually repealed in 2001, although under section 18(1A) of the Broadcasting Act 1960, inserted in 1976, RTÉ is still prohibited from broadcasting 'anything which may reasonably be regarded as likely to promote, or incite to crime, or as tending to undermine the authority of the State.'

Public order or morality

Extensive restrictions on free speech are also permitted on another ground, that of public morality. Article 40.6.1.i places great emphasis on 'public order or morality', even containing within it the extraordinary acknowledgement that, 'The publication or utterance of blasphemous, seditious or indecent matter is an offence which shall be punishable in accordance with law'. The inclusion within a guarantee of free speech of a penal clause seems, to say the least, 'inappropriate'.[6] Due to a lack of blasphemy prosecutions, this tailpiece to the Article had appeared to be of academic interest only, until the recent case of *Corway v. Independent Newspapers*, [1999] 4 IR 484.

In this case, Corway, an anti-divorce activist, wanted to take a private prosecution for blasphemous libel against the *Sunday Independent* newspaper for a cartoon published in the wake of the successful referendum in 1995 which introduced divorce. The cartoon showed a priest offering Communion to three government Ministers, each of whom was rejecting it. The caption read, 'Hello Progress – Bye-bye Father?', a play on the anti-divorce campaigners' slogan, 'Hello Divorce – Bye-bye Daddy'. The Supreme Court rejected the application, holding that, 'In the absence of any legislative definition of the constitutional offence of blasphemy, it is impossible to say of what the offence of blasphemy consists.' The effect of this decision was to remove blasphemy from the Constitution – without the need for an amendment.

More significantly than the arcane law on blasphemy, extensive statutory restrictions on free speech on grounds of public morality also exist in the Censorship of Films Acts 1923–1992 and the Censorship of

Publications Acts 1929–1967. In relation to films, under section 7(2) of the Censorship of Films Act 1923, the Official Censor may refuse to certify a film as fit for public exhibition on grounds that it is:

... indecent, obscene or blasphemous or because the exhibition thereof in public would tend to inculcate principles contrary to public morality or would be otherwise subversive of public morality.

Under the Video Recordings Acts 1989–1992, the censor has similar powers relating to the certification and classification of video recordings. Both Acts have brought about the cutting and banning of countless films, including *Natural Born Killers* (refused a certificate in Ireland in October 1994, despite having been passed uncut with an over-18s certificate in Britain), and *Monty Python's Life of Brian* (banned in 1979 on grounds of blasphemy, but released some years later following resubmission to the censor). Infamously, a prosecution was even brought to prevent the staging of Tennessee Williams' play *The Rose Tattoo* in 1957, on the grounds that it was an 'indecent and profane' performance.

Similarly, the legislation provides the Censorship of Publications Board with power to prohibit the sale and distribution of publications that are deemed 'indecent or obscene', or that advocate the procurement of abortion or miscarriage. This legislation has had a long and ignominious history, resulting in the censorship, at one time, of over 1,000 books and other publications a year, among them novels by Kate O'Brien, such as *The Land of Spices*; the English children's book *Jenny lives with Eric and Martin* in 1990; and as recently as 2000 the *In Dublin* listings magazine, which was alleged to have carried ads for sexual services and brothels.

Despite the highly restrictive nature of the legislation and the often absurd consequences of its application, especially prior to the 1960s when censorship was at its height, its constitutionality was challenged only once, in the late 1970s in a case taken by the pioneering pro-contraception campaign group, the IFPA (*Irish Family Planning Association v. Ryan* [1979] IR 295). The IFPA challenged a decision by the Censorship Board to ban an information booklet it had produced about contraception; the Supreme Court held against the Publications Board, although on the narrow ground that by failing to communicate its decision to the IFPA it had not observed the principles of natural justice.

This limited victory aside, it is clear that the censorship legislation has been applied in a particularly persistent way to prevent the distribution of publications dealing with women's sexuality and reproductive health. Mary Kelly argues that its aim is 'to curtail the representation of female sexuality and fertility within circumscribed limits, and to control access to alternative information, images and hence choices, apart from those tolerated within the relatively narrow world-view of nationalist and Catholic ideology.'[7]

In 1987, for example, the Censorship of Publications Board banned Dr Alex Comfort's educational book *The Joy of Sex*. Two years later, in 1989, the Board ordered the British women's magazine *Cosmopolitan* to withdraw its advertisements for abortion clinics or face a ban on distribution in Ireland. This latter ban led to a rash of self-imposed censorship, with another English magazine removing an information supplement on abortion from its Irish editions in 1990, and public libraries removing books on women's health from their shelves. Other censorship was judicially imposed; in the *Open Door Counselling* case, the Supreme Court held that where counsellors gave pregnant women in Ireland information about abortion services lawfully available in England, they were breaching the constitutional right to life of 'the unborn' *(AG (SPUC) v. Open Door Counselling Ltd* [1988] IR 593). This decision led to further self-imposed censorship, so that for many years students' unions were the only agencies providing such information to women. This remained the case until the law was finally changed following political campaigns around the 1992 *X* case, with the passing of a referendum in November 1992 and subsequent legislation in 1995 allowing information on abortion to be provided legally (see Chapter 5).

In more recent years, as social attitudes towards sexuality have changed and information on abortion has become more widely available, the censors have become less proactive in imposing such outlandish bans. The recent, controversial Mel Gibson film, *The Passion of the Christ*, was not only passed by the censor in 2004 but was awarded a 15PG certificate, despite its inclusion of scenes of explicit violence – perhaps because it is based on a religious story?

The issue of moral or sexual censorship has effectively gone off the political agenda, although information on reproductive health remains difficult to access for many women. However, the debate about censorship on public morality grounds resurfaced briefly in the summer of 2002, when the Butler Gallery in Kilkenny was told that, under the Censorship of Films Act 1923, it would need a censor's certificate before an exhibition of well-known installation artist Paul McCarthy's sexually explicit videoworks could be shown in public. In order to get around this problem, the Gallery closed the exhibition temporarily, then reopened it as a 'club', for members only.

This ludicrous case has very disturbing implications for the public exhibition of art in the medium of film and video in Ireland, which come under the Censorship of Films Act. The 1923 Act provides that, 'No picture shall be exhibited in public by means of a cinematograph or similar apparatus unless and until the Official Censor has certified that the whole of such picture is fit for exhibition in public.' The censor may refuse a certificate if, in his or her view, it is 'unfit for general exhibition in public by reason of its being indecent, obscene or blasphemous.'

Thus, according to a strict interpretation, the need for censor's certification applies to all public film showings, whether in cinemas or art galleries. Although the application of censorship law in arthouse cinemas had already been an issue at the time of the ban on *Natural Born Killers*, the showing of art films in galleries had simply been ignored until this incident. The Kilkenny experience disrupted this state of blissful ignorance.

This disruption did have a positive effect, however, provoking a renewed debate around outdated censorship laws. Many argued that if those working in the arts did not seize the opportunity to change the law, a dangerous self-censorship culture would develop, with galleries refusing work that might be deemed 'indecent' for fear of being denied certification. Indeed, 'challenging' shows like McCarthy's are still rare in Ireland, perhaps because such a culture already exists. It is interesting that while it is unthinkable now that Kate O'Brien's novels might be banned, or a Tennessee Williams play be the subject of a criminal prosecution, the application of censorship legislation to visual art remains an unresolved issue.

Freedom of Information

Apart from the restrictions on expression created in the name of State security, there are further restrictions imposed on the basis of 'official privacy'. The Official Secrets Act 1963 remains the principal statute in this area. It must be signed and complied with by all holders of public office or employees of the State (civil servants, gardaí, etc). Section 5 provides that such a person should not communicate to a third party any information related to their contract with the State, or expressed therein to be confidential. According to Patrick MacEntee SC, writing in 1993, this Act:

> ... is an Alice in Wonderland because, while it turns on the definition of what is official information, it provides that official information is what the Minister says it is. If the Minister says it's official information, then it is official information, and that is that. The Act is so broadly drawn that any document concerning the public service can be said to be an official document by the Minister and therefore is an official document.[8]

The passing of the Freedom of Information Act 1997 (under the rainbow coalition government of Fine Gael, Labour and Democratic Left) significantly changed the secretive, anti-information culture created by the Official Secrets legislative regime in government departments and public offices. The 1997 Act provides that persons have the right to access official records held by public bodies; the right to have personal information held on them corrected or updated where such information is incomplete, incorrect or misleading; and the right to be given reasons for decisions taken by public bodies which affect them. Section 48 of the Act allows a defence to any prosecution under the Official Secrets Act for any person who is authorised to provide information under the Freedom of Information (FOI) regime. Over three hundred public bodies are covered by the Freedom of Information legislation, including all government departments, local authorities, health boards, third-level education institutions and nearly all noncommercial State organisations.

The use of the FOI procedure by journalists, in particular, brought a great deal of important matters to public attention for the first time, for example, it gave political reporters previously unheard of access to correspondence showing disagreement between Government Ministers on spending plans for the proposed National Stadium (or 'Bertie Bowl'). Many NGOs also made extensive use of the FOI procedure. A coalition of environmental groups, for example, revealed in 2002 that the European Commission was investigating over one hundred complaints against Ireland's environmental record – more than any other country in the European Union on a *per capita* basis. Perhaps because of the uses it afforded journalists and groups such as this, after the Act had been in force just a few years it was amended significantly by the Fianna Fáil/Progressive Democrat Government through the Freedom of Information (Amendment) Act 2003.

The 2003 Act restricts the scope of the original 1997 Act by limiting the range of public documents which may be accessed, and by introducing new charges for those seeking access to records – charges often high enough to deter private individuals from seeking access to records. In addition, the Act allows the head of a public body to refuse an FOI request if it is frivolous, vexatious 'or forms part of a pattern of manifestly unreasonable requests from the same requester or from different requesters who, in the opinion of the head, appear to have made the requests acting in concert.' The introduction of the new Act was strongly criticised by the National Union of Journalists, among others, who warned that it heralded a return to the 'bad old days' before the FOI regime was in place. Notwithstanding these objections, the Act was passed, and the public right of access to information about the workings of Government has unfortunately been greatly diluted as a result.

The political debate

Freedom of speech is usually seen as a negative 'freedom' – ie, an aspect of the private sphere, upon which the State should not intervene – as opposed to a positive 'right' – ie, the exercise of which the State should actively facilitate and enable. Whether expressed as a freedom or a right, the debate around free speech tends to divide along two broad political lines. On the one hand, liberals argue for the least restrictions possible upon individual freedom of expression. In the 1960s, particularly in the USA, liberals were united around free speech, arguing against State restrictions on civil rights protests. Since then, however, free speech controversies over complex issues like pornography and political campaign advertising have had the effect of dividing liberals among themselves.[9]

On the other hand, those who might broadly be described as having a communitarian political outlook argue that freedom of speech must always be seen in a social or community context, so that limits upon the individual freedom are justified in accordance with the common good. Like liberals, communitarians are politically divided. They may share a similar view on the need to restrict free speech in the interests of the common good, but they differ strongly on how to define the 'common good'. Forty years ago, the communitarian argument for restricting free speech was often couched in paternalistic terms, on grounds of public morality, by those from a conservative political outlook. Now arguments for restricting free speech are also made by feminists, anti-racist campaigners and those on the political left – what might be called 'progressive communitarians'. The tension between the two broadly defined political positions, and within each position, on the issue of free speech reflects political tensions regarding concepts of human rights generally. Such tension is clearly apparent in the ongoing conflict between the two competing ideologies of theocracy and liberal-democracy apparent in the very language of the constitutional rights Articles (see Chapter 1).

Given the continued application of outdated censorship laws, it may legitimately be said that the ideology of theocracy has prevailed and a culture of censorship has developed in Ireland, a culture based upon a particularly theocratic notion of what constitutes the common good. The Supreme Court has previously indicated its view that the 'common good' is identified in the 'national aspirations' expressed in the Preamble to the Constitution – a text that itself begins, 'In the Name of the Most Holy Trinity ...' The challenge for progressives in Ireland is how to redefine the 'common good' so as to ensure that freedom of expression is more strongly protected, and only limited according to a set of consistent criteria. What is needed is a rational definition of what constitutes the 'common good', one which is not based on religious dogma, and does not bring about the repression of women's sexuality, or the muzzling of artistic expression or investigative journalism.

Progressive definitions of the 'Common Good'

It is very difficult to devise a consistent progressive communitarian definition of the common good. Such a task may only be possible if free speech is viewed through a prism of equality, or in a way that takes account of the imbalance of power in social structures. In this way, the law would presume that no restrictions on free speech are permitted. Where such a restriction was proposed, its implications would always be examined for their effect on upholding or challenging structural inequalities in society. This approach would test how freedom of expression affects social equality, in order to come up with a definition of the common good in each individual case, where it was proposed to use this as a basis for restricting the freedom. The question would therefore be whether the exercise of the freedom amounted to an abuse of power by a stronger group or individual. Thus, 'common good' would be defined as primarily meaning 'protecting against abuse of power'.

Such an approach would be greatly facilitated if a 'core norm' of equality was introduced into the Irish Constitution, that is, a right that would take priority over other rights, and to which the constitutional guarantee of freedom of expression could be explicitly subjected. Equality before the law is guaranteed in Article 40.1 of the Irish Constitution, but is subject to extensive restrictions and has been interpreted conservatively by the courts (for a further discussion of this, see Chapter 4).

It is useful to compare the limited nature of the Irish equality guarantee with the relevant provisions of the 1996 South African Constitution, a document drafted and recently enacted in line with a progressive communitarian ideology. Unlike the Irish Constitution, the South African charter seeks to protect socio-economic rights, some of which are as directly enforceable as the right to free speech. These include the right to basic education, the right not to be refused emergency medical treatment, and the right of a child to basic nutrition, shelter, basic healthcare services and social services. All of these rights are guaranteed in accordance with the basic principle of equality, and equality is the first substantive right guaranteed in the Bill of Rights. Article 9 of the South African Constitution provides that:

(1) Everyone is equal before the law and has the right to equal protection and benefit of the law; (2) Equality includes the full and equal enjoyment of all rights and freedoms. To promote the achievement of equality, legislative and other measures designed to protect or advance persons, or categories of persons, disadvantaged by unfair discrimination may be taken.

Article 39 of the South African Constitution provides that, when interpreting the Bill of Rights, courts 'must promote the values that underlie an open and democratic society based on human dignity, equality and freedom'. Because equality is a 'core norm', in the context of which other rights must always be seen, the freedom of expression guarantee in Article 16 explicitly provides that this protection does not extend to 'a. propaganda for war; b. incitement of imminent violence; or c. advocacy of hatred that is based on race, ethnicity, gender or religion, and that constitutes incitement to cause harm.'

But while Article 16 may answer the question as to what sort of speech should be limited by 'common good' criteria in a secular, pluralist republic, it also specifies certain forms of individual expression as particularly in need of protection. It provides a general guarantee that, 'Everyone has the right to freedom of expression'; and then states that this includes:

a. freedom of the press and other media;
b. freedom to receive or impart information or ideas;
c. freedom of artistic creativity; and
d. academic freedom and freedom of scientific research.

From a progressive perspective, and in this author's view, this formula amounts to a careful and appropriate balancing of interests. Potentially vulnerable forms of expression, the free exercise of which are essential in any functioning democracy, are explicitly protected. Equally, forms of expression potentially harmful to the common good, which may cause harm or allow invidious discrimination against certain groups, are explicitly excluded from constitutional protection. Freedom of expression is seen in the context of power in the South African text. Where a group or class of persons is disempowered and needs society's protection in some way, then stronger groups should not be permitted to use the freedom of expression to abuse the power imbalance.

Such balancing of interests can most easily be carried out in a context where equality is explicitly guaranteed as a core norm, as in the South African example, ie, where the right to equality takes precedence over other constitutional rights. But even where equality is not explicitly guaranteed as such, as in Ireland, in practice every democratic society employs an equality test to justify different types of restriction on free speech; democracy is premised on equality, and true liberty depends on equality of means to participate fully in society.

Justifying restrictions – the Equality Test

Even in the USA, where free speech but not equality is generally seen as a core norm, regulation of free speech in the form of controls on political-campaign spending and advertising is regarded as necessary. American commentator Owen Fiss describes such controls as exemplifying 'the tension between capitalism and democracy', and goes on to describe how the free speech decisions of the US courts in the 1970s allowed capitalism to win. In striking down (ie, declaring invalid) legislative controls on election spending, the decisions served to 'impoverish rather than enrich public debate and thus threatened one of the essential preconditions for an effective democracy'. In other words, controls on political access to the media during elections are necessary in order to preserve an equal and democratic system.

In the same way arguments for regulating advertising, for example, to prohibit the advertisement of tobacco-based products, can be based on the equality premise that potential harm might be caused to vulnerable or disempowered members of the community were such companies to have unfettered rights to advertise their products. It is equally possible to justify other restrictions on freedom of expression in the same way. Prohibitions on hate speech, child pornography, or on the right to march through sensitive areas in Northern Ireland may mean encroaching upon freedom of expression, but that encroachment is justified in the interests of protecting weaker members of society from harm caused by abuse of power. Conversely, the application of the equality test would not justify restrictions on freedom of expression which cause the banning of sexually explicit artwork in galleries, or prevent access by pregnant women to relevant medical information. This is because neither the display of explicit art nor the provision of abortion information encroaches upon the rights of disempowered groups. A re-framing of free speech in the context of equality and of social power is thus possible and desirable.

The equality test is often applied in practice in many jurisdictions to justify restrictions upon hate speech, ie, speech promoting or inciting racial discrimination. This type of speech is explicitly excluded from protection in Article 16 of the South African Constitution, and in the laws of many democratic states. In Ireland, although there has been little debate around hate speech, its restriction in the interests of the common good was accepted as necessary in the Prohibition of Incitement to Hatred Act 1989. This forbids the publication, distribution, or broadcast of material intended to stir up hatred against a group of persons on account of their race, ethnicity or nationality, religion, sexual orientation, or membership of the Traveller community.

CENSORSHIP AND PORNOGRAPHY

Like hate speech, pornography is also seen by many as harmful of the common good, but its prohibition is not so routinely accepted by progressive communitarians. The censorship legislation discussed in relation to films, books and art, with its emphasis on prohibiting 'obscene and indecent' material, represents a form of legal moralism or paternalism, based on concern about the moral welfare of citizens. Most progressives would argue for its repeal on the basis that it is unduly restrictive of individual freedoms which may be exercised without the risk of causing harm to others – in other words, adults may read Kate O'Brien's novels, or watch Paul McCarthy's videos, without this activity causing harm to anyone else.

Recently introduced legislation criminalising child pornography is based on a more tangible concern: that such material involves the causing of actual harm to children, and should be prohibited to protect this especially vulnerable group. The Child Trafficking and Pornography Act 1998 introduced a new criminal framework for the possession, production or distribution of child pornography (including internet porn). Until its enactment, neither possession of child porn nor the taking of indecent photographs or making of sexual video recordings of children were criminal offences, so long as no assault was involved. Again, few communitarians, or indeed liberals, would question the pressing need for, or the ideological basis of, the new legislation.

The debate about adult pornography, and whether it should be seen as actually being harmful to adult women in the same way, is more complex. Here, Irish law remains mired in a state of moral paternalism. In the USA and elsewhere, however, feminists have been seeking change in pornography laws to reflect the harm/equality perspective. In a sense, anti-pornography feminists are effectively united with the moralist/conservative position in seeking a ban on such material, although of course differing from the conservatives in their reasons for wanting prohibition. Feminist anti-pornography arguments are based upon the concept that porn causes real harm to real women; that it amounts to discrimination against women. As well-known feminist lawyer Catherine MacKinnon has said, 'protecting pornography means protecting sexual abuse as speech, at the same time that both pornography and its protection have deprived women of speech, especially speech against sexual abuse'.[10] But in truth the feminist movement is divided on this issue. Nadine Strossen, for example, has written a strong critique of what she describes as Catherine MacKinnon and Andrea Dworkin's 'pro-censorship' approach. She argues that the effect of their campaign against porn is to blame the words and images that make up porn for the social fact of violence against women, and so to overlook the root causes of 'complex, troubling societal problems'.[11]

Feminists, liberals and those on the left are often divided on approaches to pornography, or on agreement as to whether it can be restricted on the basis of applying an equality test. This is perhaps the most difficult free speech issue, since it would always be a matter of contention as to whether particular pornography amounted to discrimination against women. This complexity is compounded by the fact that the definition of pornography is itself contentious. To put it simply, one woman's erotica is another woman's porn, and every legal system has wrestled with this difficulty as to where the line may be drawn between the merely erotic and the clearly pornographic.

Future possibilities

The application of an equality test wherever restrictions on speech are proposed might not resolve satisfactorily that most difficult free speech issue of pornography, but it would go some way to solving what has always been the principal problem with free speech for progressives. The fact is that laws favouring freedom of expression have consistently permitted the dominance of the individual interest over the collective; the victory of capitalism over democracy. The political left and the women's movement need to reclaim freedom of speech by placing it within the equality context, so that it becomes a right that must always be seen in a constitutional framework where equality is the 'core norm'. To echo the words of Catherine MacKinnon, what we require is:

... a new model for freedom of expression in which the free speech position no longer supports social dominance, as it does now; in which free speech does not most readily protect the activities of Nazis, Klansmen and pornographers, while doing nothing for their victims, as it does now; in which defending free speech is not speaking on behalf of a large pile of money in the hands of a small group of people, as it is now.[12]

Those holding liberal or left-wing views, like this author, can only reclaim free speech when equality becomes the core constitutional norm – that would mean that the freedom of expression would become more than a negative freedom, more than a marking of private territory upon which the public sphere may not encroach. Rather, freedom of expression needs to be seen as a positive right, the exercise of which the State would facilitate where necessary to empower those disadvantaged in society, and would restrict only where necessary to prevent abuse of power by dominant groups. This approach to free speech would protect the interests of those who are genuinely not free to speak, due to economic or social conditions, and could ensure a greater harmony between the right to free speech and the core norm of equality in democratic societies like Ireland.

NOTES FOR CHAPTER SEVEN

1.   McGonagle, M., *A Textbook on Media Law,* p.23. (Dublin: Gill & Macmillan, 1996.)

2.   Constitution Review Group, *Report of the Constitution Review Group,* p.292. (Dublin: Government Publications, 1996.)

3.   Hogan, G. and Whyte, G., *J.M. Kelly: The Irish Constitution,* p.176 (Fourth edition). (Dublin: Butterworths, 2003.)

4.   *People (DPP) v. O'Leary* (1988) 3 Frewen 163.

5.   MacEntee, P., *Let in the Light,* p.113. (Ireland: Brandon Books, 1993.)

6.   Ranalow, S., 'Bearing a Constitutional Cross: Examining Blasphemy and the Judicial Role in *Corway v. Independent Newspapers*', p.95, in *3 Trinity College Law Review* 95, 2000.

7.   Kelly, M., 'Censorship and the Media', p.185, in Connelly, A., *Gender and the Law in Ireland.* (Ireland: Oak Tree Press, 1993.)

8.   MacEntee, P., as at note 5.

9.   see Fiss, Owen, *Liberalism Divided: Freedom of Speech and the Many Uses of State Power*. (USA: Westview Press, 1996.)

10. MacKinnon, C., *Only Words,* p.6. (USA: Harvard University Press, 1993.)

11. Strossen, N., *Defending Pornography: Free Speech, Sex and the Fight for Women's Rights,* p.279. (London: Abacus, 1995.)

12. MacKinnon, C., as at note 10.

CHAPTER 8
Ethnicity and Immigration

One of the widely held myths about Ireland is that it is ethnically homogenous: a society of 100% Irish people, all green-eyed and red-haired, with a strong probability of freckles. In fact, this was always just a myth. Even before the Anglo-Normans arrived in the late twelfth century, there had already been successive waves of visitors to Irish shores in previous centuries, with Celts, Vikings and others settling, intermarrying and becoming Irish. Since then, similar processes have occurred with other groups: Spanish, Huguenots, Jews and, in the twentieth century, Hungarians, Vietnamese and Bosnians, among others. Members of the Traveller community constitute the longest-established ethnic minority group in Ireland. Now, however, in the early twenty-first century, for the first time in our history, Ireland is experiencing more inward than outward migration.

PATTERNS OF MIGRATION INTO IRELAND

By comparison with other European states, there was relatively little immigration to Ireland in the twentieth century. This is hardly surprising given the history of extensive emigration from Ireland; for centuries our 'people traffic' was one way: out. During the years of the Great Famine (1845–1850) and directly after, hundreds of thousands of Irish people left due to poverty and conditions of starvation; 990,000 left for the USA alone between 1851 and 1860. The pattern since then and until very recently has consistently been one of net emigration, as lack of employment prospects at home drove many tens of thousands of Irish to seek work abroad, in the USA, in Britain and elsewhere in Europe.

In the 1990s, the years of the Celtic Tiger, this pattern changed dramatically. Between 1992 and 1997, 220,000 people immigrated into Ireland, while 197,000 emigrated; in 1997 alone, the net inflow into Ireland was 15,000 persons, the majority of whom were returning Irish citizens, or migrants from Britain or elsewhere in the EU. Immigration has remained a constant feature since then. In the twelve months up to April 2002, 76,000 people immigrated to Ireland, one-third of whom were Irish-born returners. *Irish Times'* journalist Fintan O'Toole remarks that of those 76,000 incomers, the total number of those immigrants from outside the EU or USA was only 15,000, ie, less than the number of Irish citizens who emigrated to other countries in the same period (18,800).[1] The 2002 Census figures present a similar picture. Non-Irish nationals make up 5.8% of the population of Ireland, but almost half of these 'non-Irish' are UK nationals (2.7% of the population) and the next most numerous group is made up of other EU nationalities. In total, 90% of people living in Ireland were born here, 200,000 were born in Britain and 50,000 in Northern Ireland. The Census indicates that the 'new communities' of recent migrants are numerically very small, and confirms that much of the net immigration is due to Irish emigrants returning home having worked abroad. Any debate on immigration must start with recognition of this fact.

In any discussion about immigration, it is also necessary to be aware that migration can take different forms; many Irish people who emigrate to the USA, for example, do so on the basis of having been awarded a work visa under one of the visa lottery programmes announced from time to time by the American Government. Similarly, other Governments operate a quota system, seeking a certain number of workers skilled in particular areas each year.

Ireland, however, lacks any coherent immigration policy and does not operate any visa lottery programme or effective skills quota system. Citizens of other EU Member States have the benefit of freedom of movement under the Treaty of Rome and EC law, and may live and work legally in Ireland or anywhere else in the EU without any visa. Similarly, citizens of Iceland, Liechtenstein and Norway (members of the EEA – the European Economic Area) do not require any visa to live and work in Ireland. But for non-EU citizens, there are basically only two ways to live and work legally in this country: by taking up a job here, in respect of which an Irish employer has obtained a work permit for them; or by claiming asylum.

Asylum-seekers

Those seeking asylum are entitled to come to Ireland under the 1951 Geneva Convention on Refugees, which provides that persons who have had to leave their country of nationality due to a 'well-founded fear of being persecuted for reasons of race, religion, nationality, membership of a particular social group or political opinion' have the right to refugee status, that is, to reside in another country and to work and receive social protection there. In order to achieve refugee status, a non-national must make an application for asylum under the Geneva Convention, and all states that are party to the Convention are obliged to examine the application of any non-national who arrives at their borders or in their territories seeking asylum. Only persons whose applications are successful are granted refugee status.

During the 1990s, there was a significant increase in the number of people applying for asylum in Ireland, reaching its highest point at 11,634 in 2002, having risen steadily since the mid-1990s. In 2003, however, there was a sharp drop of 32% in the numbers applying for asylum in Ireland, down to 7,939. Overall, the numbers had risen from an extraordinarily low base in comparison to other European countries. Just thirty-nine people applied for asylum in Ireland in 1992, a year in which journalist Paul Cullen notes that there was a peak of 700,000 applications in the rest of Western Europe.[2] The number of applications in Ireland subsequently began to rise gradually, to 424 in 1995 and then more steeply to 4,626 in 1998. The Department of Justice initially reacted very slowly to this development, failing to increase the numbers of staff needed to deal with the rise in claims until a backlog had already built up. This, in turn, perhaps generated an impression that the numbers involved in claiming asylum were much greater than in fact they were.

Asylum-seekers and the law

Irish law on asylum and refugee status has gone through quite a number of changes in recent years, both in legislation and in case law. The government reacted slowly to the increasing numbers of asylum-seekers, and when reforming legislation was finally introduced in 1996, to provide clear procedures for the processing of asylum claims, the opportunity to introduce a comprehensive reform of outdated immigration laws was, unfortunately, not taken. Instead, much of the new law was based on the old 'Aliens' legislation of the 1930s and 1940s (the Aliens Act 1935 and the Aliens Order 1946). Reliance upon hopelessly outdated statutes has ultimately created many problems for the Government.

Basic procedures for dealing with asylum claims are now set out in the Refugee Act 1996, although due to the lack of resources being applied to implement the Act, it did not come into effect fully until November 2000. Subsequently, further amending legislation was passed, namely the Immigration Act 1999, the Illegal Immigrants (Trafficking) Act 2000 and the Immigration Act 2003. Together, these Acts provide that applications for asylum must be made first to the Refugee Applications Commissioner, and on appeal to the Refugee Appeals Tribunal.

Numerous criticisms have been expressed by civil liberties organisations and refugee support groups about the procedures, in particular about the relatively high number of claims that are declared to be 'manifestly unfounded' at the first stage, and about the high numbers that are turned down at the first stage only to succeed on appeal. The Integrating Ireland organisation, for example, conducted a study of the applications for asylum processed in the first two months of 2003, in total numbering almost 2,000. They found that some 1,000 were either withdrawn or refused for procedural reasons – for instance, because the applicant did not turn up for interview. Of the remaining applicants only seventy-one were recognised as refugees, but a massive 830 were refused, with twenty others found to be 'manifestly unfounded'. A further forty applications were refused under the Dublin Convention, that is, where the applicants arrive in Ireland having travelled through another EU country; they may then be returned to that first EU country to have their application processed there.

The criteria used by officials in the Refugee Applications Commissioner's office to deem claims to be manifestly unfounded have been criticised by Amnesty International as unnecessarily broad, since they extend far beyond the accepted thresholds of the United Nations High Commissioner for Refugees (UNHCR). According to accepted norms in international refugee protection laws, manifestly unfounded claims are properly categorised as being those which are either 'clearly fraudulent', or 'not related to the granting of refugee status'. By contrast, the Irish Commissioner has a list of grounds on which claims may be considered 'manifestly unfounded', including where an applicant has given 'clearly insufficient details or evidence to substantiate his/her application', or has unreasonably failed to reveal that he/she was travelling under a false identity or using false travel documents – a very common and necessary occurrence when a person is being persecuted in, and wishes to escape from, their country of citizenship.

Other criticisms, relating to the 2003 legislation in particular, concern the imposition of criminal liability and penalties (up to €3,000 in fines) on those carriers who negligently transport asylum-seekers into Ireland. Similar criticism was expressed about the provision in the 2000 Act shortening the time period within which a judicial review action may be taken by asylum-seekers in the High Court to challenge any aspect of asylum procedures. Some suggested that the legislation might even be unconstitutional, since it discriminated against non-nationals. The Supreme Court disagreed, upholding what was then the 1999 Bill in *Re Article 26 and the Illegal Immigrants (Trafficking) Bill, 1999* ([2000] 2 IR 360, at p.382–3), noting that:

... in the sphere of immigration, its restriction or regulation, the non-national or alien constitutes a discrete category of persons whose entry, presence and expulsion from the State may be the subject of legislative and administrative measures which would not, and in many of its aspects, could not, be applied to its citizens.

The Court ruled against the arguments on discrimination, stating that by the very nature of the Bill's provisions they applied only to non-nationals. The distinction was thus not simply between citizens and non-nationals: there were also further distinctions, since the provisions would apply only to certain categories of non-national, ie, to those whose applications for asylum or refugee status have not yet been decided, or that have been decided and refused. The Court also held that the Bill's provisions served a legitimate public policy objective and facilitated the better administration and functioning of the asylum system.

Although undoubtedly the procedures for processing asylum claims are now working better than they did prior to the full implementation of the 1996 Act, concerns remain about the potential for injustice in the procedures. Amnesty International, in particular, has raised concerns that under the accelerated procedure for cases deemed manifestly unfounded there is no oral appeal hearing, and that the time limit for lodging an appeal is shorter than in the normal procedure. Amnesty has also indicated that asylum-seekers may not be able to obtain adequate legal representation within the process, since government policy is to disperse them throughout the country. It is thus increasingly difficult for them to find solicitors who are knowledgeable in asylum law, or to access the free Refugee Legal Service, which has offices in just three locations outside Dublin.

Another difficulty involves the question of interpretation and translation services. Clearly, in order to ensure a fair hearing, asylum-seekers must fully understand the proceedings, yet the refugee legislation obliges the State to provide interpreters only 'where possible', with the result that applicants may be forced to speak in a language with which they are not fully familiar; this may also mean inaccurate communication with the interviewer during the application process.

Since 1999, more than 8,000 asylum-seekers have had their applications for refugee status in Ireland turned down, and have been subsequently served with deportation orders. Just under six hundred deportation orders against failed asylum-seekers, or those otherwise deemed resident illegally in Ireland were implemented by the Garda National Immigration Bureau (GNIB) in 2003. Refugee support groups expressed particular concern about the covert manner in which sixty-five people, Romanians and Moldovans, including young families, were deported early in the morning on a specially chartered plane in February 2004. The head of the GNIB responded there would be more mass deportations on these chartered planes as more deportation orders are made and implemented – and indeed March 2004 saw a further group deportation to Romania take place.

The biggest problem for asylum-seekers in Ireland, however, is that they are not allowed to work or to take up employment while awaiting the outcome of their application for refugee status. This means they must remain dependent on social welfare benefits and are therefore afforded little opportunity to integrate with local or indigenous communities; in turn, the perception has been fostered among some sectors of the Irish population that they are 'scroungers' because they do not work. Myths about asylum-seekers have spread like wildfire through the country – myths that they get free 'phones, cars, prams, even hairdressing vouchers from the State.

While there is no truth in any of this, the dissemination of such falsehoods has helped to generate hostility among Irish people towards anyone who is, or whom they believe looks like, an asylum-seeker. In turn, such hostility can lead to actual racist assaults. Concern about the effects of rumours such as these has recently led Comhlámh (the returned development-workers' association) to produce a booklet addressing them directly – *Myths/Facts about Immigrants, Asylum seekers and Refugees*. But the best way to tackle the myths, and the racism they foster, would be to give asylum-seekers temporary work visas so that they could take up employment, use their skills and talents to good effect, and thereby integrate more easily within their local community.

Economic migrants

The truth is that although the debate on immigration often focuses on asylum-seekers, they constitute only a small proportion of immigrants to Ireland. By far the largest group of non-EU nationals who come here are economic migrants, who move to Ireland in order to take up work for an employer who has obtained a work permit for them. From the mid-1990s onwards, the growth in national economic prosperity saw a concomitant increase in inward labour migration to Ireland. For the first time in its history, Ireland became an attractive economic proposition to many living in poorer countries.

Most labour migrants come here from other EU Member States, but there has been a notable increase in numbers from outside the EU, rising from about 4,000 in 1976 to over 40,000 in 2002. In 2003, over 47,000 employment permits were granted to employers in respect of migrant workers from non-EU countries, many of whom work in low-paid and unskilled agricultural jobs, such as fruit picking and mushroom harvesting. For a large proportion of these workers, their aim is to save enough money to be able to return home to their country of origin and set themselves up there. This desire was brought into sharp focus for many Irish people by the tragic story of a young Ukrainian man, Vasyl Timinskyy, killed on the Dublin quays in February 2004 in a bus accident in which five people died. It was reported that he had been working in Dublin for three years, and before his death had just saved enough from his earnings to return to the Ukraine and build a new home for his family there.

Economic migrants and the law

The law on work permits, or 'employment permits', has been subject to significant criticism. There is a 'fast-track' work-visa scheme for non-EEA citizens skilled in areas where there is a labour shortage in Ireland, and who have a job offer from an employer here. There are currently about 10,000 people working in Ireland under this scheme, of whom around half are nurses, mainly from the Philippines. In February 2004, the holders of these special work visas secured the right for their spouses to get work permits too.

However, by far the largest group of non-EEA nationals working in Ireland are doing so under the employment permit scheme. Work permits are issued to employers by the Department of Enterprise, Trade and Employment. Due to a shortage of indigenous labour in certain sectors, there has been an increase of more than 600% in the number of visas granted since 1999.[3] Until 2003, the permits scheme was operated under the auspices of a 1946 Aliens Order, but then the Employment Permits Act 2003 came into effect, making it an offence to employ a non-national (ie, a non-EU national) without an employment permit. The 2003 Act was designed primarily to provide a legislative basis for granting full access to employment in Ireland to nationals of the ten new Member States acceding to the EU in May 2004, and was passed through all stages in the Dáil on one day, much to the concern of Opposition deputies. This haste was justified by the Minister for Enterprise, Trade and Employment, Tánaiste Mary Harney, on the basis that any legislation to underpin national measures for the transitional accession period had to be enacted before 16 April 2003 – the date for signing the Accession Treaty.

Despite the title of the legislation, neither in the Act nor in any Ministerial Order introduced under it are the procedures for the granting of employment permits set out, so that no clear statutory basis exists for the work permits scheme. That this position is unsatisfactory was recognised implicitly by Minister Harney in her speech in the Dáil on 3 April 2003 introducing the 2003 Act, when she stated that:

> Work is continuing on preparing the more comprehensive employment permit legislation agreed by the Government last year and I intend that the legislation will be published shortly after Easter. The current proposals [for the 2003 Act] are in no way a substitute for that Bill.

No such comprehensive employment permit legislation has yet been published, and the work permits system continues to be governed by 'operational arrangements' decided by the Department of Enterprise, Trade and Employment. The process by which such permits are granted is cumbersome. The work permit is given to an employer for a specific job, to employ a named employee. The permit is valid for up to twelve months, at which time it can be renewed. However, in order to secure the permit in the first instance, the employer must advertise the position with FÁS for a period of four weeks and must give priority to applications from EU citizens. The conditions for granting work permits have been subject to change on a number of occasions, and different occupational sectors are regularly declared to be ineligible for work permits, presumably on the basis that labour shortages no longer exist in those sectors. The ineligible sectors in March 2004, for example, included clerical and administrative staff, general labourers and builders, sales staff, hotel tourism and catering staff, and childcare workers. These complex and awkward procedures governing work permits cause problems for both employers and their non-national employees. There are obvious changes which could be made to improve the system and make it both fairer and more efficient.

Crucially, employment permits should be issued to migrant workers, not to employers; the present system amounts to a type of 'bonded labour' since workers cannot move jobs, and reports of exploitation of migrant workers by unscrupulous employers abound. Other rights for migrant workers, such as the right to family reunification, should also be introduced, and the validity period for work and residency permits extended beyond the current one-year maximum. Another obvious reform would be to introduce a single residence/employment permit to replace the present separate employment and permanent-resident permits system, which is unnecessarily bureaucratic. Finally, the rights of migrant workers who become unemployed need to be clarified, and better protections provided for those who are dismissed from their jobs.

Problems with immigration law

Largely because of the absence of a clear statutory basis for many procedures, the operation of immigration legislation, both on asylum-seekers and work permits, has been highly problematic and has generated a great deal of case law. Much of the case law has concerned the way in which the power to make immigration law has been left to Ministers, without sufficient intervention from the Oireachtas. In a number of cases this has been found to breach the doctrine of separation of powers, a vital doctrine in any democracy, which recognises the need to separate the functions of the legislature, ie, to make laws, and the functions of the Executive/Ministers, ie, to implement laws. The doctrine means that primary legislation – laws introducing important 'policy and principle' changes – must be passed through the full legislative process, and be debated before the Dáil and the Seanad before being signed into law by the President. There will always be the need for other, less important laws dealing with administrative matters, and these can be delegated to Ministers to implement through what are known as Ministerial Orders, which do not get debated by the Dáil or Seanad. But trouble arises when Ministers start making important policy decisions through Ministerial Orders because then there is no opportunity for democratic debate on the changes being made; they are effectively making law by the back door.

This is exactly what was found to have happened in the context of immigration law in the 1999 decision in *Laurentiu v. Minister for Justice, Equality and Law Reform, Ireland and the Attorney General* ([1999] 4 IR 26). Here, a Romanian footballer whose asylum claim had been rejected challenged the power of the Minister to deport him from Ireland. He won his case before the Supreme Court on the grounds of the separation of powers doctrine. At that time, deportation powers were provided for under Article 13 of the Aliens Order 1946, but the Court ruled that it was not permissible for the legislature to delegate to a Minister the power to legislate for deportation. The Court pointed out that only administrative, regulatory and technical matters could be delegated to Ministers to implement through Ministerial Order; laws which concerned 'principles and policies' had to be passed through the Oireachtas.

Subsequent legislation (the Immigration Act 1999 and the Illegal Immigrants (Trafficking) Act 2000) was then hurriedly passed in order to clarify the Minister's power to deport non-nationals found to be residing illegally within the State. But on 22 January 2004, the Government again received a rap on the knuckles regarding its immigration policy, this time from the High Court. Section 2 of the Immigration Act 1999 provided that Ministerial Orders relating to immigration would be given the status of primary legislation, as if they had been passed through the Oireachtas. Orders thus made had dealt with non-nationals on vital matters like registration, accommodation, travelling, employment, and so on. High Court Judge Finlay Geoghegan declared section 2 to be unconstitutional for its breach of the separation of powers doctrine (*Leontjara and Chang v. DPP*, 22 January 2004).

As a result of this High Court decision, immigration procedures were again thrown into disarray, and again the Minister for Justice announced hasty plans to pass amending legislation. Accordingly, a new Immigration Bill 2004, aimed at controlling entry into the State and regulating the duration and conditions of a stay in the State by non-nationals, was rushed through the Seanad and the Dáil in a matter of days in late January and early February 2004, amid vociferous protests from Opposition Deputies and Senators, many of whom walked out of the debating chamber in disgust. They were highly critical of, among other things, the provision giving power to deport or to refuse entry to persons with a mental disorder or people who have served more than a year in jail – a provision which would have ruled out the entry of Nelson Mandela, as one Senator pointed out. Like some of its predecessors, the Act (now passed) may yet create problems for the Government in future challenges before the courts.

Immigration and Irish citizenship

On one important matter, however, the courts have upheld the Government's power to restrict immigration. The Supreme Court had ruled in the landmark case of *Fajujonu* (1989) that unless there were compelling circumstances, it would be unconstitutional to deport the non-national parents of children born in Ireland. This decision was based upon Article 41 of the Constitution, which guarantees the rights of 'the Family' and recognises the Family as the 'natural, primary and fundamental unit of society', which has rights that are 'inalienable and imprescriptible'. The effect of that decision was confirmed by the amendment to Article 2 inserted by the 1998 referendum on the Belfast Agreement. That Article now provides that: 'It is the entitlement and birthright of every person born in the island of Ireland ... to be part of the Irish nation.' Accordingly, many of those who came to Ireland to claim asylum, or to find work, were able to stay in the country by virtue of having had a child born on the island.

The numbers of those able to reside legally in Ireland on this basis was reported to number about 10,000 by January 2003. In that month, the Supreme Court overturned the *Fajujonu* decision in another landmark ruling in cases taken by a Galway-based Nigerian family, the Osayandes, and by the Lobe family from the Czech Republic, who were living in Ballineen, County Cork (*Osayande and Lobe v. Minister for*

Justice [2003] 1 IR1). Both families had Irish-born children and sought the right to remain in Ireland on the basis that those children were Irish citizens. The Court held against the families, ruling by a 5:2 majority that the non-national parents of Irish citizens do not have the right to reside in their children's country of citizenship. The majority accepted that under Article 2 of the Constitution, any child born in Ireland is entitled to Irish citizenship, but they ruled that although the citizen has a right to reside here, they do not have the right to the care and company of their families in this State. This right is overridden by the need to protect the integrity of the asylum and immigration process, and by the sovereign right of the State to dictate its own immigration policy. One of the judges in the majority remarked that even if the children do not reside in Ireland, they retain their rights as citizens of Ireland and may exercise these rights at a later date; postponing the effect of their citizenship.

To any rational observer the conclusions of the majority appeared to defy logic. Surely the right to reside in the State of one's citizenship is the most basic right of citizens? Does it not make a mockery of Article 2 to suggest that citizens may be forced to postpone their entitlements until they are old enough to survive without their parents? What happens when a citizen living abroad decides, at age 10 or 12, to return to their country of origin? And what is to happen if some non-national parents decide that although they are being deported, it is in their child's best interests to stay in Ireland? Who is going to take on the care of those child citizens? These questions all remain unanswered in the wake of this momentous decision.

The two dissenting Supreme Court judges in the *Osayande and Lobe* case, Judges Fennelly and McGuinness, took these and other questions very seriously. They concluded that the need to preserve the integrity of the asylum and immigration system was not a sufficiently powerful reason for the State's rights to prevail over those of the child. Judge Fennelly said that the notion that a child's citizenship rights could be postponed was 'offensive to logic'. He pointed out that, 'The deportation of a child of tender years, in practice often in the early months of life, automatically and unarguably deprives that child of the possibility of being nurtured and educated in the country of his or her citizenship.' Thus, he held that it was not possible to reconcile the Minister's argument for deportation with the rights declared and guaranteed and by Article 2 of the Constitution. Judge McGuinness reached the same conclusion, and raised another important issue, based upon Article 41. She noted that over the years the Supreme Court had emphasised the nature, weight and importance of family rights. In that context, she could not be satisfied that respect for the maintenance of the immigration and asylum system was sufficiently grave and substantial a reason to justify the denial of the constitutional rights of these children and their families.

Despite the admirably logical reasoning of the two dissenting judges, the majority allowed abstract, administrative arguments, based upon the notion of the integrity of the State's immigration system, to outweigh the most basic rights of children and of families. It is no wonder that many responded to this decision with disappointment and concern. Its effect is to deny full rights of citizenship to children born to non-nationals. The judgment has brought about a two-tier citizenship system: one group of Irish citizens are able to live here with their families, as they have always done; but another group of child citizens, those with lesser legal status, are only able to exercise their right to reside in Ireland if they do so in orphanages or foster homes, deprived of the care and company of their family.

The majority decision also raised serious concerns about the treatment of non-nationals in Ireland generally. Although the two families concerned in the Supreme Court ruling were asylum-seekers, the decision will apply to anyone from outside the EU or EEA who is resident in Ireland and has a child born here. Yet there was reference in some majority judgments to a factor that should have been irrelevant to the decision: the numbers of persons claiming asylum in Ireland. This sort of 'flood- gates' argument is often used to justify tougher Government policy on deportations, ie, to justify laws that have the effect of depriving non-nationals resident here of rights or benefits. The effect of such policies can be to encourage the growth of racism, and to foster the development of hostility towards foreign nationals.

This sort of irrational argument needs to be challenged; we should remember too that the decision has immediate implications for only a few thousand people, the parents of Irish citizens, many of whom have been living in Ireland for years and have contributed to the economy and enriched society. A generous approach to Irish citizenship, one which did not deny the rights of one group of children or their families, would have the effect of further enriching our society in many ways. Instead, since the *Osayande* decision the numbers being deported have risen, and some families have even had to go into hiding in order to escape being uprooted – often after years of living legally in Ireland. A new lobby group, the Coalition Against the Deportation of Irish Citizens (CADIC), was recently established to campaign for the rights of Irish citizens with non-national parents, and has also organised protests against the deportation of families with Irish-born children.

Despite this campaign, the Minister for Justice has indicated that he proposes to hold a referendum to restrict citizenship rights of Irish-born children further. The proposed referendum, apparently, at the time of writing, due to be held in 2004, would amend Article 2 of the Constitution to deny automatic citizenship rights to those children born in Ireland to non-national parents. The amendment would allow citizenship to such children only where one of their parents has lived in Ireland for a significant period of time, such as two or three years. This is a hugely contentious proposal, justified initially by the Minister on the basis that the Masters of the maternity hospitals had complained that too many non-national mothers were giving birth in their hospitals; in reality many of these non-national mothers are in fact from other EU countries, and many may have no desire to seek Irish citizenship for themselves, or for their children. The best answer to any concerns the Masters might have had would be to provide increased resources to maternity hospitals.

All sorts of questions would be raised by the proposed referendum, such as its effect for people born in Northern Ireland to parents who are not Irish citizens. Unfortunately, the sort of vague assertions made by the Minister, about mothers arriving in Ireland late in pregnancy just to obtain citizenship for their children, may even have the effect of encouraging the spread of racism and promoting a false view of our population of foreign nationals. Instead of hinting about sinister motives of non-national mothers, we should be welcoming the much-needed immigration that has boosted our economy and enriched our society. A logical approach to Irish citizenship, which does not create a two-tier system denying the rights of some citizens and their families, would be an infinitely preferable basis for our immigration law. Further, a more rational approach to law-making in this area, requiring actual justifications for any legal change, would be an infinitely preferable basis for a constitutional referendum on such an important issue.

Planning a policy on immigration

Instead of tampering with the Constitution to make unnecessary changes to our citizenship law, the Government should seek to adopt a coherent and logical immigration policy that would allow asylum-seekers the right to work on a temporary basis; and that would provide for legal labour migration without the need for prior contact with an employer. This measure would go a long way to resolving the problems which have arisen in so many cases and for so many unfortunate individuals now facing deportation. A new model for just such a logical and coherent labour migration policy has been put forward by the Immigrant Council of Ireland, which has criticised current immigration policy as being 'ad hoc and piecemeal'. Among the recommendations is the proposal to adopt a more integrated approach to immigration, with improved coordination between the many Government departments currently responsible for different aspects of policy in this area.

An immigration policy must be developed that is located within a clear human rights framework, conforming to UNHCR guidelines; a policy that emphasises the positive benefits of inward migration and that sends a clear message that immigration is not a problem but a solution, particularly to labour market shortages. Unfortunately, in the absence of such a policy we are likely to see the growth of racism and hostility towards Ireland's vibrant new communities.

Racism and Irish society

Given Ireland's long history of emigration, and with the experience of living and working abroad a continued reality for many Irish people today, it might be expected that once levels of immigration into Ireland began to rise, a welcome would be extended to those arriving here, either fleeing political persecution or economic deprivation. Unfortunately, that has not proved to be the case. Despite our traditional reputation as a friendly kind of place, the reality is that visitors here often perceive Ireland as a very unwelcoming country. Even for tourists from Europe and North America, for example, holidaying in Ireland can be a less than positive experience due to high prices, inept service and poor value for money, leading to consumer organisations coining the phrase 'rip-off Ireland'. But for those who are visibly 'different', or from more vulnerable communities, Ireland can represent a seriously hostile environment.

Few welcomes are offered to those who come here seeking asylum, or to those who simply have a different skin colour from the majority 'white' population. The myth of the hundred, thousand welcomes masks what different guidebooks to Ireland have memorably summed up, in a warning to those intending to visit these shores, as 'peculiarly naïve' and even 'particularly lurid' brands of racism. In recent years there has been a deeply worrying increase in racist incidents, and sometimes even violent attacks. UCD academic Bryan Fanning has documented the 'shrill tenor of media coverage of asylum-seekers' from around 1997, evident in headlines like, 'Floodgates open as a new army of poor swamp the country' and 'Refugee Rapists on the Rampage' which were commonplace for a time.[4] Apart from the openly racist rhetoric, there have been horrific racist attacks. In January 2002, Zhao Liu Tao, a young Chinese man, together with two Chinese friends, was attacked by a group of Irish youths on a street in Drumcondra, Dublin. The youths subjected the Chinese students to racist verbal abuse, and then Zhao Liu was hit on the head a number of times with an iron bar. He died in hospital three days later from his injuries, and his death was widely reported as 'Ireland's first racially motivated murder'.

This tragic incident cannot be dismissed as an isolated event. The March 2003 issue of *Spectrum*, the journal of the National Consultative Committee on Racism and Interculturalism (NCCRI), noted a 60% increase in the number of racist incidents reported to them, compared to their two previous reports. Racist abuse, assaults, harassment and other forms of cultural disrespect were the most common forms of incident, and the NCCRI commented that some of these were of a particularly serious nature. For example, they recorded a suspected arson attack on a Nigerian family in a city-centre location; a serious assault combined with racist insults upon a Zimbabwean man in the cloakroom queue at a nightclub in Dublin; and a vicious night-time attack on twenty Traveller families living in a temporary site near Laytown, County Meath, by a person driving agricultural machinery. Other incidents reported to the NCCRI included complaints by persons who had received racist abuse not only from immigration officials at Dublin Airport but even from officials in the Department of Justice. Finally, in a new development which suggests a more organised and sinister form of racism, the NCCRI found that there has been a significant increase in the number of racist and offensive emails, letters and texts being sent to organisations working against racism in Ireland.

Politicians who speak out publicly on anti-racism platforms regularly receive hate mail; inflammatory pamphlets are circulated by groups like the Immigration Control Platform (ICP) – a small outfit set up by Cork schoolteacher Áine Ní Chonaill with the aim of achieving a 'tight immigration policy' and 'a determined response to all illegal immigration'. More seriously, physical attacks and verbal abuse on blacks and Asians on Irish streets occur with depressing frequency. There is little leadership from the Government on the issue, with foot-dragging over the introduction of any proper immigration policy compounding the issue, and widespread use of anti-asylum-seeker language to justify restrictive immigration policies. The Government has even decided to restrict access to social welfare entitlements for citizens of the ten new EU accession states by imposing a 'habitual residency' test – a move widely seen as a response to tabloid media-generated frenzy about 'welfare tourism'.

Yet on a more optimistic note, there has been no overt attempt by any mainstream political party to play the 'race card', and every mainstream political party has signed up to an anti-racism electoral protocol. Apart from the small and effectively irrelevant ICP, which gains only a few hundred votes on any occasion when it puts forward candidates at elections, no anti-immigration organisation has been formed with the aim of placing race on the political agenda. Discrimination on grounds of race is forbidden in the equality legislation, and the most extreme racist rhetoric is criminalised in the Prohibition of Incitement to Hatred Act 1989. There is also a great deal of activism taking place within the new communities, with asylum-seeker and migrant worker organisations emerging; a vibrant, multicultural newsletter, *Metro Eireann*, being published monthly; and individuals from Nigerian communities in Galway and Dundalk, among other places, standing as candidates in local elections. These are all very positive developments.

There is no room for complacency about this, however. Opinion polls generally tend to show that the subject of immigration provokes strong feelings and hostility, particularly in disadvantaged urban areas. Moreover, an examination of Irish policy, attitudes and laws on immigration relating to the 'new communities' shows the danger inherent in not tackling racism upfront and at the highest political levels. Most importantly, there is a need for a coherent immigration policy that facilitates economic migration to Ireland and that emphasises the positive contribution of immigration to Irish economy, society and culture.

THE TRAVELLER COMMUNITY IN IRELAND

For a long time another, equally pervasive form of racism has been part of Irish society, pre-dating the current experience of hostility directed against new communities. Those born into the Traveller community in Ireland have long been treated as second-class citizens. Everywhere in Ireland today, prevailing lay definitions of Travellers as deviants and misfits may be found, definitions which deny Travellers' history, language and cultural contribution to society. This is ironic given that they are the oldest ethnic minority group in Ireland, having lived here for many hundreds of years. References to Travellers and to the nomadic culture date back many centuries. It is clear that Irish society has always had a nomadic strand, held distinct from the majority and regarded by them as outcast.

Nomadism is essentially the principal difference between Travellers and settled people, as the language itself suggests. Nomadism is central to the way of life of Travellers, affecting every aspect of their lifestyle and influencing the development of their language: it is a core value for Travellers. While many Travellers are settled or living in permanent accommodation, many continue to practise nomadism on an occasional or regular basis. This practise has historically been used as the justification for the exclusion of Travellers from the sorts of rights and benefits available to the settled community. Social policy on Travellers in Ireland has always been linked to their nomadism and it has been used against them. For example, the 1963 Commission on Itinerancy pursued a firmly assimilationist policy, stating that, 'it is not considered that there is any alternative to a positive drive for housing itinerants if a permanent solution to the problem of itinerancy, based on absorption and integration, is to be achieved.'

Twenty years on from that, in the *Travelling People Review Body Report*, the term 'itinerant' had been dropped. The language had changed in other ways too: instead of describing nomadism as a problem, part of the Body's brief was to address 'the needs of Travellers who wish to continue the nomadic way of life'. But the Report also stated that, 'Travellers who are not accommodated [in houses] cannot hope to achieve an adequate education. Nor can they avail satisfactorily of services such as health and welfare.'

Arguably, much social policy regarding Travellers is still based on this essentially false and misguided premise, ie, that nomadism is a problem, that it is a deviation from 'normal' settled life, and that those Travellers who continue to pursue a nomadic way of life are wilfully placing themselves beyond the support and provision of State services.

As long as nomadism is viewed disparagingly by the settled community, Travellers' lives will be made more difficult overall. Census figures for various aspects of Travellers' lives show clearly the level of disadvantage currently suffered by this section of our community. The 2002 Census shows that of the 23,700 Travellers enumerated, of those who indicated at what age they had left full-time education, two-thirds had left before the age of 15 (compared with 15% of the overall population). Furthermore, unemployment among male Travellers is 73%, compared with 9.4% for the male population overall. Mortality rates, literacy rates and general standards of health are also significantly lower for Travellers than for the settled population. Given that the numbers of Travellers overall are very small – at less than 1% of the whole population – it should be perfectly possible for the State to ensure they are provided with decent accommodation, and to improve standards of living and of health among the community.

Travellers and the law

David Joyce of the Traveller Legal Unit has recently written that Travellers may generally be seen as 'outsiders' in terms of Irish society. In his article[5], Joyce demonstrates how, even after Independence, the pathological perception of Travellers' way of life has continued in legislation. Since Travellers are a mainly oral community, recorded history is quite scarce, yet the common view of Travellers as recorded through centuries of legislation tells its own story. The core concept running right through this legislation has been the categorisation of the nomadic way of life as criminal.

This historic criminalisation of Travellers is not a phenomenon unique to Ireland and England, and similar laws may be found in most other European States. Unfortunately, with the establishment of a national Irish parliament, national legislators adopted the same approach evident from previous colonial statutes. Early post-1922 legislation often had a severe impact on different elements of Travellers' lives, and certain laws have been disproportionately used against Travellers. Examples of such legislation include the Local Government (Sanitary Services) Act 1948, section 31 of which provides for the prohibition and exclusion of 'temporary dwellings' from local authority areas. Even some modern legislation has continued to follow this trend; for example, section 69 of the Roads Act 1993 deals with the erection and maintenance of temporary dwellings, and gives the power of seizure to Gardaí and authorised persons to remove caravans from certain types of road.

On the other hand, some modern legislation, often introduced after specific lobbying by Traveller groups, has taken a different approach. Over the last thirty years, Traveller representative groups have pursued a campaign for the promotion of equality, especially with the establishment in 1990 of the Irish Traveller Movement, a national network of eighty organisations and individuals working within the Traveller community. This strategy has been relatively successful.[6] For example, discrimination against Travellers has been prohibited in different contexts, both in the Prohibition of Incitement to Hatred Act 1989, and in the Unfair Dismissals (Amendment) Act 1993. More particularly, positive changes to the law on equality have occurred in recent years. The introduction of the Employment Equality Act 1998 and the Equal Status Act 2000 was perhaps the most significant legislative development aimed at the promotion of legal protection for Travellers on an individual level. A broad legal definition of 'Traveller community' is provided in section 2 of the Equal Status Act 2000:

> ... the community of people who are commonly called Travellers and who are identified (both by themselves and others) as people with a shared history, culture and traditions including, historically, a nomadic way of life on the island of Ireland.

However, Travellers groups and civil liberties organisations were critical of section 15 of the Equal Status Act, which allows service providers (eg, publicans) to refuse service where they reasonably believe that the provision of services would create a substantial risk of criminal or disorderly conduct or damage to property. Thus, where a pub-owner had a pub full of members of the Immigration Control Platform, he or she could legitimately refuse to serve a black customer on the grounds that the other customers present might create disorder in the pub as a result. It was envisaged by critics that this provision could significantly undermine the purpose of the Act.

As it turned out, the implementation of the Equality Acts and the mechanisms provided to ensure their effectiveness were at first relatively successful in addressing the socially ingrained practice of maintaining 'Traveller-Free premises', in particular licensed premises. A series of cases taken by individual Travellers challenging such practices resulted in a number of high-profile awards of compensation being made by publicans who had previously barred people from their pubs on grounds of ethnicity. An example was the case of Travellers Bridget and Michael Connors, who were each awarded IR£2,200 (€2,793) because they were refused service in Molly Heffernan's public house in Tallaght in November 2000. The publican was also ordered to erect a sign in the pub stating a commitment to equality.

In response to these equality claims, the publicans mounted a strong offensive, taking a no-holds-barred approach in their opposition. Tadg O'Sullivan of the Vintners' Federation of Ireland (VFI), who led the charge, stated that 'publicans have been under siege since this legislation came in, with a state of extortion and blackmail by a section of the Traveller community.' He asserted that members of one extended Traveller family had an average of eight to ten cases each against more than twenty pubs.[7] In response, the national Travellers' centre, Pavee Point, countered that the number of claims being taken reflected how widespread discrimination against Travellers seeking service in pubs had been. The Office of the Director of Equality Investigations (now the Equality Tribunal) also defended its record on making decisions in the Traveller claims, pointing out that not all had been won by the claimants. In fact, the amount of compensation awarded was also typically very small; the Connors' award was one of the highest.

Ultimately, the vintners' lobbying campaign was successful in bringing about a change in the law, demonstrating that there remain powerful interests opposed to providing equal access to Travellers. When the Minister for Justice introduced the Intoxicating Liquor Act 2003, he included within it a provision removing jurisdiction for discrimination claims relating to incidence on licensed premises from the Equality Tribunal and transferring the power to hear such cases to the District Court. In other words, while discrimination cases involving shops, cinemas, schools and any other providers of services are dealt with under the Equal Status Act procedures through the Equality Tribunal, from now on cases involving discrimination claims against pubs are to be heard by a different court (perceived by publicans as being more favourable to their interests). So much for equality.

The provision of accommodation for Traveller families has always fallen far short of what is necessary. In 1995, the *Task Force Report on Travellers* recommended that 3,100 units of accommodation be provided for Travellers by the year 2000, but only 127 new units were provided in that time. According to figures from the Department of the Environment, 1,207 Traveller families are currently still living on the roadside.

Progress on accommodation for Travellers has been made through legislation, notably the Housing (Traveller Accommodation) Act of 1998. This Act established the National Traveller Accommodation Consultative Committee (NTACC) and local Traveller Accommodation Consultative Committees, which advise local authorities and are made up of Traveller representatives, local councillors and local authority officials. However, the legislation contains no sanctions should these accommodation plans not be implemented. This is its major weakness, evident in the fact that since the Act came into force the actual provision of serviced halting sites by local authorities has still failed to meet the obligations contained in law. The Department of the Environment stated that 3,600 new units of accommodation for Traveller families were required between 2000 and 2004, but this target is far from being met. Of 2,200 new halting-site bays promised by 2004, according to the first report of NTACC, just 129 had been provided as of December 2002. More recent figures supplied by local authorities in 2004 show that the number of halting-site bays increased by 206 to 1,398 between 2001 and 2003 – still well below the target – and that group housing units increased by eighty-nine to 545. However, the Irish Traveller Movement has accused the Minister of 'massaging' the figures, and claimed that nowhere near 1,300 families had been accommodated by local authorities between those years.

In this context recent legislative change again represents a significant step backwards. The introduction of an amendment to the Criminal Justice (Public Order) Act 1994, by way of section 24 of the Housing (Miscellaneous Provisions) Act 2002, amounts to an effective criminalising of occupiers of temporary dwellings. The new provisions inserted into the public order legislation make it an offence to enter onto, occupy, or place an object on land without the owner's consent, where 'object' is defined to include a 'temporary dwelling' and to include animals. It is very clear just whom the legislation is targetting. New powers have also been given to gardaí to request that persons move on when they are found to be occupying land in this way; and to arrest people without a warrant if they find them in breach of the Act. These provisions were introduced following widespread condemnation of a Travellers' encampment at Rathfarnham in South Dublin, which left a public park and local beauty spot in a littered and grossly damaged condition. The state in which the public park was left by those individual members of the Traveller community involved was appalling; but the effect of their behaviour has been to cause the criminalisation of other Traveller families with nowhere else to go, whom the State has failed in its duty to provide serviced halting sites.

Despite the equality legislation, negative attitudes to Travellers and Traveller culture persist and continue to be expressed openly in many fora. In 1996, for example, journalist Mary Ellen Synon's article in the *Sunday Independent*, 'Time to get tough on tinker terror culture', provoked huge controversy.[8] Her article reflected a commonly held perception that the Traveller way of life is deviant. This view continues to result in the exclusion of Travellers from society, an exclusion frequently reinforced by law and resulting in the criminalising of individuals simply because they are part of nomadic communities.

The launch of the Traveller Legal Unit by the Irish Traveller Movement in June 2003, with the declared aim of advancing Traveller human rights under various legislative frameworks, has been a very welcome development. So too is the publication of a research project jointly commissioned by the Irish Traveller Movement and the Traveller Movement of Northern Ireland, entitled *Misli, Crush, Misli (Irish Travellers and Nomadism)*. Its purpose was to examine nomadism in contemporary Ireland and to find out what nomadism means to Travellers today. The research came at an important time: Travellers' nomadic lifestyles are under serious attack, both from outside the law, through physical attacks on Traveller families around the country, and also from within the legal system itself, through the passing of anti-Traveller legislation. The research project also clearly presented nomadism as a human right rather than a deviant lifestyle, a very positive perspective.

Yet, despite reports like this, and despite all the work done by Traveller representative groups, Traveller culture remains effectively marginalised, just as it was historically. It is vital therefore to place legislation and policy on Travellers on a secure rights basis. This would have the effect of enabling Travellers to seek redress before the courts for the State's failure to provide accommodation. It would also have the effect of providing Travellers with a more secure place in Irish society as citizens and full members of the community, with all the rights and responsibilities that would necessarily entail.

NOTES FOR CHAPTER EIGHT

1. O'Toole, F., *After the Ball*. (Dublin: New Island, 2003.)
2. Cullen, P., *Refugees and Asylum Seekers in Ireland*. (Ireland: Cork University Press, 2000.)
3. *Labour Immigration into Ireland: Report and Recommendations on Work Permits, Working Conditions, Family Reunification and the Integration of Immigrant Workers in Ireland.* (Immigrant Council of Ireland, May 2003.)
4. Fanning, B., 'The Political Currency of Irish Racism: 1997–2002', in 91 *Studies*.
5. Joyce, D., in (2003) *4 Irish Criminal Law Journal*.

6.   For a more detailed discussion of litigation by Traveller groups aimed at securing equality, see Whyte, G., *Social Exclusion and the Law*. (Dublin: IPA, 2002.)

7.   *Sunday Business Post*, 21 April 2002.

8.   Synon, Mary Ellen, *Sunday Independent,* 28 January 1996.

CHAPTER 9
Social Policy and Environment

Over the last twenty-five years or so, different campaigns to liberalise Irish society have achieved significant legal change in a whole range of areas: from the relations between State and Church; to family planning laws; to the shape of our education system. Despite the limitations inherent in the text of the fundamental rights Articles 40-44 of the Constitution, litigation and lobbying have given effect to social change, both in law and in social policy, around many of those rights.

In relation to Article 45, however, much still needs to be done. Entitled 'Directive Principles of Social Policy', this Article sets out a series of principles intended as guidelines for the Oireachtas in the making of laws (for full text, see Appendix). Those principles are clearly informed by a social democratic perspective, constituting directions to our legislators that the State should seek to ensure that 'the ownership and control of the material resources of the community may be so distributed ... as best to subserve the common good'; and that the operation of free competition shall not be allowed to develop so as 'to result in the concentration of the ownership or control of essential commodities in a few individuals to the common detriment'. The State is also directed to 'safeguard with especial care the economic interests of the weaker sections of the community' and to ensure that the 'strength and health of workers' is not abused.

These are noble aspirations, which should form the basis for all areas of social policy development in a modern, liberal and secular European country. But the social guidelines contained in Article 45 are expressed as principles rather than as enforceable rights, which means, in effect, that they are merely aspirations. They may be contrasted, for example, with the right to education guaranteed in Article 42. This is the only Article that confers 'rights' status on any aspect of social or public services. Accordingly, an individual may sue the State for failure to provide them with an education. By contrast, there is no enforceable, constitutional right to housing, social security or healthcare. One might believe that there is nevertheless an onus on the State to fulfill these aspirations envisaged in Article 45, but it has in fact failed to do so in a whole range of ways; we will examine some of those areas of failure here.

The current laws regulating social policy and the living environment are problematic and, in places, inadequate. In order to abide by its responsibilities as laid out in Article 45, the State – albeit not bound by a legal duty in these areas – does have a moral duty to regulate with compassion and to make due provision for the weaker sections of the community. Unfortunately, the State is not meeting its moral obligations in many aspects of this duty – from inadequate legislation on waste and limited enforcement of waste policies, to lack of provision of decent public housing, public transport facilities, and care services for children, people with disabilities and older people.

Of course, rights carry with them responsibilities, and it can be argued that if social and economic rights, like the right to housing, were guaranteed in the Constitution, individuals would have to take on corresponding social responsibilities. We do not, as citizens, have a great record on communal responsibility, as evidenced by ongoing problems with littering, illegal dumping, and extensive tax evasion scandals – therefore a culture must be developed in which social rights are conferred on people, but social responsibilities also expected of them. This would clearly take time to develop, but would ultimately be worth the struggle.

However, there is strong political resistance to any incorporation in the Constitution of social and economic rights, like the right to housing or healthcare. The Labour party put forward a bill in 1999 (the Twenty-First Amendment to the Constitution Bill (No. 3) 1999) that proposed to provide specific constitutional recognition for social, economic and cultural rights, including the right to adequate housing or shelter. If passed, the bill would have provided that the exercise of individual rights would be regulated by principles of social justice. In fact, the bill was not adopted. The idea of enshrining social and economic rights in law has encountered strong ideological opposition. Those against this idea argue that the separation of powers doctrine means that the implementation of social and economic policy must be solely a matter for the legislature and Executive (Government), not for the judiciary. They take the view that the courts should not rule on the way in which public money should be spent, or the way in which public services should be run. If enforceable rights were granted, they argue, then social policy would be decided in the courts because every time an individual felt they had not received an adequate public service they would sue the State – and this would reduce the ability of governments to govern effectively.

This is an ongoing and vitally important debate. The present Supreme Court also opposes making social and economic rights legally enforceable. But proponents of such rights, like Donncha O'Connell of NUI Galway, have argued that the result of separating rights into two groups – the enforceable civil and political rights in Articles 40-44, and the unenforceable social and economic rights in Article 45 – is a weakening of the democratic process. As O'Connell says:

> If we believe in the rule of law then we cannot avoid some judicial involvement in the resolution of disputes that inevitably arise between citizens and the state, as well as between citizens themselves. The end of the rule of law is served by doctrines such as separation of powers, not the other way around ... If the judiciary are not to retain a role as guarantors of fundamental rights and enforcers of statutory entitlement, we, as a citizenry, are leaving ourselves rather exposed to the capricious whim of authoritarian government ... Numerous countries have given constitutional protection to social and economic rights, and this has not resulted in the end of the democratic world as we know it.[1]

O'Connell's arguments make sense. If we were to make the Directive Principles contained in Article 45 enforceable as rights, litigation would still take place only as a last resort, where legislators and government had failed to deliver on adequate public services. Moreover, the Constitution is an aspirational document which should identify a set of socially desirable goals, a picture of the kind of society we *want* to have; it should also provide a means of achieving that end. Only a rights-based approach to social policy can ensure that aspirations become reality.

WASTE MANAGEMENT

There is a large gap between aspirations and reality as far as waste management is concerned. A distinct lack of regulation and failure to develop a coherent waste policy has long been a problem in Ireland. Every year this country produces hundreds of thousands of tonnes of rubbish – 2.3 million tonnes in 2001 – yet we recycle only 13% of it. Like Britain, but unlike just about every other European neighbour, we take a 'bin, burn and bury' approach to waste management.[2]

The twenty-first century has brought a new awareness of waste and waste-management globally. Despite Ireland's poor record on rubbish, things are now slowly changing, largely as a result of international and European pressure. The adoption of the Framework EEC Directive on Waste (75/442/EEC) and other subsequent Directives has had a major impact on law and practice here. Until the 1990s, the main piece of legislation governing waste management was the Public Health Act 1878 – an Act that obviously belonged to a very different time with very different problems. Thankfully, that anomaly was finally acknowledged, and in 1996 the Waste Management Act was introduced, ushering in a new regime for policy development. Under this Act a series of regulations has been adopted which has helped to set the agenda for literally cleaning up waste policy in Ireland. There was a lot of ground to make up; according to the Government's own 'Race Against Waste' website:

> Waste management is one of the most problematic and challenging environmental issues in Ireland at the present time. Historically, we have had no proper waste management planning, were almost completely dependent on

poorly managed, cheap landfill, and had little or no awareness that individuals should take responsibility for their own waste. When Ireland was ignoring the waste issue, our European neighbours were developing and implementing sustainable integrated waste management practices. These practices have used a variety of waste solutions, and achieved very high levels of recycling. In fact recycling began in earnest in Europe soon after World War Two, yet it remains an unfamiliar activity in some parts of Ireland.[3]

Certainly, we can no longer afford to ignore our massive waste problem, especially as latest figures indicate clearly that the situation is getting worse each year. The total quantity of municipal (household, commercial and street-cleansing) waste increased by over 31% between 1998 and 2001: from 2,056,652 tonnes in 1998 to 2,704,035 tonnes in 2001. This huge increase in just a short space of time has placed severe pressure on existing (and already inadequate) waste-management facilities and infrastructure, and has forced a rethink of waste-disposal measures.

Landfill has traditionally been the main disposal method in Ireland: we bury over 80% of all our waste; by contrast, the Swiss bury just 7% of theirs. In fact, between 1998 and 2001 there was a disturbing increase of 20.3% overall of waste consigned to landfill in Ireland. Continued reliance on this method is now regarded as unsustainable because we are rapidly running out of landfill space. Many landfill sites in Ireland are nearly full, with six out of ten waste-management planning regions having less than three years' landfill capacity remaining. Finding new sites is difficult given that every proposed landfill site has encountered stiff opposition from local communities. Among the reasons cited by communities for their opposition is the unsightliness of the landfill sites, the attendant odour and the potential public health risks. Although landfill design may have improved in recent years, it is considered an outdated method of waste disposal upon which Ireland remains over-reliant. The Government has therefore turned its attention to other methods of disposal – particularly incineration and recycling.

Unfortunately, the same problems arise with the alternative of incineration: like landfill sites, no community wants to have an incinerator located anywhere nearby, and the campaigns by local residents against proposed incineration plants, such as that planned for the Poolbeg Peninsula at Ringsend in Dublin, have assumed epic proportions. The main concern expressed by local communities about incinerators is the fear of dioxin, a chemical by-product of incineration that people believe will cause cancer in humans and animals. There are different opinions on the dangers posed by incinerators, but in spite of government attempts to reassure communities about them, and in spite of strict limits set on emission levels through EU legislation, local opposition to incinerator plants has thus far prevented any being built in Ireland.

Recycling, then, is everybody's professed favoured waste-disposal method – in theory. In practice our recycling rates are absurdly low compared with other European countries, where coherent waste-management policies have been in place for decades. Compare our rate of 13% with, for example, Austria's 64%, Belgium's 52%, or the rate of 47% in The Netherlands. To bring Ireland in line with its EU counterparts, national waste-management targets were set in 1998 by the current Government, for example, to divert 50% of household waste from landfill, and to achieve a recycling rate of 35% for municipal waste by 2013. Although there has been some progress towards increased recycling – household and commercial waste recycling rates having increased from 9% in 1998 to just over 13% in 2001 – we are still a long way off from the target rate of 35%. Moreover, poor progress and even regression have been noted in other areas, as evidenced by the increased use of landfill in recent years.

When you add to these problems the increased preponderance of visible rubbish – litter strewn everywhere, in city centres, on streets in rural towns, thrown over hedges in the middle of nowhere; illegal dumps widespread in some rural areas – it paints a pretty grim picture for the next generation. Worse still, it is this bad simply because we won't face up to our waste problem and take responsibility for it: nobody wants a dump, an incinerator, a sewerage plant, or anything that might actually dispose of unwanted detritus anywhere near where they live. The classic NIMBY ('not in my backyard') attitude prevails as far as rubbish is concerned.

Of all the attempts by the Government to curb the waste problem, the most effective initiative was the introduction, in 2002, of a 15c. levy on plastic bags. This has resulted in a dramatic decrease in that aspect of waste creation. Although many people grumbled and complained beforehand, we have all become used to bringing a reusable bag with us when shopping: it was, in the end, a pain-free transition. Department of Environment figures show that the levy raised more than €9 million for the Exchequer during its first four months in operation, and reduced the use of plastic bags by 90% in the same period. This success aside, other attempts to discourage waste generation have been ill thought-out, like the bin charges introduced recently in Dublin, which generated such strong public opposition and resulted in short jail sentences for a dissenting TD and a number of other protestors. It is true that bin charges introduced elsewhere in the country generated far less opposition, but before any environmental tax of this kind can be implemented, people need to be convinced that it is part of a workable, national waste-management policy – and there was no indication at the time the Dublin tax was initiated that this was the case.

The announcement that a 'pay-by-use' system of waste charges will be introduced in January 2005 is welcome – it will mean a change from a flat fee to a charge based upon weight or volume of waste generated – and will hopefully encourage people to recycle more. But in order to be equitable, this system would require allowances to be made for those with larger families, and some form of waivers for those on low incomes. Again, the key requirement for success is to produce a fully researched, coherent, well-presented plan of action before the introduction of any new charges.

Overall, as far as waste management is concerned, national policy currently lacks any real sense of equity, any coherence or sense of civic pride, and is characterised by an 'ostrich' approach. We have not established any creative alternatives to dumps or incinerators, illegal dumping still continues to be a real problem in many areas and we are miles behind most of our EU neighbours in our use of recycling.

In order to change waste culture, a properly resourced national strategy is needed, preferably coordinated by a national waste-management agency (still to be created) and policed by a greatly strengthened Environmental Protection Agency with an increased number of inspectors. Legislative changes will also be required to support a comprehensive strategy. Such laws would have to set mandatory minimisation and recovery targets to ensure increased use of recycling; require manufacturers of electrical and computer goods to take responsibility for their products at the end of their lifespans; give incentives to households to produce segregated waste – not just charged by volume; and make provision for a significant increase in recycling facilities nationwide. Put quite simply, we have no choice other than to make radical changes in our waste-management policy, otherwise the apocryphal scenario in the 'Race against Waste' advertisements, featuring a plague of rats and an avalanche of rubbish, will become a reality in towns and rural areas around Ireland.

HERITAGE AND PLANNING

Waste-management issues aside, the myth of Emerald Ireland is alive and well, and the John Hinde images of luridly green fields are still being used to flog holidays in the 'unspoilt' south and west, but the reality for the tourists who are lured here on these false pretences is often very different. What they see is not an idyll of greenness, craggy cliffs and rolling hills, but a nest of unplanned, one-off developments, the product of short-sighted tax breaks which have resulted in 'bungalow blight', a rash of interpretive centres, and rolling fields full not of peacefully grazing cattle but of endless regiments of holiday homes.

The truth is that heritage and environmental protection have always been weak in Ireland. The recent absorption of the heritage agency, Dúchas, into the Department of the Environment, Heritage and Local Government has emphasised the low placing that preservation of historic sites occupies in the list of the Government's priorities. For some time we have been subjected to the drip-feed spin of developers telling us that our heritage and planning laws have slowed down development and hampered the building of the necessary infrastructure – for which we can generally assume they mean roads (see further, below). Their spin has created the impression that the expendable old is unnecessarily, and expensively, being preserved at the expense of the new and improved. Government decisions in these areas often seem to suggest they have been swayed by this argument.

The gaps in heritage protection are compounded by the absence of funding for adequate numbers of conservation officers in different county and city councils. As Peter Cox of the International Council on Monuments and Sites has said, the lack of resources demonstrates that the Government has 'no commitment to the protection of our heritage'. This lack of commitment was evident in the decision by the State, in 2003, not to purchase the nineteenth-century Sligo mansion *Lissadell House*, the childhood home of Constance Markievicz, to which W.B. Yeats was a regular visitor; the house was instead bought privately. The State's failure to purchase *Lissadell* attracted condemnation from organisations like An Taisce, the independent National Trust group, and from the Mayor of Sligo, who had argued that the house, like Muckross House in Killarney, could have attracted tens of thousands of tourists annually and generated significant income for the local community and the exchequer. The *Lissadell* case shows the need for heritage trust legislation, which would empower voluntary sector organisations (like the National Trust in England, which, as a registered charity, is completely independent of Government) to undertake the ownership and management of such properties in the future, for the benefit of all citizens.

As with heritage protection, planning also requires stronger regulation. Both urban and rural planning policies have generated huge controversy across Ireland for many years. As the capital city with an ever-expanding population and infrastructure, Dublin has been one of the worst-hit areas in terms of lack of heritage protection and poor planning practices. The citizens of Dublin have fought long and hard to preserve some of the city's older façades – something which can be interpreted positively as proof of a strong sense of civic responsibility. In the 1980s, for example, public campaigns were mounted to preserve Georgian buildings in Dublin and save them from demolition by speculators, while huge demonstrations were held to protest the building of local authority offices on an important archaeological site at Woodquay on Dublin's south city quays. Despite all this activism, large swathes of housing in the centre of Dublin were demolished at the time, roads widened, and the civic offices were built on top of important Viking remains – all with utter disregard for public concerns about heritage and proper planning practices.

Many rumours and counter-rumours abounded in Dublin about the use and abuse of the planning process in the outer Dublin suburbs during the 1980s and early 1990s, but the extent of this scandal is only now coming to light. The Flood (later Mahon) Tribunal, the Tribunal of Inquiry into Certain Planning Matters and Payments, was established by the Oireachtas in October 1997, under the chairmanship of Mr Justice Feargus Flood, to investigate the general issue of planning corruption and payments to politicians; and in particular the planning history of 726 acres of land in North County Dublin. Revelations and allegations have emerged about corruption among (mostly Fianna Fáil) councillors and some city officials, and about backhanders being paid to key people to change votes on rezoning in order to line the pockets of developers. The country has been riveted by the proceedings at the Tribunal, and also deeply shocked at the level of corruption that defined the period in question, and the damage wrought by those seeking only personal financial gain. The information emerging from the Mahon Tribunal has demonstrated the potential for abuse due to the poor state of planning policy in suburban Dublin at the time, and has highlighted how many councillors wilfully ignored the living conditions of the residents of the areas affected by their decisions.

The effect of insufficient regulation in the planning process is easy to see. Dublin now suffers severely from urban sprawl, with a 'footprint' that is two or three times that of some other European cities with similar-sized populations. According to one estimate, were current trends to persist until 2010, Dublin could end up consuming as much land as Los Angeles in order to accommodate only a quarter of the population of that city.

Planning is not just an urban issue. In rural Ireland, one of the most controversial planning problems is that concerning the construction of one-off houses. These are essentially houses which are built individually without reference to developments in the surrounding area, or to access to water and sewerage systems, public transport services, etc. There is currently a real controversy about this practice, since the building of houses nationally on a one-off basis is seen as incompatible with any sort of sustainable development; it contributes to commuting times, and to urban sprawl generally. Although planning laws have been strengthened, and each local authority is now supposed to grant planning permission according to its own local development plan, councillors may still vote to override these plans in specific cases, to permit, for example, the building of these 'one-off' houses in rural areas. According to the Minister for Housing, up to 60% of new homes in some local communities are one-off houses.

An Taisce has led a campaign against this practice, arguing that in order to ensure sustainable development, new houses should ideally be built in existing settlements or villages, even though this may not be what many individuals want. According to An Taisce, 43% of all houses built in Ireland are one-off houses, and 85% of applications for planning permission for such houses are granted by local authorities. An Taisce appeals less than 2% of applications for one-off houses nationally, usually on the grounds that the building of such houses would endanger public health, or local water quality through inadequate provision for sewage disposal. However, their campaign against this form of building has generated great hostility in countryside communities, where many farming families resent having restrictions imposed on how they use their land, particularly where they wish to build new homes adjacent to existing farmhouses for grown-up children.

Further controversy has been generated recently by the announcement of draft guidelines on housing in the countryside, published by the Minister for the Environment in March 2004. In these guidelines, the Minister did not impose any ban on the building of one-off housing; critics have accused him of giving developers the green light to proceed with such housing, without any indication as to how the requirements of EU law under Ground Water and Drinking Water Directives, and on public transport commitments, could be met.

The effect of inadequate planning regulation in rural areas is far-reaching, giving rise to many problems, such as pollution of rivers and lakes due to overloaded sewerage infrastructure. At the same time, many small communities are highly aggrieved at the spread of multitudinous holiday cottage schemes, spawned by short-sighted rural incentive taxation programmes. As a result, some local councils are now calling a halt to the construction frenzy and seeking to control rural development by imposing certain conditions on any new building. However, this approach is not without its problems either.

For instance, in 2003 permission was granted to a County Galway developer to build a scheme of just twelve houses in the highly sought-after location of Carraroe village in the Connemara Gaeltacht. Nothing unusual about that – except that Galway County Council inserted a condition into the permission that the occupants of the new scheme had to be fluent in Irish, and the houses were stated to be for 'the exclusive use of occupants who have an appropriate competence/fluency in the Irish language'. By so doing, they were seeking to ensure that the cultural identity of the area was respected. The County Galway Development Plan allows conditions to be imposed on planning permission to ensure the protection of Irish as a community language, but this was the first time that a local authority had granted planning permission subject to this sort of specific language condition, a move that was welcomed by Irish-language groups.

Arguably, proactive measures like this are required in order to preserve the linguistic and cultural identity of particular communities. But despite the very legitimate purpose that this planning condition meets, its practical application is likely to be more problematic. For instance, how does one judge an 'appropriate competence or fluency' in Irish? And what happens if an Irish speaker who buys a house in the scheme then wishes to sell it to somebody who lacks an appropriate level of fluency? The reality is that planning conditions imposed on small communities require a considered, cautious approach.

Some years ago, the Commissioners of Public Works were given the power, through legislation, to compulsorily purchase land on the Great Blasket Island in order to establish a national park there. However, they could only exercise this power over land that had been bought after 1953. In other words, islanders whose families had occupied land on the island before that year could keep their land. This power was successfully challenged by disgruntled landowners who had bought island property after 1953. In a landmark judgment, the Supreme Court ruled in 1999 that the law was discriminatory. The Court held that to make a distinction between 'native residents' of the island and others was to introduce an 'unusual and dubious classification with ethnic and racial overtones.' The Court further stated that the legislation had been based on a 'principle of pedigree', which should have no place in a 'democratic society committed to the principle of equality' (*Blascaod Mór Teo v. Commissioners of Public Works* [2000] 1 IR 16).

The condition imposed in the Great Blasket case was not exactly analagous to that imposed more recently in Carraroe by Galway County Council, but the case highlights some of the same issues. The key problem for planners is how to balance the need to preserve the identity of a community with the interests of a modernising society. In this balancing exercise the most obvious threat to the integrity of many traditional communities is financial. The rising cost of houses in 'C4' – as the more affluent part of Connemara is now described since TG4, the Irish-language TV station, set up its headquarters there – has priced out many of those whose families have lived there for generations.

The imposition of language conditions, while often welcomed by local communities, may not help to make houses more affordable, nor impose sufficient controls on the building of one-off houses in rural areas. What would vastly improve the planning process and increase the prospects of achieving sustainable development is the effective enforcement of local development plans, and an end to the practice of building one-off houses – except where they are genuinely required to accommodate family members. In planning for the future and protecting the environment, Irish citizens, particularly aspiring home-owners, need an effective and properly regulated planning process, from which there is no unnecessary deviation, and a coherent national housing policy aimed at providing an adequate amount of social housing and affordable homes for all.

HOUSING

Quite apart from problems with planning, there is a serious problem with the shortage of social housing for those who cannot afford to buy their own homes – an increasing number, given the rapidly increasing house prices; as recently as 1996, the average cost of a new house in Dublin was €97,056, today, it is over €300,000.

Those on low incomes or dependent on social welfare are forced to live in insecure and often sub-standard rented accommodation for years at a time, while they slowly edge their way up the housing waiting lists. A staggering 48,413 households are now on waiting lists for social or public housing, with the number growing monthly. On top of this, there are now 5,581 individuals estimated to be homeless nationwide. The Dublin Simon Community estimates that almost 3,000 adults are homeless in the Greater Dublin Area alone. Under the National Anti-Poverty Strategy (2000–2006), the Government committed to providing 41,500 local authority housing starts, but the homeless agency/NGO Focus Ireland say that, to date, only 10,900 units have been built and that there is now a crisis in social/public housing, which has deepened in recent years. This crisis is due to a number of factors, notably a slow-down in the construction of social housing by local authorities in the late 1980s and early 1990s. Other contributory factors are the rise in the cost of renting private accommodation and, most obviously, the huge price increases for houses generally.

The lack of any enforceable right to housing or shelter has meant that there is no way to ensure that individuals have access to good quality, affordable housing. Yet in Irish society, property or land-ownership retains immense cultural significance – something our European neighbours often find hard to understand. The Irish focus on property ownership is reflected in the legal protection granted to the right to own private property, which is one of the fundamental rights guaranteed in the Constitution (Article 43). Accordingly, Ireland has a higher proportion of homeowners than any other country in Europe. According to the Irish Council for Social Housing (figures for the year 2000), there is an 81% rate of owner-occupation in the Irish housing sector, compared to a home-ownership rate of around 62% in Finland, 50% in

France and 45% in The Netherlands. But for the first time this pattern of home-ownership as the cultural and practical norm in Ireland is changing. It is estimated that over 150,000 households now live in the private rented sector, which translates as 12% of all households in the country – a 50% increase from the mid-1990s when just 8% of all households were occupying rented accommodation.

The importance of private rental accommodation is pivotal for the future provision of housing in Ireland, yet it remains an unattractive option for many people, not least because tenants currently have few if any statutory rights. All too often individuals and families, often the most vulnerable, must uproot from their homes and find alternative accommodation at the whim of their landlord or landlady. In recognition of the serious insecurity facing tenants, the Residential Tenancies Bill was introduced in 2003 to provide some basic protections for tenants, most notably specifying, for the first time, that they have security of tenure for a period of four years, and setting out minimum notice periods depending on the length of tenure. If enacted, the Bill would also place the mutual obligations of tenant and landlord on a statutory basis, and would establish a Private Residential Tenancies Board to hear and rule on landlord/tenant disputes.

While welcoming the Bill in principle, the national housing association, Threshold, has pointed out that its impact will be limited if the Board is empowered to hear only those disputes involving registered tenancies; currently less than one in five landlords comply with existing registration requirements, despite their statutory obligation to register as landlords under the Housing (Registration of Rented Houses) Regulations 1996. Clearly, greater enforcement of landlords' obligation to register is required.

The current lack of adequate protections for those in the private rented sector is in direct contrast with the strong protection for the right to own private property, as laid out in Article 43 of the Constitution. This, however, is not an absolute right. Article 43.2, in particular, provides that the exercise of this right ought to be 'regulated by the principles of social justice' (ie, in accordance with the good of the community rather than simply the benefit of the individual); in similar terms, the Article allows the State to restrict property rights in order to reconcile their exercise with 'the exigencies of the common good'. Thus, for example, local authorities have the power to acquire land compulsorily for development in the public interest. This State power has proved controversial at times, as landowners have managed on occasion to make a great deal of money out of authorities in such circumstances. It would be advisable, therefore, to place a cap on the level of compensation that can lawfully be paid when land is compulsorily acquired. This would obviously constitute a restriction on landowners' rights, but a restriction adopted in the interests of the 'common good', and therefore constitutional.

However, constitutional amendment is required in order to bring about real change for those who remain homeless or in need of housing; to provide them with rights that may be enforced against the State where there is a failure in Government housing policy. In short, the State's commitment to protect private property rights should be balanced by a commitment to provide social housing to those in need through the adoption of a constitutional right to shelter. Of course, this does not mean that individuals would then have the right to be given property by the Government – but it would oblige the Government to make adequate provision for those currently homeless or on housing waiting lists. This could be achieved by adopting measures such as the construction of social housing units which could be rented out to families on low incomes at reduced rates, and by exploring other means of providing shelter, such as facilitating the establishment of housing associations, and supporting homeless agencies in the provision of hostels and supported accommodation.

TRANSPORT

Housing policy, and the way in which new homes are being built, has had a highly adverse effect on transport patterns. The ESRI has carried out a study showing that as many as one-third of homes built since the late 1990s are out of reach of basic amenities, such as schools, shops and sports centres, except by car. This has resulted in hugely increased use of cars generally, but especially in urban areas. Car ownership has increased exponentially in recent years: in 1993, there were 64,278 new car sales, which more than doubled to over 200,000 in 2000, the peak year for new car registrations. (Figures for new car sales since then have dropped each year, to 156,115 in 2002 and 145,331 in 2003, although used-car sales have risen commensurately.) Figures released for 2003 show 600,000 cars registered in Dublin alone – almost one per adult; the Minister for Transport has not ruled out introducing congestion charges for the capital city, following the lead of London's Mayor, Ken Livingstone.

According to the National Roads Authority (NRA), roads are the primary mode of internal transport in Ireland, accounting for 96% of passenger traffic and 93% of freight transport. The most recent Census figures (2002) similarly show that going to work by car is the principal means of travel for Irish workers. Just over 55% of all workers drive private cars to work, up from 46% just six years ago. Combined with those who travel to work as passengers in someone else's car and those who drive to work in vans or lorries, over two-thirds of people now use private vehicles to get to work.

Road-building is thus central to any discussion of planning and environmental policy in Ireland. The Government's ongoing motorway-building programme is now estimated to cost as much as €21 billion, and will reinforce the dominance of Dublin as the hub from which all transport networks radiate outwards. No decentralisation policy – like that proposed for civil servants – can work effectively while this remains the case, yet no major review of the motorway-building programme is planned.

The routeing of the motorways has come in for a lot of criticism, with accusations of inflexibility levelled against the Government. The most contentious of the disputes has centred around Carrickmines Castle in South County Dublin, a major archaeological site due to be destroyed to make way for the last stretch of the M50 motorway. A series of court challenges taken by a protest group, the 'Carrickminders', to prevent destruction of the site has highlighted the many short-cuts taken by the Government in seeking to green-light the project, including making Ministerial Orders that were actually invalid. Not only that, but it now appears from revelations at the Mahon (formerly Flood) Tribunal that the company from whom the lands at Carrickmines were purchased, Jackson Way, was never the owner of those lands. For its part, the European Commission has produced a draft report that identifies the Carrickmines Castle dispute as 'the *cause célèbre* of Irish archaeology', and that criticises the lack of any effort to change the road scheme once the true significance of the site was appreciated. Interestingly, the M50 road-building scheme is EU-funded – and is going ahead in spite of the controversy.

The next battle is likely to be fought over the NRA's plan to replace the existing N3 between Clonee and Kells in County Meath with a new motorway, likely to cost an astounding €680 million, which like all the others will feed into the M50. Conservationists are outraged that the proposed motorway is planned for a route that will take it within a kilometre of the outstanding historic site, the Hill of Tara, scarring the beautiful Boyne Valley area.

All this road-building and emphasis on provision for car-drivers has adversely affected the numbers of those who cycle to work regularly. The numbers have almost halved between 1986 and 2002 – so that now only 2.1% of people cycle to work (2002 Census figures) – a decrease from 60,750 to 34,250 persons, despite a rise in the labour force between the same years from one million to 1.6 million people.

The drop in numbers of pupils cycling to secondary school has been even more marked; from 50,648 in 1996 to 11,118 in 2002. Changes in housing design must be seen as one of the most significant causes of this decline in popularity of the bicycle, alongside increased reliance upon the car generally. The spread of housing developments into the suburbs, particularly the continuing expansion of Dublin into surrounding counties, has meant increased numbers of long-distance commuters and, of course, has contributed hugely to traffic congestion.

There would be obvious advantages – in terms of the environment and public health – attendant upon an increase in the numbers cycling to work, but local authorities have not generally adopted policies to encourage this. Indeed, many commonplace work policies actively discourage workers from relying on bicycles. For example, employees using cars for work can clock up untaxed mileage expenses, and employers can buy tax-free public-transport tickets for their staff. Bicycles, by contrast, attract no such financial concessions – and 21% VAT is payable on all bike accessories, including safety essentials like lights and helmets (except children's helmets). The Dublin Cycling Campaign has won some improvements for cyclists in Dublin City, with many more bicycle-parking facilities and vastly increased stretches of cycle tracks. Nonetheless, the more radical Critical Mass Cycling Movement points out the disproportionately high number of accidents between cyclists and HGV lorries in Dublin city centre; and the absence of cycle lanes on some crucial routes, such as along the south quays, are real causes of concern for those of us who, against the odds, continue to use the bicycle as our principal means of transport.

For those who rely on public transport, the picture is not much brighter. Public transport usage (bus and train) fell from 9.3% in 1996 to 8.8% in 2002; this was part of an ongoing fall-off in bus and train travel as a proportion of all journeys. For instance, public transport's share of passenger trips in the Dublin area, both DART and bus, declined from 36% in 1991 to 27% in 1997. To try and reverse this decline, there has been significant investment in public transport infra-structure under the National Development Plan (NDP) 2000–2006, notably with the building of the Dublin LUAS tram network. Heralded as the great saviour of Dublin's traffic problems, the LUAS system has already run into difficulties. The management of the LUAS develop-ment programme has been severely criticised, both for extensive budget overruns and for the botched planning involved in designating routes. Few believe it will prove to be the elixir that will breathe life back into Dublin's choked streets, but that remains to be seen; its intro-duction does have the potential to reduce greatly the reliance of many commuters on their cars – and one day it may even be complemented by a metro system.

In spite of this much-needed investment in public transport, it is overshadowed by the huge sums of money being poured into the road system. Roughly two-thirds of transport funding in current budgets has been allocated to road-building programmes. Under the NDP, the extent of motorway and dual carriageway networks will be increased from about 300 kilometres (at the end of 2000), to about 1,200 kilome-tres by mid-2007.

Instead of focusing on road-building to this extent, the emphasis in our transport policy should be on encouraging greater use of environ-mentally friendly means of travel. Amid growing concerns about lev-els of childhood obesity, incentives should be put in place to ensure that far greater numbers of children and young adults start walking or cycling to school or college. Restrictions on car parking in city centres have helped to reduce reliance on the car for some short journeys, but innovations long adopted in other European cities, such as extensive cycle-lane networks, separate traffic lights for bicycles and contra-flow cycle lanes on busy one-way streets, should be introduced into Irish cities to stem the rising tide of car usage. Development of the LUAS network in Dublin and greater investment in railway lines around the country, many of which are now in a frankly appalling condition – I could mention the Sligo train – are an absolute necessity in order to drive people away from their cars and get them back onto public transport. Standards need to rise if we are to be able to present people with a real, workable alternative to the car. Otherwise, the limitations of a transport policy with an overemphasis on road-building will have serious implications for the living environment, for our heritage and for the lifestyles of Irish people into the future.

SOCIAL POLICY AND DISABILITY

The failure of Irish society to live up to the noble aspirations embodied in Article 45 of the Constitution is particularly notable in relation to State treatment of vulnerable groups like persons with disabilities, children and older people.

Persons with disability make up a sizeable minority in Ireland today – 8.3% of the population (2002 Census figures). Throughout most of the twentieth century services for people with disabilities were provided through charitable groups, often religious-run. As with many other areas of social service provision, the voluntary sector supplanted what in many other societies was seen as the role of the State in this regard (see Chapter 2). For decades, service provision in this area remained woefully inadequate. For example, there was no legislation to provide for any minimum standards as to accessibility issues for those with physical disabilities. In 1960, the Irish Wheelchair Association was formed to fill this gap and to improve the provision of services for people with physical disability. The Association now provides a range of services nationwide, from training to housing support, respite and holiday assistance, and is one of a whole range of voluntary organisations now providing vital services to those with different forms of disabilities.

In 1990 a new group was formed with the aim of taking a radical, rights-based approach to disability matters. The Forum of People with Disabilities was established to seek recognition for the rights of people with disabilities as citizens and not just as individuals in need of services. The first campaign organised by the Forum, for example, focused on reform of voter-registration procedures for people with disabilities, alongside other legal reform.

It was not until the late 1990s, following lobbying by groups like the Forum, that the Government took proactive steps in relation to rights for those with disabilities. Discrimination on grounds of disability is prohibited, along with other grounds such as gender and age, under the Employment Equality and Equal Status Acts of 1998 and 2000. Unfortunately, both Acts are based upon the concept of formal equality, which means little provision is made for positive action, and enforcement depends upon individuals taking claims against employers, clubs, or other establishments, since few positive duties are imposed upon employers, service providers, or the State. The original draft of the legislation was slightly more radical in terms of imposing positive duties, but it was struck down by the Supreme Court on the basis that imposing duties on employers to reasonably accommodate persons with disabilities amounted to an interference with the employers' right to make profit. This decision – at odds with the principles of equality and social justice – clearly placed the interests of profit above those of people, at the expense of citizens with disabilities.

Since the watered-down version of the equality legislation was introduced, campaigns by disability groups have generally focused on the form of long-awaited legislation dealing specifically with disability. In 1996, the Commission on the Status of People with Disabilities, chaired by Judge Flood, advised the government to introduce a rights-based Act which would provide a means of redress for those with disabilities whose rights are denied. However, eight years later, the legislation has still not been produced, and the Commission has expressed concern over the delay. In 2002, the Government did seek to introduce a Disability Bill, but it failed to provide for any right to independent redress from the courts where services provided were not adequate – in short, it was not rights-based, and indeed specifically ruled out any right of recourse to the courts. As a result it was widely criticised by disability groups and eventually withdrawn after great controversy. New legislation is now promised, but the Minister for Justice Michael McDowell TD has made it clear that he does not personally favour rights-based legislation. He is against the introduction of enforceable social and economic rights generally, adhering to the view that policy in such areas should remain the preserve of the legislature and Executive alone.

Campaigners on disability rights are familiar with fighting long and hard to secure change. For example, persons with disabilities have had to persevere for a long time to secure access to adequate education facilities – and that campaign is far from over. Numerous cases have been taken to court under Article 42 of the Constitution (the education Article) seeking redress for those denied the opportunity to develop the skills necessary for them to participate fully in society. The best-known of these cases was that taken by Cork-based disability rights campaigner Kathryn Sinnott on behalf of her son Jamie, a young adult with severe autism. She had battled with health and educational professionals for over twenty years to try to persuade them to recognise autism and provide appropriate education and training for her son. All of her efforts were met with what the trial judge described as 'official indifference and persistent procrastination which continued up to and through this trial.'

Jamie Sinnott was 11 years old before he first participated in a course of education, and thereafter his mother continued to encounter intense difficulty in obtaining appropriate educational facilities for him, eventually taking the State to court for the failure to provide such facilities, in a case which she ultimately lost before the Supreme Court (*Sinnott v. Minister for Education* [2001] 2 IR 545).

While the Supreme Court accepted that of all the social services 'education is, uniquely under our constitutional arrangements, the only one in respect of which the State are subject to a specific obligation in relation to its provision', the majority held that the right to education is not an open-ended right, and that the legislature is entitled, under the separation of powers doctrine, to set an age beyond which a person may not be entitled to provision of education. Here, Jamie Sinnott's entitlement had ended when he became 18 years of age, so the Executive was not obliged to provide him with education after that age. The decision, in Hogan and Whyte's view, may 'signal the ascendancy of classical liberal democracy over more communitarian values in the judicial interpretation of the Constitution, while at the same time reflecting an excessive judicial conservatism on the question of whether the judiciary could ever command the other branches of government to take certain positive steps.'[4] Following this decision, the Education for Persons with Disabilities Bill 2003 was introduced, aimed at filling the ongoing and lamentable gap in service provision; at the time of writing, it is being debated in the Oireachtas.

Legislative reform may have taken place, to some extent, concerning intellectual or learning disability, but unfortunately procedures introduced in 1945 governing the involuntary detention of psychiatric patients still remain in force today, despite being hopelessly outdated. The Mental Treatment Act 1945 provides for the structures and governance of 'mental hospitals', and sets out procedures whereby spouses, family members, or others may seek to have persons detained involuntarily in psychiatric institutions. The Act does not provide for proper criteria for the detention or assessment of patients, nor for adequate detention review mechanisms, nor for an independent body to oversee conditions in institutions, which are often appalling in practice. In short, it has no regard for the rights of patients. Its main flaw is the absence of any mechanism whereby a patient who has been involuntarily admitted to a mental hospital could have his or her admission reviewed. There is no way for the patient to initiate a discharge from the institution, even where the psychiatric opinion was that they should be discharged.

In recognition of the huge problems within the psychiatric care system, in 1995 a government *White Paper* promised fundamental reform to bring Irish law on mental health into line with Council of Europe rules and other international principles. The Mental Health Act 2001 was finally passed, repealing most of the 1945 Act and establishing an independent, statutory Mental Health Commission. However, the most important part of the Act, Part II, which reforms the procedure for involuntary admissions, has not yet been brought into force. Thus, in a most unsatisfactory state of affairs, patients continue to be admitted involuntarily into institutions under the 1945 legislation. The Commission has declared that Part II of the new Act will be brought into force as soon as possible, and has expressed concern that Irish rates of involuntary admissions are high by international standards; in 2001, for example, 2,667 people were admitted to psychiatric hospitals against their will, and worryingly there are considerable variations in detention rates across different regions in Ireland. Underfunding also remains a core concern. The budget for mental healthcare has decreased from 10.6% of the total healthcare budget in 1990 to 6.8% in 2003, resulting in a shortfall in funding for the development of community-based mental healthcare services.[5]

In 2003, the Year of People with Disabilities, the Special Olympics was held in Ireland – the first time this event had taken place outside the USA. Thousands of people volunteered to work on the event, which was an unqualified success, generating huge amounts of good will and a true sense of an inclusive social community. Yet a year later, Ireland has not moved on in terms of rights-based legislation for those with disabilities, with a protracted wrangle expected over the new Disability Bill when it finally emerges. It is clear from even this brief examination of the treatment of people with disabilities that recourse to the courts – as an option of last resort where there has been a failure in provision of services – is essential to ensure that the real needs of this vulnerable group in Irish society may at last be met.

SOCIAL POLICY OF CARE: CHILDREN AND OLDER PEOPLE

Just as social policy on disability rights remains inadequate to address the needs of people with disabilities, so too does social policy on care in Ireland fall far short of addressing the needs of children and older people – and of their carers, mostly unpaid and mostly women. In relation to childcare, Ireland has one of the lowest levels of childcare provision in the EU. The National Women's Council estimates that parents in Ireland spend around 20% of their earnings on childcare, compared to an average of 8% across other EU countries. Parental leave was introduced in 1998, but it is unpaid and the manner in which it may be availed of lacks flexibility. There is no right to paternity leave for fathers upon the birth of a child; even the Adoptive Leave Act 1995 discriminates against fathers, in allowing leave for adoptive mothers only. Clearly, legislation is needed to provide for affordable, accessible and high-quality pre-school and after-school childcare facilities; and to give tax relief to parents paying for childcare privately. As Trinity College Dublin researchers Grainne Collins and James Wickham have reported, 'Almost uniquely in Europe, Ireland has virtually no State provision of pre-school childcare and no tax credits for childcare expenses.'[6]

Within the area of childcare, particular resources are required to provide family supports, where necessary, for children growing up in abusive homes, or who have come into contact with the criminal justice system. Although there is major reforming legislation dealing with children in the criminal courts (the Children Act 2001), this has not yet been enacted in full. Until the relevant provision of the 2001 Act comes into force, the age at which children may be found criminally responsible in Ireland will remain the youngest in the EU, at 8 years of age. That this is still the case is unjustifiable. It simply makes no sense to criminalise children that young, or to send them to secure penal institutions. Instead, resources should be ploughed into early intervention processes; family supports; and small, high-support units instead of penal institutions.

One of the major problems with providing care for such children is the lack of resources made available to investigate the causes of youth crime. Unfortunately, the automatic political response to the tragic killings of two gardaí in Dublin by young 'joyriders' in 2002, for example, was to create more secure places for under-18s within St Patrick's – the penal juvenile detention unit. While the young offenders involved clearly deserved serious criminal sanction, a more effective long-term political response would entail examining what had caused the appalling tragedy, with a view to taking action at an earlier stage by identifying the warning signs which may signal the beginnings of a criminal career, even in very young children. Although this can be an area fraught with difficulties and conflicting emotional and intellectual responses, we have a duty of care towards all children. Ultimately, we also serve victims of crime better by taking steps to prevent crime, by adopting policies of early intervention and by providing adequate resources to social services in the provision of family supports, in order to divert young offenders away from a criminal career.

The most commonly cited social care problem, however, is that of the unpaid care work carried out in the home, whether for persons with disabilities, for children or for older persons. Such work is simply not valued in Irish society, despite the fact that it saves the State millions of euro per year. The Carers' Association – the national voluntary organisation of family carers in the home – estimates that there are at least 120,000 carers in Ireland providing care to family members, both children and adults, who are incapacitated due to old age, ill health, or disability. Extremely limited State supports are available to these people; the National Women's Council has pointed out that only 10% of carers are eligible for carers' allowance. The plight of carers is compounded by the lack of official recognition of their work. Furthermore, the majority of those engaged in unpaid caring work are women and the concomitant lack of child-care and eldercare facilities, and the lack of financial supports to pay for childcare and eldercare, block these women's participation in employment, education and training.

Care for the elderly is also a neglected area, despite its growing significance given the increasing number of elderly people in the population. Age Action Ireland estimates that by the year 2011, persons aged 65 and over will represent 14.1% of the population in Ireland (the percentage was 11.13% in 2002). But again, little provision is made by the State for those engaged in unpaid caring work for elderly relatives in the home.

Greater recognition of the work that carers do, whether it is childcare or eldercare, is essential. The household means test for carers, which currently determines eligibility for a carer's allowance, should be abolished, and existing benefits should be combined into a State-funded wage for carers. Equally, pension provisions need to be changed to recognise and give credit for years of unpaid caring work; more than 70% of older women do not have occupational pensions, despite often having worked for many years in a caring capacity. The State must take more responsibility for childcare and for eldercare, both in providing supports to those who are engaged in such care within the home, and in providing care services directly where necessary.

Care provision is undoubtedly one of the biggest issues affecting individuals and families in twenty-first-century Ireland. Campaigns to afford greater recognition to carers, and the development of social policy on care services and supports, may well be a defining feature of political debate in years to come. Unfortunately, in the absence of a rights framework for carers, or for those requiring care, the noble aspirations in Article 45 appear largely toothless – to the detriment of society as a whole.

get an adequate education; the number of homeless people continues to rise; nurses, teachers, clerical workers and public servants cannot afford homes of their own in our capital city. Time and again the Government has chosen to cut taxes and give benefits to the wealthy, without making any provision for the needs of health, education and welfare programmes. The truth is that even after the Celtic Tiger years, we have simply never invested adequate resources to create a properly functioning public services system.

The last election, in 2002, saw the Progressive Democrat/Fianna Fáil Government re-elected with promises to put massive investment into health, education, housing and transport. Those promises were swiftly broken, and instead cutbacks across the range of public services, including the healthcare system, were implemented, with sixteen particularly savage cuts in social welfare benefits. It is no wonder that people are now confused about the Irish economy, having been told that we could pay lower taxes and yet have first-class public services – that we could take the best from both 'Boston' and 'Berlin', so to speak. Now maybe we might realise that it is not so simple, and that our economic values must shift in favour of 'Berlin' and the social democratic model if we are to have a more equal society, with access to public services provided for all.

Secondly, I am horrified at the spread of racism in this newly prosperous Ireland, at the increasing incidence of racist attacks and the widespread prevalence of racist myths being perpetuated about the new communities from other countries that have already contributed so much to making this island a more interesting, diverse and multicultural place. We should welcome 'non-nationals' (even the word is negative), and recognise the enrichment, both cultural and economic, that immigration provides. Instead, Government Ministers speak in apocalyptic terms of 'floods' of immigrants, and propose further restrictions on Irish citizenship for children born here to non-national parents. The Government's hastily conceived referendum on

NOTES FOR CHAPTER NINE

1. O'Connell, D., 'A Failure of Dáil, not Courts', *Sunday Business Post*, 28 March 2004.
2. Jane Withers, *Observer*, 25 January 2004.
3. www.raceagainstwaste.com
4. Hogan, G. and Whyte, G., *J.M. Kelly: The Irish Constitution*, preface (Fourth edition). (Dublin: Butterworths, 2003.)
5. Mental Health Commission, *Annual Report for 2002; Strategic Plan for 2004–2005*.
6. Collins, G. and Wickham, J., *What Childcare Crisis? Irish Mothers Entering the Labour Force*. (Dublin: TCD Employment Research Centre report, 2001.)

CONCLUSION

This has been, of necessity, a highly selective overview of some key campaigns in recent years which have sought to change the law, and which have liberalised Irish society. It is evident even from such a brief review that laws are slow to change and that legislators are often resistant to reform campaigns and movements, but it is also clear that values and social mores in Ireland are now evolving rapidly. The economic boom has made us a more confident and outward-looking society. Our social and cultural values have become more pluralist as a result, and we have become a more tolerant and open-minded people, enriched by greater prosperity and by greater cultural diversity.

When it comes to any discussion of these changes, however, many people are inclined to take a 'doomsday' view of modern Ireland. The decline in religious attendance, the apparent loss of trust in institutions like the Catholic Church and the Government, under-age drinking, apparent growth in violent crime figures, even corruption in the planning process – all of these are referred to as signs of dangerous social fragmentation. Some commentators have gone so far as to argue that with the loss of old certainties has come a 'gaping void', a loss of all values and a general disintegration of society.

I disagree strongly with this doomsday view, which stems, I believe, from a misplaced sense of nostalgia; I do not believe that we should hark back to times past in a misguided attempt to rediscover a richer set of values. Twenty years ago, Ireland was an infinitely more miserable place: insular, narrow-minded, with little tolerance of diversity. High unemployment and high emigration created a pervading sense of gloomy resignation and low expectation; we conveniently forget that even our crime figures were higher then. Depression, suicide and alcohol abuse were widespread problems in those days, just as they are now; and many older people thought the social fabric was breaking down irrevocably, just as they do now. We were not better people then – just poorer.

Far from regretting the loss of past values, I believe that recent change has mostly been very positive. We are a much more public-spirited, tolerant, community-minded society now than we were then. This belief is confirmed by recent, magnificent public endeavours, such as the Special Olympics in 2003 and the mass demonstrations against the war in Iraq, when over 100,000 people marched through Dublin in protest against the USA/British invasion of Iraq. Such events showed a well-developed sense of civic pride and civic responsibility, suggesting that strong social values and a refusal to accept social injustice remain defining characteristics of the Irish community.

Obviously, not all change has been positive, and there are still many problems and inequities within our society. In two important aspects our value system has not improved in recent years, and I think there is cause for concern about the future direction of Irish society.

First, like many others, I cannot accept the economic values which have generated such immense wealth for a relatively small number of individuals and have reduced the numbers of those in poverty overall, yet have made this Tiger society so deeply polarised, allowing the gap between rich and poor to widen as the cost of living creeps ever higher. The reckless application of right-wing economic policies – hasty privatisations, cutbacks in public spending – has left us with unjustifiable levels of poverty, a creaking health system and grossly underfunded public services. By any standards, we have first-world *per capita* average income levels, yet we have a third-world public service infrastructure: hospital patients die on trolleys; babies are born in ambulances due to inadequate maternity facilities; children with disabilities cannot citizenship bodes ill for the future of Ireland as a tolerant society; it is short-sighted and narrow-minded. We should be positively welcoming of inward migration if we are serious about wanting 'Irishness' to have an inclusive, dynamic and progressive meaning in the future.

To help us in developing this more inclusive conception of 'Irishness', we need to move beyond the narrow construction of rights currently recognised in the Constitution towards a true human rights culture, in which the needs of those who are marginalised are recognised, and which empowers disadvantaged groups and communities to seek change themselves. To date, as discussed in previous chapters, we have not really measured up as a society, even in terms of protecting those limited civil and political rights guaranteed in Articles 40–44, our constitutional Bill of Rights. We have certainly come nowhere near to fulfilling the aspirations for a more equal society contained in Article 45.

This failure to implement rights cannot be laid at the door of the courts. In the absence of any real principled or ideological debate in the legislature, and with the reluctance of politicians to take on difficult issues, the judiciary has been left to step into a vacuum which has developed in many areas – such as reproductive rights, immigration policy, disability rights. In some instances, the judiciary has been forced to create policy in areas neglected by those charged with making law.

To address this unsatisfactory situation, a more effectively functioning legislature, more assertive and less prone to domination by the Executive, is needed to facilitate principled political debate. Through such debate it might ultimately be possible to generate a genuine human rights culture, through the development of a new conception of rights, based on an economic and social model. The dynamism of the anti-neo-liberal globalisation movements elsewhere, and the arguments which have been made here for a change in rights-thought, could provide a basis from which to progress this new vision. Otherwise, the limited guarantees of civil and political rights in the Constitution can at best improve the lot of individuals, but not of disadvantaged classes or groups. Before a new human rights culture can emerge, a new concept of human rights must be developed. The prevailing conception of rights as exclusively civil-political should be challenged, so that greater emphasis is given to the social and economic guarantees, like the rights to healthcare and to housing, which have more potential for real change. Of course the entrenchment of economic rights would not actually guarantee economic equality, but it would at least address the scale of poverty and inequality and provide those on the political left with some scope to address problems of economic inequality within present constitutional structures.

There is ground for optimism on this shift in rights culture. Some recognition of the need for change in rights language is apparent in the content of the draft EU Charter of Rights contained within the proposed EU Constitution. Unlike the European Convention on Human Rights or the Irish Constitution, the EU Charter includes guarantees of social rights, like the right to healthcare and to social security. The need for change has also influenced an emerging new discourse about rights, based on what are sometimes called third-generation or group rights, such as the right of the community to an environment free of pollution, or the rights of particular groups to self-determination. These group rights have formed an ideological basis for the campaigns of ecological activists, and more recently for the dynamic international movement against global neo-liberalism. This exciting new movement, manifesting itself in demonstrations in Seattle in 1999 and Prague in 2000, seeks to undermine the international neo-liberal capitalist consensus, represented by the International Monetary Fund and the World Bank, by challenging the hegemony of these powerful international financial institutions.

One of the key ideologists of the new movement, Naomi Klein, has described a new concept of rights that is emerging from the largely underground system of internet-generated information, protest and planning, a system coursing with ideas crossing many national borders. The new rights talk is all about anti-corporatism, from the Zapatistas of Mexico, to students in Toronto, to activists in Dublin, Cork and Galway. And yet this new movement, with its developed analysis of the workings of the global economy, is part of a much older struggle; it can be seen as the heir to centuries-old campaigns against feudal landlords, military dictators and autocratic rulers.

The campaigns of the anti-corporatists are easily dismissed because their targets sometimes seem absurd: they boycott Nike products, refuse to eat at McDonalds, sabotage Microsoft products. Yet these brandnames are merely metaphors for a global economic system the anti-corporatists and their allies in the NGO community worldwide condemn as unjust and unsustainable. Their movement is breathing new life into rights language, investing it with an energy that has been lacking over the years as the existence of countless international human rights instruments had patently failed to tackle global injustices. Through the NGO community at international, national and local level, rights discourse is being invested with new meaning.

As a result of this ongoing re-evaluation, documents such as our own Constitution and the European Convention, while based on a traditional civil-political model of rights, retain the potential to provide an opportunity to allow the perspectives of disadvantaged persons to enter the law. Recent incorporation of the European Convention into Irish law may help to heighten awareness of the conflicts within society, and may have the potential to generate debate about rights concepts and to politicise disempowered groups, thereby helping to bring about social change.

In conclusion, I believe we need to create a society based on the values of humanism, tolerance and pluralism. A society in which human rights are taken seriously, in recognition and in enforcement, rather than just the negative freedoms, or traditional civil-political rights, like the right to vote and the right to freedom of speech – vital though those are in any democratic system. Social and economic rights, such as the right to housing, to healthcare, to equality, must also be recognised in law to enable us to build a society based on a socialist or social democratic economic model. Ideally, this would be a society based on humanist and communitarian values; a society in which there is real commitment to tackling poverty; in which public services are properly and adequately funded through a fair and equitable taxation system; in which diversity is respected and tolerated; in which no organised religion holds undue power and influence; in which women can and do participate equally with men at every level; and which is liberated and progressive, not closeted and repressive. We have the potential to do this – the future is ours to change.

APPENDIX
IRISH CONSTITUTION, ARTICLES 40–45

FUNDAMENTAL RIGHTS

Personal Rights: Article 40

1.

All citizens shall, as human persons, be held equal before the law.

This shall not be held to mean that the State shall not in its enactments have due regard to differences of capacity, physical and moral, and of social function.

2.

1° Titles of nobility shall not be conferred by the State.

2° No title of nobility or of honour may be accepted by any citizen except with the prior approval of the Government.

3.

1° The State guarantees in its laws to respect, and, as far as practicable, by its laws to defend and vindicate the personal rights of the citizen.

2° The State shall, in particular, by its laws protect as best it may from unjust attack and, in the case of injustice done, vindicate the life, person, good name, and property rights of every citizen.

3° The State acknowledges the right to life of the unborn and, with due regard to the equal right to life of the mother, guarantees in its laws to respect, and, as far as practicable, by its laws to defend and vindicate that right.

This subsection shall not limit freedom to travel between the State and another state.

This subsection shall not limit freedom to obtain or make available, in the State, subject to such conditions as may be laid down by law, information relating to services lawfully available in another state.

4.

1° No citizen shall be deprived of his personal liberty save in accordance with law.

2° Upon complaint being made by or on behalf of any person to the High Court or any judge thereof alleging that such person is being unlawfully detained, the High Court and any and every judge thereof to whom such complaint is made shall forthwith enquire into the said complaint and may order the person in whose custody such person is detained to produce the body of such person before the High Court on a named day and to certify in writing the grounds of his detention, and the High Court shall, upon the body of such person being produced before that Court and after giving the person in whose custody he is detained an opportunity of justifying the detention, order the release of such person from such detention unless satisfied that he is being detained in accordance with the law.

3° Where the body of a person alleged to be unlawfully detained is produced before the High Court in pursuance of an order in that behalf made under this section and that Court is satisfied that such person is being detained in accordance with a law but that such law is invalid having regard to the provisions of this Constitution, the High Court shall refer the question of the validity of such law to the Supreme Court by way of case stated and may, at the time of such reference or at any time thereafter, allow the said person to be at liberty on such bail and subject to such conditions as the High Court shall fix until the Supreme Court has determined the question so referred to it.

4° The High Court before which the body of a person alleged to be unlawfully detained is to be produced in pursuance of an order in that behalf made under this section shall, if the President of the High Court or, if he is not available, the senior judge of that Court who is available so directs in respect of any particular case, consist of three judges and shall, in every other case, consist of one judge only.

5° Nothing in this section, however, shall be invoked to prohibit, control, or interfere with any act of the Defence Forces during the existence of a state of war or armed rebellion.

6° Provision may be made by law for the refusal of bail by a court to a person charged with a serious offence where it is reasonably considered necessary to prevent the commission of a serious offence by that person.

5.

The dwelling of every citizen is inviolable and shall not be forcibly entered save in accordance with law.

6.

1° The State guarantees liberty for the exercise of the following rights, subject to public order and morality:

i. The right of the citizens to express freely their convictions and opinions. The education of public opinion being, however, a matter of such grave import to the common good, the State shall endeavour to ensure that organs of public opinion, such as the radio, the press, the cinema, while preserving their rightful liberty of expression, including criticism of Government policy, shall not be used to undermine public order or morality or the authority of the State.

The publication or utterance of blasphemous, seditious, or indecent matter is an offence which shall be punishable in accordance with law.

ii. The right of the citizens to assemble peaceably and without arms.

Provision may be made by law to prevent or control meetings which are determined in accordance with law to be calculated to cause a breach of the peace or to be a danger or nuisance to the general public and to prevent or control meetings in the vicinity of either House of the Oireachtas.

iii. The right of the citizens to form associations and unions.

Laws, however, may be enacted for the regulation and control in the public interest of the exercise of the foregoing right.

2° Laws regulating the manner in which the right of forming associations and unions and the right of free assembly may be exercised shall contain no political, religious or class discrimination.

The Family: Article 41

1.

1° The State recognises the Family as the natural primary and fundamental unit group of Society, and as a moral institution possessing inalienable and imprescriptible rights, antecedent and superior to all positive law.

2° The State, therefore, guarantees to protect the Family in its constitution and authority, as the necessary basis of social order and as indispensable to the welfare of the Nation and the State.

2.

1° In particular, the State recognises that by her life within the home, woman gives to the State a support without which the common good cannot be achieved.

NOTES FOR CHAPTER NINE

1. O'Connell, D., 'A Failure of Dáil, not Courts', *Sunday Business Post*, 28 March 2004.

2. Jane Withers, *Observer*, 25 January 2004.

3. www.raceagainstwaste.com

4. Hogan, G. and Whyte, G., *J.M. Kelly: The Irish Constitution*, preface (Fourth edition). (Dublin: Butterworths, 2003.)

5. Mental Health Commission, *Annual Report for 2002; Strategic Plan for 2004–2005*.

6. Collins, G. and Wickham, J., *What Childcare Crisis? Irish Mothers Entering the Labour Force*. (Dublin: TCD Employment Research Centre report, 2001.)

CONCLUSION

This has been, of necessity, a highly selective overview of some key campaigns in recent years which have sought to change the law, and which have liberalised Irish society. It is evident even from such a brief review that laws are slow to change and that legislators are often resistant to reform campaigns and movements, but it is also clear that values and social mores in Ireland are now evolving rapidly. The economic boom has made us a more confident and outward-looking society. Our social and cultural values have become more pluralist as a result, and we have become a more tolerant and open-minded people, enriched by greater prosperity and by greater cultural diversity.

When it comes to any discussion of these changes, however, many people are inclined to take a 'doomsday' view of modern Ireland. The decline in religious attendance, the apparent loss of trust in institutions like the Catholic Church and the Government, under-age drinking, apparent growth in violent crime figures, even corruption in the planning process – all of these are referred to as signs of dangerous social fragmentation. Some commentators have gone so far as to argue that with the loss of old certainties has come a 'gaping void', a loss of all values and a general disintegration of society.

I disagree strongly with this doomsday view, which stems, I believe, from a misplaced sense of nostalgia; I do not believe that we should hark back to times past in a misguided attempt to rediscover a richer set of values. Twenty years ago, Ireland was an infinitely more miserable place: insular, narrow-minded, with little tolerance of diversity. High unemployment and high emigration created a pervading sense of gloomy resignation and low expectation; we conveniently forget that even our crime figures were higher then. Depression, suicide and alcohol abuse were widespread problems in those days, just as they are now; and many older people thought the social fabric was breaking down irrevocably, just as they do now. We were not better people then – just poorer.

Far from regretting the loss of past values, I believe that recent change has mostly been very positive. We are a much more public-spirited, tolerant, community-minded society now than we were then. This belief is confirmed by recent, magnificent public endeavours, such as the Special Olympics in 2003 and the mass demonstrations against the war in Iraq, when over 100,000 people marched through Dublin in protest against the USA/British invasion of Iraq. Such events showed a well-developed sense of civic pride and civic responsibility, suggesting that strong social values and a refusal to accept social injustice remain defining characteristics of the Irish community.

Obviously, not all change has been positive, and there are still many problems and inequities within our society. In two important aspects our value system has not improved in recent years, and I think there is cause for concern about the future direction of Irish society.

First, like many others, I cannot accept the economic values which have generated such immense wealth for a relatively small number of individuals and have reduced the numbers of those in poverty overall, yet have made this Tiger society so deeply polarised, allowing the gap between rich and poor to widen as the cost of living creeps ever higher. The reckless application of right-wing economic policies – hasty privatisations, cutbacks in public spending – has left us with unjustifiable levels of poverty, a creaking health system and grossly underfunded public services. By any standards, we have first-world *per capita* average income levels, yet we have a third-world public service infrastructure: hospital patients die on trolleys; babies are born in ambulances due to inadequate maternity facilities; children with disabilities cannot get an adequate education; the number of homeless people continues to rise; nurses, teachers, clerical workers and public servants cannot afford homes of their own in our capital city. Time and again the Government has chosen to cut taxes and give benefits to the wealthy, without making any provision for the needs of health, education and welfare programmes. The truth is that even after the Celtic Tiger years, we have simply never invested adequate resources to create a properly functioning public services system.

The last election, in 2002, saw the Progressive Democrat/Fianna Fáil Government re-elected with promises to put massive investment into health, education, housing and transport. Those promises were swiftly broken, and instead cutbacks across the range of public services, including the healthcare system, were implemented, with sixteen particularly savage cuts in social welfare benefits. It is no wonder that people are now confused about the Irish economy, having been told that we could pay lower taxes and yet have first-class public services – that we could take the best from both 'Boston' and 'Berlin', so to speak. Now maybe we might realise that it is not so simple, and that our economic values must shift in favour of 'Berlin' and the social democratic model if we are to have a more equal society, with access to public services provided for all.

Secondly, I am horrified at the spread of racism in this newly prosperous Ireland, at the increasing incidence of racist attacks and the widespread prevalence of racist myths being perpetuated about the new communities from other countries that have already contributed so much to making this island a more interesting, diverse and multicultural place. We should welcome 'non-nationals' (even the word is negative), and recognise the enrichment, both cultural and economic, that immigration provides. Instead, Government Ministers speak in apocalyptic terms of 'floods' of immigrants, and propose further restrictions on Irish citizenship for children born here to non-national parents. The Government's hastily conceived referendum on citizenship bodes ill for the future of Ireland as a tolerant society; it is short-sighted and narrow-minded. We should be positively welcoming of inward migration if we are serious about wanting 'Irishness' to have an inclusive, dynamic and progressive meaning in the future.

To help us in developing this more inclusive conception of 'Irishness', we need to move beyond the narrow construction of rights currently recognised in the Constitution towards a true human rights culture, in which the needs of those who are marginalised are recognised, and which empowers disadvantaged groups and communities to seek change themselves. To date, as discussed in previous chapters, we have not really measured up as a society, even in terms of protecting those limited civil and political rights guaranteed in Articles 40–44, our constitutional Bill of Rights. We have certainly come nowhere near to fulfilling the aspirations for a more equal society contained in Article 45.

This failure to implement rights cannot be laid at the door of the courts. In the absence of any real principled or ideological debate in the legislature, and with the reluctance of politicians to take on difficult issues, the judiciary has been left to step into a vacuum which has developed in many areas – such as reproductive rights, immigration policy, disability rights. In some instances, the judiciary has been forced to create policy in areas neglected by those charged with making law.

To address this unsatisfactory situation, a more effectively functioning legislature, more assertive and less prone to domination by the Executive, is needed to facilitate principled political debate. Through such debate it might ultimately be possible to generate a genuine human rights culture, through the development of a new conception of rights, based on an economic and social model. The dynamism of the anti-neo-liberal globalisation movements elsewhere, and the arguments which have been made here for a change in rights-thought, could provide a basis from which to progress this new vision. Otherwise, the limited guarantees of civil and political rights in the Constitution can at best improve the lot of individuals, but not of disadvantaged classes or groups. Before a new human rights culture can emerge, a new concept of human rights must be developed. The prevailing conception of rights as exclusively civil-political should be challenged, so that greater emphasis is given to the social and economic guarantees, like the rights to healthcare and to housing, which have more potential for real change. Of course the entrenchment of economic rights would not actually guarantee economic equality, but it would at least address the scale of poverty and inequality and provide those on the political left with some scope to address problems of economic inequality within present constitutional structures.

There is ground for optimism on this shift in rights culture. Some recognition of the need for change in rights language is apparent in the content of the draft EU Charter of Rights contained within the proposed EU Constitution. Unlike the European Convention on Human Rights or the Irish Constitution, the EU Charter includes guarantees of social rights, like the right to healthcare and to social security. The need for change has also influenced an emerging new discourse about rights, based on what are sometimes called third-generation or group rights, such as the right of the community to an environment free of pollution, or the rights of particular groups to self-determination. These group rights have formed an ideological basis for the campaigns of ecological activists, and more recently for the dynamic international movement against global neo-liberalism. This exciting new movement, manifesting itself in demonstrations in Seattle in 1999 and Prague in 2000, seeks to undermine the international neo-liberal capitalist consensus, represented by the International Monetary Fund and the World Bank, by challenging the hegemony of these powerful international financial institutions.

One of the key ideologists of the new movement, Naomi Klein, has described a new concept of rights that is emerging from the largely underground system of internet-generated information, protest and planning, a system coursing with ideas crossing many national borders. The new rights talk is all about anti-corporatism, from the Zapatistas of Mexico, to students in Toronto, to activists in Dublin, Cork and Galway. And yet this new movement, with its developed analysis of the workings of the global economy, is part of a much older struggle; it can be seen as the heir to centuries-old campaigns against feudal landlords, military dictators and autocratic rulers.

The campaigns of the anti-corporatists are easily dismissed because their targets sometimes seem absurd: they boycott Nike products, refuse to eat at McDonalds, sabotage Microsoft products. Yet these brandnames are merely metaphors for a global economic system the anti-corporatists and their allies in the NGO community worldwide condemn as unjust and unsustainable. Their movement is breathing new life into rights language, investing it with an energy that has been lacking over the years as the existence of countless international human rights instruments had patently failed to tackle global injustices. Through the NGO community at international, national and local level, rights discourse is being invested with new meaning.

As a result of this ongoing re-evaluation, documents such as our own Constitution and the European Convention, while based on a traditional civil-political model of rights, retain the potential to provide an opportunity to allow the perspectives of disadvantaged persons to enter the law. Recent incorporation of the European Convention into Irish law may help to heighten awareness of the conflicts within society, and may have the potential to generate debate about rights concepts and to politicise disempowered groups, thereby helping to bring about social change.

In conclusion, I believe we need to create a society based on the values of humanism, tolerance and pluralism. A society in which human rights are taken seriously, in recognition and in enforcement, rather than just the negative freedoms, or traditional civil-political rights, like the right to vote and the right to freedom of speech – vital though those are in any democratic system. Social and economic rights, such as the right to housing, to healthcare, to equality, must also be recognised in law to enable us to build a society based on a socialist or social democratic economic model. Ideally, this would be a society based on humanist and communitarian values; a society in which there is real commitment to tackling poverty; in which public services are properly and adequately funded through a fair and equitable taxation system; in which diversity is respected and tolerated; in which no organised religion holds undue power and influence; in which women can and do participate equally with men at every level; and which is liberated and progressive, not closeted and repressive. We have the potential to do this – the future is ours to change.

APPENDIX
IRISH CONSTITUTION, ARTICLES 40–45

FUNDAMENTAL RIGHTS

Personal Rights: Article 40

1.

All citizens shall, as human persons, be held equal before the law.

This shall not be held to mean that the State shall not in its enactments have due regard to differences of capacity, physical and moral, and of social function.

2.

1° Titles of nobility shall not be conferred by the State.

2° No title of nobility or of honour may be accepted by any citizen except with the prior approval of the Government.

3.

1° The State guarantees in its laws to respect, and, as far as practicable, by its laws to defend and vindicate the personal rights of the citizen.

2° The State shall, in particular, by its laws protect as best it may from unjust attack and, in the case of injustice done, vindicate the life, person, good name, and property rights of every citizen.

3° The State acknowledges the right to life of the unborn and, with due regard to the equal right to life of the mother, guarantees in its laws to respect, and, as far as practicable, by its laws to defend and vindicate that right.

This subsection shall not limit freedom to travel between the State and another state.

This subsection shall not limit freedom to obtain or make available, in the State, subject to such conditions as may be laid down by law, information relating to services lawfully available in another state.

4.

1° No citizen shall be deprived of his personal liberty save in accordance with law.

2° Upon complaint being made by or on behalf of any person to the High Court or any judge thereof alleging that such person is being unlawfully detained, the High Court and any and every judge thereof to whom such complaint is made shall forthwith enquire into the said complaint and may order the person in whose custody such person is detained to produce the body of such person before the High Court on a named day and to certify in writing the grounds of his detention, and the High Court shall, upon the body of such person being produced before that Court and after giving the person in whose custody he is detained an opportunity of justifying the detention, order the release of such person from such detention unless satisfied that he is being detained in accordance with the law.

3° Where the body of a person alleged to be unlawfully detained is produced before the High Court in pursuance of an order in that behalf made under this section and that Court is satisfied that such person is being detained in accordance with a law but that such law is invalid having regard to the provisions of this Constitution, the High Court shall refer the question of the validity of such law to the Supreme Court by way of case stated and may, at the time of such reference or at any time thereafter, allow the said person to be at liberty on such bail and subject to such conditions as the High Court shall fix until the Supreme Court has determined the question so referred to it.

4° The High Court before which the body of a person alleged to be unlawfully detained is to be produced in pursuance of an order in that behalf made under this section shall, if the President of the High Court or, if he is not available, the senior judge of that Court who is available so directs in respect of any particular case, consist of three judges and shall, in every other case, consist of one judge only.

5° Nothing in this section, however, shall be invoked to prohibit, control, or interfere with any act of the Defence Forces during the existence of a state of war or armed rebellion.

6° Provision may be made by law for the refusal of bail by a court to a person charged with a serious offence where it is reasonably considered necessary to prevent the commission of a serious offence by that person.

5.

The dwelling of every citizen is inviolable and shall not be forcibly entered save in accordance with law.

6.

1° The State guarantees liberty for the exercise of the following rights, subject to public order and morality:

i. The right of the citizens to express freely their convictions and opinions.

The education of public opinion being, however, a matter of such grave import to the common good, the State shall endeavour to ensure that organs of public opinion, such as the radio, the press, the cinema, while preserving their rightful liberty of expression, including criticism of Government policy, shall not be used to undermine public order or morality or the authority of the State.

The publication or utterance of blasphemous, seditious, or indecent matter is an offence which shall be punishable in accordance with law.

ii. The right of the citizens to assemble peaceably and without arms.

Provision may be made by law to prevent or control meetings which are determined in accordance with law to be calculated to cause a breach of the peace or to be a danger or nuisance to the general public and to prevent or control meetings in the vicinity of either House of the Oireachtas.

iii. The right of the citizens to form associations and unions.

Laws, however, may be enacted for the regulation and control in the public interest of the exercise of the foregoing right.

2° Laws regulating the manner in which the right of forming associations and unions and the right of free assembly may be exercised shall contain no political, religious or class discrimination.

The Family: Article 41

1.

1° The State recognises the Family as the natural primary and fundamental unit group of Society, and as a moral institution possessing inalienable and imprescriptible rights, antecedent and superior to all positive law.

2° The State, therefore, guarantees to protect the Family in its constitution and authority, as the necessary basis of social order and as indispensable to the welfare of the Nation and the State.

2.

1° In particular, the State recognises that by her life within the home, woman gives to the State a support without which the common good cannot be achieved.

2° The State shall, therefore, endeavour to ensure that mothers shall not be obliged by economic necessity to engage in labour to the neglect of their duties in the home.

3.

1° The State pledges itself to guard with special care the institution of Marriage, on which the Family is founded, and to protect it against attack.

2° A Court designated by law may grant a dissolution of marriage where, but only where, it is satisfied that:

i. At the date of the institution of the proceedings, the spouses have lived apart from one another for a period of, or periods amounting to, at least four years during the five years,

ii. There is no reasonable prospect of a reconciliation between the spouses,

iii. Such provision as the Court considers proper having regard to the circumstances exists or will be made for the spouses, any children of either or both of them and any other person prescribed by law, and

iv. Any further conditions prescribed by law are complied with.

3° No person whose marriage has been dissolved under the civil law of any other State but is a subsisting valid marriage under the law for the time being in force within the jurisdiction of the Government and Parliament established by this Constitution shall be capable of contracting a valid marriage within that jurisdiction during the lifetime of the other party to the marriage so dissolved.

Education: Article 42

1.

The State acknowledges that the primary and natural educator of the child is the Family and guarantees to respect the inalienable right and duty of parents to provide, according to their means, for the religious and moral, intellectual, physical and social education of their children.

2.

Parents shall be free to provide this education in their homes or in private schools or in schools recognised or established by the State.

3.

1° The State shall not oblige parents in violation of their conscience and lawful preference to send their children to schools established by the State, or to any particular type of school designated by the State.

2° The State shall, however, as guardian of the common good, require in view of actual conditions that the children receive a certain minimum education, moral, intellectual and social.

4.

The State shall provide for free primary education and shall endeavour to supplement and give reasonable aid to private and corporate educational initiative, and, when the public good requires it, provide other educational facilities or institutions with due regard, however, for the rights of parents, especially in the matter of religious and moral formation.

5.

In exceptional cases, where the parents for physical or moral reasons fail in their duty towards their children, the State as guardian of the common good, by appropriate means shall endeavour to supply the place of the parents, but always with due regard for the natural and imprescriptible rights of the child.

Private Property: Article 43

1.

1° The State acknowledges that man, in virtue of his rational being, has the natural right, antecedent to positive law, to the private ownership of external goods.

2° The State accordingly guarantees to pass no law attempting to abolish the right of private ownership or the general right to transfer, bequeath, and inherit property.

2.

1° The State recognises, however, that the exercise of the rights mentioned in the foregoing provisions of this Article ought, in civil society, to be regulated by the principles of social justice.

2° The State, accordingly, may as occasion requires delimit by law the exercise of the said rights with a view to reconciling their exercise with the exigencies of the common good.

Religion: Article 44

1.

The State acknowledges that the homage of public worship is due to Almighty God. It shall hold His Name in reverence, and shall respect and honour religion.

2.

1° Freedom of conscience and the free profession and practice of religion are, subject to public order and morality, guaranteed to every citizen.

2° The State guarantees not to endow any religion.

3° The State shall not impose any disabilities or make any discrimination on the ground of religious profession, belief or status.

4° Legislation providing State aid for schools shall not discriminate between schools under the management of different religious denominations, nor be such as to affect prejudicially the right of any child to attend a school receiving public money without attending religious instruction at that school.

5° Every religious denomination shall have the right to manage its own affairs, own, acquire and administer property, movable and immovable, and maintain institutions for religious or charitable purposes.

6° The property of any religious denomination or any educational institution shall not be diverted save for necessary works of public utility and on payment of compensation.

Directive Principles of Social Policy: Article 45

The principles of social policy set forth in this Article are intended for the general guidance of the Oireachtas. The application of those principles in the making of laws shall be the care of the Oireachtas exclusively, and shall not be cognisable by any Court under any of the provisions of this Constitution.

1.

The State shall strive to promote the welfare of the whole people by securing and protecting as effectively as it may a social order in which justice and charity shall inform all the institutions of the national life.

2.

The State shall, in particular, direct its policy towards securing:

i. That the citizens (all of whom, men and women equally, have the right to an adequate means of livelihood) may through their occupations find the means of making reasonable provision for their domestic needs.

ii. That the ownership and control of the material resources of the community may be so distributed amongst private individuals and the various classes as best to subserve the common good.

iii. That, especially, the operation of free competition shall not be allowed so to develop as to result in the concentration of the ownership or control of essential commodities in a few individuals to the common detriment.

iv. That in what pertains to the control of credit the constant and predominant aim shall be the welfare of the people as a whole.

v. That there may be established on the land in economic security as many families as in the circumstances shall be practicable.

3.

1° The State shall favour and, where necessary, supplement private initiative in industry and commerce.

2° The State shall endeavour to secure that private enterprise shall be so conducted as to ensure reasonable efficiency in the production and distribution of goods and as to protect the public against unjust exploitation.

4.

1° The State pledges itself to safeguard with especial care the economic interests of the weaker sections of the community, and, where necessary, to contribute to the support of the infirm, the widow, the orphan, and the aged.

2° The State shall endeavour to ensure that the strength and health of workers, men and women, and the tender age of children shall not be abused and that citizens shall not be forced by economic necessity to enter avocations unsuited to their sex, age or strength.